Patty's
Promise

Bob —

Treasure Your memories !

Patty

Phil 4:8

LIVELY PUBLICATIONS
7925 King Road
Spring Arbor, MI 49283

ISBN 1-889808-02-4
Library of Congress Control Number: 2002092523

Photography by Mel Lively
Layout and Design by Leisa Meggison
Printed and bound in the United States of America

Patty's Promise

Patricia A. Lively

Acknowledgements

To my husband Mel
For his unconditional love and devotion.
My love and thanks are conveyed in each word.

To our Son Gary and daughter Leisa
For the pride and joy they bring.

To my brother Gee, sisters Wilma and Ailene
For their concern and stability.

Many thanks to my writer friends and those
Who offered words of encouragement.
Perhaps the greatest inspiration to complete
This project was due to my grandchildren.

Chapters

The Departure

The room had a cool, clammy feeling. The air almost shivered. Muffled notes of the organ wafted up through the wooden floorboards.

If only someone had prevented my five-year-old sister and me from seeing a picture that is forever engraved in my mind. We stood at the second floor window. My arms were tightly folded. My face felt cold and hot at the same time. Ailene's chin was propped on her hand as if overcome with great weariness.

A black hearse was backed into the entrance of Grandma Pittman's big white house. Six men wearing black overcoats and black hats clutched the handles of a silver casket and cautiously walked with their heads down, making footprints in the snow.

The driver opened a wide back door and the casket disappeared inside. The engine roared into life and the black machine with my thirty-eight-year-old mother inside rounded the curve and dropped out of sight. Many cars followed the hearse at a slow space. Strong north winds chased the vehicles and hurled snow into wide crescents.

From a distant neighbor's chimney, columns of smoke mounted into the air and became lost in the gray sky. Withered hollyhocks poked through tall snowdrifts. The enormous sweet-smelling snowball bush in the front yard where the girls played dolls had died. The roses had died and a vase sitting on the mahogany player piano held the dried petals. My whole world had died.

Usually on cold winter days a pleasing wood smell came from the crackling fireplace. On Sundays such as this, the hillside would be dotted with a kaleidoscope of snowsuits and winter gear, cousins sledding and snowboarding. Grandma's house had many gables, five bedrooms upstairs, and two down. Mom used to sit on the huge wrap-around porch and watch the happenings of the small mining town below. Every Sunday this house came alive with the sound of children playing board games or hide and seek. The back yard became a battlefield for cowboys and Indians. Today there was silence. My cousins looked sad.

When Daddy sent us and the other children upstairs to play, my eyes wrote clinical details of what I had seen in the parlor.

EARLIER DOWNSTAIRS, Daddy looked handsome in a dark suit. He lingered at Mom's casket for a long time. I overheard Uncle Roy say, "Sid, you can't let your little ones see their mother this way. It's too difficult for them to understand."

"Oh, yes I can and I will. It's the last time they'll see their mother," Daddy said as he gathered Ailene and me in his arms. Staring into the white satin-lined casket left a painful image. Mom's shiny dark brown hair and round face with high cheekbones rested on a white satin pillow. She wore a light pink dress. Her right hand was placed by her side, her left hand across her stomach. She had smooth, soft hands and a plain gold wedding ring.

Mom's sister told Daddy, "She was beautiful." I thought so too. I wanted to touch her. But I didn't. I wanted to believe she was sleeping. But I knew she wasn't. I wanted to breathe life into her. But I couldn't. My mother had died, any child's worst dread, terror in the night. My hands stiffened and my heart pounded. I tried to think about how beautiful Ailene looked in her pretty blue dress. We wore white patent leather shoes with a gold buckle on the side and cotton socks with white lace. I tried to think about my first new clothes, a pink dress, moist from Daddy's tears.

Ailene became restless and Daddy put her in a chair. She reached in her coat pocket and found a small doll with a blue diaper held in place by a tiny silver pin. She pressed the doll to her chest and squeezed it tight. Even though I was seven, I understood that death was final. I put my arms around my little sister. "Ailene, no one told me, but I just know our mother will go to heaven and become an angel. Just a week ago she told me it was all right to cry."

The mantle clock chimed. The organ's harmonious sound became ruffled. The people took their places in rows of folding chairs. Ailene and I sat on each side of Daddy. My sisters and fifteen-year-old brother Gee sat in silence. Paul, thirteen, cried above all the other uneven sobs. Whispers scattered throughout the crowd. Throats cleared. Someone with an annoying voice sat on my left. "I feel so sorry for the two small children. They're not aware of what's happening." I knew what was happening, and sorry didn't help.

An elderly lady sitting behind me smelled like lilacs. She spoke in a quiet, almost apologetic voice. "Aunt Mattie cared for her mother until she died. They placed Grandma Pittman's casket in that same corner. The funeral was held in this same room."

The preacher's small shoulders appeared lost in a dark plaid suit jacket. He read from large sheets of paper and stacked them in various sections of the Bible. His short staccato words echoed off the high ceiling. "I pray for blessings on this dear lady's children. I'm thankful for her life that doctors couldn't save." Those last few words made me escape the childhood fantasy that I had caused her death.

Several cousins, acting as flower girls, placed bouquets and potted plants around the casket and sat down in the front row. I glanced around the room. Double doors led to two long hallways that extended from the front of the house to the back. A

11

huge coal stove in the main hall made a clicking noise. No one lingered because you always felt a cold draft. On the south wall stood a big walnut bookcase with knobby trim, and a bureau with thirteen panes in the glass doors. A whatnot stand with jigsaw-cut scalloped edges held glass figurines. On the top shelf was my favorite made-in-Japan statuettes, prone babies with various facial expressions and bare bottoms peeking from open pajama flaps. On the second shelf was several never-used souvenir ashtrays with GERMANY stamped on the side, and a see-no-evil monkey that glowed in the dark.

Near the stairway was a Queen Anne chair, a black and white Persian rug, mellowed like Mom's sister who lived in this house. I didn't like this house any more. I couldn't think about the good times. I wanted to leave and never return.

The preacher closed his Bible, bowed his head and offered a prayer. He nodded and two men made their way toward the casket. A gray-haired, well-dressed man shut the lid. His hands were delicate, almost feminine. The wheels squeaked as the casket rolled out of the room and Mom out of my world.

Today, Friday, December thirteenth, six children stood in this room and took a final look at the one who gave them life.

Brunk Hollow

*C*omedian Bill Cosby once said, "You're more likely to remember your childhood than the place you left your glasses." He's right. Six children recall six distinctive memories of our brief time with Mom.

Gee remembers when the family lived in a company-owned house in Brooklyn, West Virginia. He told me, "Our home was a gathering place for neighborhood children. Daddy made a wood gym set, swings and a slide, the first one the kids had ever seen. The small mining town had an abundance of bullies. One of them loved throwing rocks and sticks. The back of my head must be indented like a Chinese checkerboard. Daddy wasn't concerned. 'You'll have to fight many battles. Might as well learn now,' he said. I learned. That bully never won.

"The house was crowded, with two girls, two boys and parents. I was quite surprised to learn that we would have another sibling. I worried about finances and wondered how Dad would manage to take care of any more children. Patty, you looked so sweet and tiny. Two years later Ailene came into our world. She had thick, blond hair. 'Precious additions,' Mom said."

Yvonne often mentioned her first birthday party. "On a moonlight night I went for a walk with my boyfriend. While we were gone Mom set a card table near the tall pine tree. A linen tablecloth, a vase of roses, a cake and one present, along with each family member made for a beautiful evening; one I'll always remember."

I was five and Ailene three when Daddy paid his sister, Aunt Hannah, one dollar for several acres of land. Twelve-year-old Gee, Paul age ten, Daddy and several relatives disassembled an old tobacco barn. With the help of our horse Dan, they hauled the weather-beaten logs down the hill and built our rustic log cabin using the half-dovetailing method, the "false clicking" with a spacer of cement between the logs. We had three rooms and a path, a path to the two-holer outhouse with a "Z" on the door. Our home at Knob Branch was known as "Brunk Hollow."

Daddy stood with his head tilted, his hands on his hips. He looked at the finished product and told my brothers, "Log cabins build character. You know we're darn lucky to have this place. There's just one problem. The fee to pipe water from Weirwood, two miles away, is too costly. There's a spring that has produced water for fifty years. We'll make a reservoir and pipe water into the house. Someday we'll have what they call inflation. We'll have money, but the money won't buy much." With a twinkle in his eye he added, "Remember, the quickest way to double your money is to fold it in half and put it back in your pocket."

He obtained a loan, built a chicken house and purchased farm animals: two cows that gave an abundant supply of milk, two pigs that became pets, and lots of chickens. Ailene and I petted the furry baby chicks. He built a springhouse on the rock-lined stream that flowed from deep within the airy mountain. Icy water refrigerated eggs and butter. The milk was so cold it hurt your teeth. Refreshing on a hot summer day.

We had no electricity and very little furniture. The combined living, dining area had an open space for the pot-bellied stove. A big bedroom at the top of the wooden stairs had two beds for the girls and a bed for my brothers. On hot nights in the summer a single window was opened to catch the scent of wildflowers and an occasional breeze. In the winter ours was the coldest room in the house. We had nothing to keep us warm except huddling together under layers of quilts.

The attic eaves became my quiet corner, a place to call my own and a place to stash treasures. I had a way of making everything "friendly," and didn't worry about matching fabric when choosing pillows and a cotton blanket to assemble a make-believe studio. A small table held a book, catalog, pen and paper and a red cigar box for my great secrets. I had a head full of dreams and a house full of loving family.

I had a special love for my big brothers. Paul Sidney was named after Daddy. Gee was named after both grandfathers, George Griffith, the third child in the Brunk clan. Mom's love for flowers demanded "Iris Yvonne" and "Lily Ailene." Daddy chose "Patricia Ann" and I've thanked him a million times for saving me from answering to "Daisy" or "Delphinium."

My older sisters gave Gee a hassle, especially about tracking dirt into the house. I'd never seen a movie, but I remember scenes: Yvonne is swinging a broom in Gee's face. "I've told you a million times. I have lots of work to do and I don't intend to mop this floor fourteen times a day just because you can't remember that you've been in the barn. I don't need that stuff in the kitchen." She locked the door. He said he would remember, but I knew he'd forget about the clean floor. He remembered many other things about growing up.

Our land produced plenty of fresh vegetables. Gee's job was plowing gardens. He told about the boring springtime job. "My friend Mel delivered papers for twenty-five cents a week and saved the money for a new bike. One day on my way to plow a garden plot, I told him, 'Let me ride your bike, you take Old Dan and plow your garden.' Mel was twelve, and knew nothing about plowing. After a long ride around the neighborhood, I checked on his adventure. The plow threw him every which way. He decided that delivering papers was an easier job. The horse didn't understand what was happening."

Daddy didn't understand why Wilma and Yvonne found pleasure sitting on the canvas top of his most precious possession, a Model T Ford. Gasoline was ten cents a gallon. He came home from work one day and discovered that Wilma had created an enormous opening. Grandpa was a tailor and Daddy inherited the talent; he patched up the damage. That night he lectured my sisters about destroying dreams and causing unhappiness. He diligently wanted education, and often mentioned the fact that he was forced to leave school in the eighth grade.

I remember my seventh birthday. The muted humming of insects and honking of southbound geese marred an afternoon stillness. I was trying to teach Ailene to play checkers, but she kept falling asleep. Our dog howled and I glanced out the west window. Rex seemed to be staring at the mountain. "Mom, what if those big round bales of hay on the hill would roll down and cover our house?"

"That's something you don't need to worry about. The hay will stay there until we need it." Rex gave a long, wailing cry. A neighboring farm dog answered.

A canopy of trees formed an umbrella of fall color. Golden leaves floated to the ground, but the red orange color at the top of the mountain caught my eye. "Mom, come here! I see stripes on the mountain. The haystacks have turned orange."

She pushed the curtain aside and looked out the window. "It's just a brush fire on the hill above the hay. I'll tell your dad to check it out." Within minutes Daddy, my brothers, uncles and cousins left their smoke house construction project and armed themselves with shovels, hoes and rakes. They began digging ditches at the base of the mountain.

Ailene slept while Mom and I stood at the kitchen window. I'm sure her heart ached with the thought of the fire advancing toward our house. After renting for years she knew how much owning a place meant to the family. "Maybe the wind will blow it the other way. We'll be all right." Rex, who had made us aware of the raging forest, shrieked in terror and cuddled near Mom's feet. She gasped and clutched her chest. I covered my eyes. Our house could burn. What if we all die?

The field was ablaze. The enraged monster, an orange-colored line pushed across steep hillsides that were dry from the hot summer. Stiff breezes spread fiery clouds toward the south. Pine trees produced the haunting fragrance of boiling resin.

Smoke billowed heavily as the men struggled to put out the flames. Currents of fire sliced toward them. They put wet handkerchiefs over their nose and mouth. Daddy's prediction came true. "The fire is racing down the north hill. Soon it will reach the bottom, and the wildlife will suffer." A deer barreled down the mountain. Birds flew in senseless directions.

My brothers cut wide strips of dry grass. Other workers continued to dig trenches. The blaze was sucking in air, bursting upward. The fire became bigger and more dangerous. By the light of flames that leaped and cavorted through scrub maples and broken ground, I could see Daddy, Gee, Paul and my cousins sweat rivers channeled through dirty faces. They breathed in labored gasps. Their throats were so dry they could barely speak. I feared for their lives.

After exhausting their effort on the mountain, they attempted to save our home by covering the dry weeds with dirt. Daddy looked down the lane to see a pick-up truck filled with helpers, who began digging a trench that encircled the house. With mounting anxiety, they retreated and waited.

All of a sudden we heard the voice of thunder, a threatening roar. Dark clouds knuckled in and towered above. Blue-white lightning flashed. The wind direction changed. The rains came. Purple smoke pressed upward as the orange line disappeared. A miracle.

Night fell. Daddy took Mom's hand and they walked arm-in-arm to the big oak table in the kitchen. She whispered a prayer of thanks. He lit the oil lamp and turned the flame down low. I flopped on the couch and cried myself into an uneasy sleep.

The next morning the soft autumn sunlight slanted amber shadows on the oil lamp. "It's a perfect day," I told Ailene. We dog-eared several pages of the Sears catalogue. "I love this wish book." My birthday "shopping" was interrupted by Paul's screams.

We hurried outside and found my brother leaning against the house. Blood dripped from his head and covered the white shirt collar. "I trapped a 'possum and built a cage so I could take him to school. That dumb hatchet slipped right out of my hand."

Mom wrapped a towel around his head to collect the blood gushing from a four-inch gash. We ran the one-mile trek to the office of Dr. Hitchman, who thirteen years ago had delivered Paul, a small cyanotic "blue baby," destined to a life plagued with numerous health problems. I remembered overhearing family discussions that Paul's condition related to blood flow. His deep blue eyes showed a dozen shades of distress. His face looked more pale than usual. *Will he bleed to death?*

Dr. Hitchman told Paul, "See, you didn't mind those stitches, did you? Here's a quarter for good behavior. Be careful with your next building project."

Paul grinned. "Experience is something you don't get till you need it."

When we got home Paul opened the cage, and raised his arm to the sky as though the animal could fly away. "You've caused me pain, my friend. Be gone."

"I wouldn't call him my friend," I said.

"But I have a generous spirit," he bragged. Paul had a loving concern for those around him. One day he came home from school wearing just an undershirt. "I gave my shirt to a poor boy." We didn't realize *we* were poor.

Because of his underlying difficulties, Paul forced himself to be charming and alluring. I envied the shiny dark curls that hung on his forehead. He smiled often. During family outings, he and I kept everyone laughing. Paul was the life of the party. He told me, "The brain is a good source for thinking up rotten things to do to your siblings."

"You talk too much."

He retrieved a biscuit from his pocket and started chewing. "A closed mouth gathers no food." Even though he ate a lot, his hunger was never satisfied. Everyone that knew him became familiar with the biscuit-in-the-back-pocket act. Even in church he munched an uncrushed biscuit. Because of complications resulting from Paul's birth the doctor told Mom not to have any more children.

Children were not allowed at my parents' Saturday night dance party. Mom and Daddy turned up the volume of the old RCA and danced away their cares. Famous ballroom professionals wouldn't have thrilled me more than my good-looking parents, smiling, whirling to the music.

The Appalachian spring brought dogwood, rhododendrons and the flowery scent of honeysuckle that filled my days with delight. Robins seemed to say, "Cheerily cheer up, cheer up." Chickadees added a spring song, "See me, see me." Wild grapevines the size of my arm, twisted through chestnut and maple trees; perfect swings for my brothers.

Sunflowers grew six to seven feet high. Some had flowers as big as faces. The brownish center looked purple in bright sunlight. The slender, outward-radiating petals in bright yellow and oranges resembled Crayola crayons.

Sitting on the bank of the creek that drifted along the driveway, I watched tadpoles swim, and listened to the green frogs' banjo-sound twang and the bullfrogs' rumbles, "under the loop, under the loop." Paul and Gee fished and speared the helpless creatures for dinner. Sometimes they let me go along. Once a catfish came fully out of the water, twisting in midair. It snapped Gee's homemade line and vanished into the chocolate milkshake-covered Paint Creek.

When fishing became boring Paul and Gee searched the house for blankets and kitchen utensils for caving expeditions. They built a fire at the end of the rock formation so bears and other animals wouldn't come in. The resin from pinecones burned for hours and produced plenty of light. Daddy said that Abraham Lincoln used the same idea as a source of light.

Daddy talked about Mom's personality. "Lillian's life was simple and streaked with melancholy. After picking berries all day, the family came home to the smell of homemade bread and her satisfying grin. After supper we used to sit in the porch swing and crowd the children on our lap. She developed her own remedial treatment: gardening, cooking, and music. She never had a lesson, yet the dilapidated piano that set in the corner lost its poverty at her touch. The family gathered around and sang loud and strong."

Grandpa brought a mammoth pump organ to our house. Mom played hymns, and our pet Rhode Island Red hen perched near the kitchen door. She carried a good tune in a chicken sort of way. Wilma set "Scarlet" on the keyboard. The hen sang while strutting across the keys.

We learned to create our own entertainment. Each child could play the battery-operated radio for thirty minutes. I remember the day Ailene and I were playing house. Mom was propped between two pillows. "Go to the kitchen and get that box of macaroni and a small pan with a little water in it. I'll teach you how to cook. Set the pan on the ledge of the potbelly stove. When the water comes to a boil, you should drop the macaroni in."

After waiting much too long I groaned, "I don't *ever* want to be a cook if it takes all day," Mom bragged about the "best dinner" she ever ate. A special constitution allowed her to keep a good outlook on life while realizing that she faced death. Each morning I combed her hair, put lotion on her thin, parchment-like skin. Absorbing these special moments reminded me of ducklings in rows of togetherness. Thoughts of her illness made me feel blue, but spending time with Mom was just what I needed.

Occasionally we had company. I sat in the big green rocker, mesmerized by adult conversations. They talked about the weather. The visit covered several subjects and ended with another cup of tea and Mom's advice that "opportunity knocks only once." I lowered my head onto my hand. I hope they wake me if someone says something meaningful. The next time I'll listen to see if they say, "Now, let's talk about the weather, then about work," as a way of getting from one subject to another. At the age of seven, I became acquainted with transitions, and they've remained a troublesome but successful part of me.

The family had mutual regard and affection for our workhorse who loved attention. He never objected to lumbering about with three or four children astride his broad back. When he wasn't chasing one of the cats, Rex trudged close by. Sometimes he ran ahead of Dan, moving southward toward the lion-colored fields, luminously golden with after-harvest stubble. Near the bank of the river stood enormous oaks and a transparent apple tree, where Dan waited to eat the cores.

That fall Daddy took Mom to Johns Hopkins Hospital in Baltimore for radium treatments. He moved her bed to the living room. At the same time every afternoon, the horse poked his head in the window. Mom patted Dan's head and extended a skinny hand filled with sugar. "Here's your treat."

Mom required periodic hospital visits so Daddy took her to Grandpa's big, beautiful house to live with Aunt Mattie, her sister. Each day the horse came to the window. He looked for his treat, saw the empty bed, and turned away. After two weeks he gave up. Daddy took him to the market. I wondered if Dan found a loving family who gave sugar treats and Mom's kind affection.

Her loving and patient temperament changed. Once she raised her hand to strike Gee. He ducked. She started to cry. "I'm sorry, son." She reached upward. He knelt at her bedside, and she clung to him for quite a long minute. Within a short time after the cancer diagnosis, the monster had enveloped her life.

Yvonne and Wilma's life consisted of true love and great concern. They missed half of the senior year in school to care for Mom. My sisters knew nothing about nursing, but every morning they would paste a smile on their faces and begin the daily grind. Mom needed morphine shots on time or the pain was too horrible to bear. She needed her teeth brushed because her mouth was dry, her lips cracking. She needed a change of clothing and bedding. She needed a bath, juice, a small breakfast and a cup of coffee.

It was on a cold, winter night when Daddy piled every family member into the car. "We're going to the hospital to see your mom. We'll walk quietly down the hallway, two-by two. When we pass the nurses station, you should be very quiet," he whispered. "Children aren't allowed in the hospital, but maybe they won't notice."

The spark in Mom's eyes had faded. She had lost weight. I tried to smile to make her feel better. After fixing her eyes on Mom for a long minute Ailene made a sighing sound on a downward note, grabbed my hand and headed for the door. "Will—Mom—die?"

"Don't think so. Daddy says he has faith and we should have it too."

"What is that?"

"It's something we can't see."

"If we can't see it, how do we know we have it?"

"I don't know. But I want to have it."

Mom was too weak to talk. I held her hand. My internal tears whispered a final goodbye. I sensed that something other than Mom's condition was troubling my sisters.

I don't know why, but after the funeral Ailene and I spent the next week at Aunt Mattie's house that had flowered wallpaper, a certain smell of antiquity, and wide hallways. I wondered what was behind the tall bedroom doors that remained shut. The bedroom at the end of the hall is where Yvonne and Wilma used to sleep. They told about cuddling up near the marble fireplace. Wilma said, "We snuggled into the tall bed with a goose-down feather tick. When Mom's mother was alive she joked a lot. I went to sleep with the feeling that I was so fortunate to have a Grandma full of laughter and love."

Even though Aunt Mattie tried to make Ailene and me comfortable, each morning we took the back hallway to avoid the one that led to the parlor and the pain of remembering

Mom's funeral. Nothing made sense.

On Christmas Eve we returned to our log cabin home. My brothers hardly spoke, Daddy walked around in a daze. My sisters tried to maintain a sense of normalcy. On Christmas morning, under a cedar tree decorated with popcorn garlands and homemade ornaments, we saw tiny cups and saucers on a small round table, a tea party for two dolls sitting on pine wood chairs. My doll had soft light brown hair. Wilma found yellow cotton fabric and showed us how to make doll clothes using the toy sewing machine. A small washing machine, with an agitator handle on the side, held three cups of water. Shining through the sparse tree was a bright red sled with steel runners. Snow had drifted several feet high, and large snowflakes continued to blanket the area. There was something magical about the snow and the relatives' generosity that helped chase away the sadness, but all too soon we encountered a cascade of circumstances that none of us was ready for.

The Separation

A narrow creek meandered along the dirt road that led to Herberton Elementary School. I hiked about a mile in the thick forest that shut out much of the sunlight. My heart fluttered with excitement, but life seemed confusing, a strange combination of contentment and happiness that I had a chance to learn, but sorrow that Mom couldn't be part of my special day. I leaned against a hollow tree, picked up a dead branch, broke off small pieces and watched the stream carry them away. "I must hurry to school," I said aloud. "Miss Wiley will be a good teacher and school will be wonderful."

I thought my first week would include mostly playtime, but after everyone wrote the alphabet, the teacher gave a brown reader to each first-grader. She leafed through pages and wrote spelling words on the blackboard. Although the other students started in September, three months earlier, catching up was not difficult. School was pleasant and all that I dreamed it would be.

Miss Wiley wore silky blouses, flowered skirts, and a pleasing smile that displayed white teeth. She taught children in three grades simultaneously, pumped water, started the fire in the pot-bellied stove and swept the floors. I cherished learning, quickly finished my work and listened to the upper grades' lessons. I volunteered to clean the blackboard and help tidy up the room.

One misty morning, the third week of school, my happy

thoughts vanished. The journey past an enormous herd of cattle resulted in a deplorable bovine panic. I stood frozen alongside the road, somewhere between my nearest neighbor and the schoolyard, and caught my first glimpse of a hundred huge dark-brown cows. "Does going to school mean I have to go through this?" I asked myself.

Far down the road I spotted a tractor creeping into view. But that was no help. I felt a positive wrench in my stomach. I tried to sort out the reason for my throbbing heart and troubled spirit. I closed my eyes, but the problem didn't go away. *Why am I afraid of cows? I have no reason to be afraid. They have never bothered me.*

The curious creatures came closer. "Please," I pleaded, just go away. I wish your owner would fence you in." I tried to pretend they weren't there. One road led to school, the other led home. I decided to take the home route. I wished a blizzard would come and cover me until spring. The warm sun beat down on my back. Dry leaves rattled. More cows? From nowhere, my doll-faced sister appeared with a bouquet of goldenrod in her hand. "Ailene!" Those flowers stink, but I'm sure glad to see you."

"Why aren't you in school?"

"Thousands of big cows are standing in the road. I'm going home."

"Oh, come on. I'll go to school with you." Every morning my five-year-old sister and Rex ushered me to school. About lunchtime I began dreading the trip home. "Oh dear, I have to walk past those cows with mammoth eyes," I whispered to myself.

At the end of the day I trudged through the narrow wooden door with thirty other students. Ailene's smiling face brought delight and relief. "Life has some mysterious stuff for someone who can't figure out why airplanes fly or how voices travel through wires," I mumbled.

The next week my teacher read a story about a boy named Hercules who overcome gigantic fright and became a brave warrior. With new courage, I decided that I could win the battle of fear. After class dismissed, I skipped along with my thoughts, my constant companion.

Winter came early that year. Miss Wiley asked the boys to go outside and get wood. Johnny, the skinny short-legged one with a well-scrubbed face and shifting eyes said, "Hey, let's have some fun." They grabbed several logs, climbed up a tree and jumped onto the roof. After stacking the logs on the chimney they returned in time for writing class. The teacher thanked them for bringing in a good supply of wood.

After lunch we noticed the air getting smoggy. Miss Wiley called the janitor who fixed the problem. We discovered that the teacher had a not-so-gentle disposition. She took a large paddle from her desk and turned each offender into a sobbing mess. In those days, parents also sentenced the guilty party.

Miss Wiley provided my educational foundation and introduced me to a new book. Dick and Jane hopped and laughed on the pages of my reader. Dick was a manly, closely barbered boy, and Jane was a smiling girl with blond curls, who let her brother take the initiative. They lived in lovely watercolor scenes with Spot, their Springer Spaniel, and Puff, their kitty.

I moved on to second grade and rarely thought of them until my teacher Miss Akers introduced me to "Growing Up With Dick and Jane." They became my best pals. I had several best pals, my family and Rex.

Rex was born to hunt. Sometimes he went solo on a fox track. Two days later he dragged his body home and slept for the next two. But on school days he became the family sentinel. My older siblings told about Rex accompanying them to school, four miles through the dense woods, past the big hollow tree where they played hide-and-seek. Dogs weren't allowed on school grounds, so Rex perched on the first step that led up Schoolhouse Hill and waited until each child entered the brick building. At 3:30 he waited for the bell to ring. Yvonne and Wilma walked ahead of Paul and Gee. Rex paced back and forth. When small children romped and wrestled, he had to be restrained because he didn't allow anyone to touch children.

Gee seemed to be his favorite pal. My brother couldn't have guessed, not in a season's best kill, that the rabbit Rex chased into a snowy brush pile would persuade Gee, with gun in hand, to climb on top of the dead limbs to scare out the rabbit. His hand slipped off the cold hammer and the bullet created a hole in the roof overhang, all because of the collie's fascination with the sport. Daddy never saw the hole, my brother never told about these adventures that soon came to an end. The inevitable happened.

Six months after Mom's death, my sisters found contentment. Following their graduation, Yvonne and Jerry had a small wedding ceremony. In September Wilma and Herbert were married. The high school sweethearts, who shared happiness mingled with sadness, moved into a duplex apartment. Daddy knew someone in Delaware, so he went there to find work. Gee and Paul left. My younger sister, entwined as a twin, disappeared from my world. No one told me where she went. The main characters in my life had been snuffed out. Our house, surrounded by Mom's morning glories and purple iris, was now vacant and deserted.

As I adjusted to a new home, I tried to forget Mom's death and remember the pleasant happenings of Brunk Hollow. Aunt Hannah was candid about her emotions. She lived in the moment, and didn't waste precious effort on stupid things like cleaning. All you had to do was look at grease on the kitchen stove or clothes thrown across the living room chairs to realize that she was above petty concerns. Her bedroom smelled earthy, of natural body smells. The first morning she saw me jumping on the bed, I stressed out. "I'm sorry. I shouldn't be doing this. But I just *had* to."

"Go ahead and jump. The feathers need stirred anyway." On weekday mornings she sat on the front porch and shared my excitement about entering a new school. The yellow school bus rounded the curve. She walked me to the bus and chatted with the driver. Taking short, quick steps she hurried away to do the farm duties. I could hardly wait to open the brown paper lunch bag to find something different each day.

Three weeks later Daddy and Ailene pulled into the driveway. Ailene leaped into my arms. "I've missed you so much. Seems like *years* since I saw you." She squealed when I squeezed her. I think I crushed her chest.

"And I've been wondering about you. Wishing for you. Didn't know where you were." Daddy, can you stay a long, long time?"

"Well, not too long. Have a job to do, and this area doesn't have much to offer." Ailene sat on his lap, hugged him every five minutes, and wouldn't let go. She hung on his arm when he went to the kitchen to get a drink of water. "Let's take a ride up to Beckley to visit your Aunt Bela," he said.

During the thirty-five mile drive, Daddy talked about my family. "Paul and Gee have been wandering in and out of relatives' homes. I visited Gee who worked at the Shoemaker farm. That boy is crazy about girls. One night the town had an old-fashioned boxed supper benefit. Gloria Dunn brought delicious food. Several guys struggled for her attention and placed bids, but Gee placed a higher one. He made $16 a month, and wasted that money buying the girl's lunch for $15." *Daddy would never be that foolish.*

"After dessert Gee walked the girl home. As they advanced to the kiss-me-goodnight stage, her father met them at the gate. He pointed a 12-guage Remington in the air and yelled, 'Get off my property and don't ever come back again.' Gee decided that life was too short to worry about one boxed supper. He left her house and while traveling the dark lonely road home, two of the low bidders jumped from behind a tree. Yes, sir, Gee's tough farm-boy experience, pitching hay and thrashing wheat, gave the advantage. A fistfight followed and Gee came out on top." *I think Daddy is proud of Gee.*

As we started to leave Aunt Bela's house, Daddy said without any explanation, "Patty, you will stay with Aunt Bela for a few months."

I bit my lip, grabbed a gob of my hair and twirled it in my hand. "What do you mean? I don't understand. Why do I have to stay here, Daddy?"

"You'll understand later. Trust me. I'm doing the right thing."

"But I don't have anything to wear, except what I have on."

Daddy nodded toward my fourteen-year-old cousin who sat across the room staring at me. "Joycelyn isn't too much bigger than you. She might share her clothes."

"What about Ailene? Where will she go? I *need* her."

"Just trust me."

Part of me died when Daddy and Ailene left. I shivered and felt out of touch with reality. My face tingled. My stomach screamed. I sat on the couch and hugged a pillow. *Daddy told me to trust him. I don't even know the meaning of trust. All I know for sure is that I'm afraid to live, afraid to die, and afraid of Aunt Bela.*

Aunt Bela had a small wrinkled face, pinched nose, and close-together brown eyes. Her gray hair was stretched into a bun. Her sharp, shrill voice spoke and everyone listened. She crammed more words into a single breath than a machine gun could shoot bullets. Aunt Bela was tall, like Mom, but that was the only resemblance. [Mom had six sisters and four brothers.] I had to make the best of the situation, but her home was so different.

My "bedroom" was a glass-enclosed porch. Strange things surrounded the half bed in the center of the room. She tossed a multi-colored quilt and pillow on the bed, shut the door and left me in the stillness. I pulled the covers over my face more for shelter than warmth, and peeked out to become acquainted with my new surroundings.

A streetlight shined through faded gray curtains. Dusty figurines with sad ugly animal faces filled one window. On the dresser was a collection of thirteen bottles, and twelve vases. Empty. That's how I felt. Empty.

Near the ceiling, from a shelf that encircled the room, eight coconuts with greenish-black eyes and long black hair kept a watchful eye. The carved faces emitted images from manic boldness to angry pouts. The frowns overpowered my ability to think clearly. *Why do they stare at me? What have I done that coconuts hate me? Will they come to life after I go to sleep?*

Tears flow. I can't stop them. *I know the world doesn't have me in mind; it has no mind. It's only a collection of things and people. I'm something that can be unnoticed. I'm a child afraid to go to sleep. I'll try to stay awake, and nap in the daytime.*

Each night attempts to sleep failed. Something oblong came into the room by flattening itself against the door and sliding in. I dared not breathe or move. The thing painted the wall with a luminous glance and stuck in the corner before it got to me, then made a strange noise and vanished. Night after night the oblong thing burst into the room where I lay awake, frozen and spellbound.

Every morning Aunt Bela opened the door and screeched, "Patty, get your lazy bones out of that bed. I've called you three times." I rubbed my eyes, and shoved the blanket aside. The dampness felt mushy. I leaped out of bed and felt a chill race through my body. *Oh, no, not again. I wish I could die! Why can't I wake up if I need to go to the bathroom?*

I saw calamity coming. Aunt Bela's left eye twitched. She breathed long and hard. "Five strokes of this ping pong paddle will remind you to never do that again!" She walloped my behind, and jerked at the soggy bedding. "Spread these across the banister to dry." Casting a frown over her shoulders, she headed for the kitchen. "After school you will go directly to your room," she yelled. I repeated the performance nightly. I couldn't seem to eradicate the situation or the humiliation.

On Friday my cousins Del and Daniel got off the school bus; their arms bulging with pinewood play furniture. Del set the small cupboard, stove and refrigerator near my bed. "Patty, I'm sorry that you and my mother don't get along. Your Aunt Bela doesn't really dislike you. You're a special cousin. We made these in shop class. Toys make you feel better." They gave me a bear hug. I had almost forgotten how my brothers' hugs felt.

Saturday evening brought an unusual kind of embrace. I went with Aunt Bela and her children to Grandma's big house on the hill. It was a cloudless, clear night. As we were leaving we stood in the driveway waiting for Aunt Bela to gave her sister Mattie some last-minute advice. Without warning, neon-colored curtains of glowing light appeared. For about ten minutes, we saw patches of color: white, brilliant yellow-green, blue and purple. The aurora rotated into a giant green ball, blinked and faded. The violent storm of plasma showered the earth's magnetic field with overheated electrons. Electrical charges seemed to fling back to the ground. The entire sky danced with lights. The impressive solar-powered light show mesmerized viewers.

Aunts, uncles, and children dashed into each other's arms. Aunt Bela screamed, "It's the end of the world. Prophecy is being fulfilled." I thought the colors were beautiful. I thought Mom was telling me that she was happy, and that I should be happy. But my body couldn't go where my heart was. Uncle Herman said it was the aurora borealis, commonly known as the northern lights.

[As I look back, I wonder how my relatives would have handled the story about the mass suicide of the Rancho SantaFe cultists who believed the Hale-Bopp comet summoned them to heaven. Three years ago I returned to the vicinity. The inscription on the building, BELA ELEMENTARY SCHOOL reminded me of sitting in the classroom feeling ashamed for having received a whipping that morning. They had named a school after my Aunt Bela. Even though she suffered terrible anxiety during the northern lights display, throughout her life she remained powerful.]

A wispy-white moon rose in the bright sky the next Saturday night, the most pleasurable and enchanting night I remember. My cousin Betty had a slumber party. Only we didn't slumber. Betty didn't know the meaning of tranquility. She was a pretty girl, with short-bobbed hair, a soft-polished complexion, freckled and rose-brown from the summer sun. She was boyishly agile and her imagination never rested. She and her family lived in Grandpa Pittman's big house on the hill. Aunt Mattie, after caring for her mother and my mom until their deaths, now had the job of caring for Grandpa, along with Betty and her three brothers.

Behind Grandpa's thick salt-and-pepper mustache, he popped his false teeth out, three times, before he decided to keep them where they belonged. Whenever he smiled, I dashed from the room and avoided the scene. Grandpa's big jar—with a "Horlick's Malted Milk" label on the front—seemed to manufacture quarters, that he generously gave to the grandchildren. Six other cousins, who lived nearby, were there for the handout. "He's rich," Betty said.

Before bedtime, Betty robbed four piggy banks. We were loaded. It was the most money to ever jingle in our pockets. We said goodnight and went upstairs. For an hour, we kept one eye pealed on the neon lights and carnival action in the valley below, and one eye on her parents' bedroom window. The lights went out, their shadows disappeared, and we knew they had gone to bed. We tiptoed out the window and onto the roof below, then jumped to the big wrap-around porch roof. We slid down the white pillar, and headed for the traveling carnival world.

"Hey, where are we going?" I asked my leader. "The entrance gate is over there."

Betty knew all about the carnival. "We can save a quarter if we crawl through the hole in the fence." We passed several children, with rumps extended, their eyes glued to peepholes in the wooden enclosure that encircled the carnival. "They're looking at a sideshow that costs fifty cents. There's a two-headed fat lady with sausage fingers and twelve toes. " She grinned. "C'mon."

The hole had been repaired, so we dragged ourselves over

the tall fence. The whole world changed. The flashing lights were brilliant, and music was everywhere. The Ferris wheel resembled pictures of the Empire State Building. There were food stands, penny tossing for glassware, everything a carnival should have. I had my first taste of pink cotton candy that stuck to everything it touched, including my short hair.

High-pitched shrieks came from the rides that hurled us round and round. Betty rode every throw-up ride, but after the Teacup Madness, my stomach met my throat. I decided to spend my quarters tossing rings for a teddy bear. But I walked away empty-handed. The carousel started and the horses looked alive. Past the kiddy rides filled with smiling faces was a tent with orange and yellow stripes. I posed in front of a metal mirror and let out a deep belly laugh. "Look. I'm fat." I almost liked myself.

It was nearing midnight. When the loudspeaker announced the beginning of the "spectacular one-of-a-kind tightrope act," my heavy eyes widened. I stood in amazement as the big spotlight followed the cyclists. Pole-balancing girls, dressed in glittery bathing suits, formed a pyramid three stories high. If they fell, their only protection would have been hundreds of spectators crowded below.

After the grand finale, fireworks like I'd never seen before, we ended our midnight excursion. While the household slept, we scaled the porch post, climbed the roof, and scurried through Betty's bedroom window. Hot dogs churned in my stomach. My cousins ate more junk food and told ghost stories. Feeling secure and relieved that we wouldn't get punished for our adventure, I fell into bed with memories of my first trip to the land of awe.

The next evening I sat on Aunt Bela's front porch wondering what would happen next. A car with a loud muffler passed by and the streetlight reflected on the windshield. *That's the same sound I hear every night! I finally figured it out. I feel much better now that I know where the oblong light came from.*

On a cloudy Saturday morning, I decided that nothing

would change, that I'd never find a rim of happiness or a pinnacle of hope. My cousin Daniel said, "Hey Patty, want me to take you for a bike ride?" I dashed to the bedroom, grabbed my sweater and returned to find him leaning against the porch railing. "Oh heck," he said. "Look who's coming. Aunt Macel is okay, but Uncle Roy talks non-stop. Can't leave now because we have to visit with relatives. That's Mama's house rule."

Daddy had eight sisters and three brothers. His brother, Roy, married Mom's sister, Macel. Three such marriages in my parents' family produced several double first cousins. As Uncle Roy shut the car door, a small truck pulled in behind them. Daddy climbed out and slammed the door. He gave me a big hug. "Honey, why don't you go play for a few minutes. I have to talk with the folks."

"I haven't seen you for months, Daddy. All of you show up at the same time. You head for the kitchen to talk and tell me to go play. What happens next?"

I hid behind the door. Aunt Bela spoke first. "Something's got to be done. Patty is a self-centered kid who needs medical attention. She's never happy. She's nothing but trouble, and she's more than I can handle."

Aunt Macel took a handkerchief from her purse and removed her dark-rimmed glasses. I think she was crying. "In my opinion, Patty is a normal child." She hung her head. "I wonder if you hate her. I've got plenty of room. I'll take her, but I can't take both kids."

Silence. Daddy gulped his coffee. "Come here, Patty." I hurried into the room. He ran his fingers through my short brown hair, stood up, and pushed the chair under the table. "Honey, uh, you're going to live with Macel and Roy." As quickly as he had appeared, Daddy was gone. Aunt Bela turned her nose up and waved. Aunt Macel picked up my small suitcase. The screen door squeaked shut behind us. I looked back and realized that my life resembled Aunt Bela's house: gray, shadowy, with flaking paint. I hadn't noticed the clear blue-white sky and the brilliant October display of tangerine and bright yellow.

But I noticed that Aunt Macel had a pleasing personality. She lived in the city. I'd never lived among so many houses. A curved sidewalk led to the brick bungalow with a tilted roof and a dark-oak door. I rang the doorbell, just because we never had a doorbell. Light filled the spacious living room. Interesting hallways and nooks revealed secrets such as a round window hidden behind a closet door. The kitchen had built-in cupboards, a small stove and refrigerator. Aunt Macel squeezed me tight. "Let's go see your bedroom." A pink and white bedspread covered a large bed. The walls were painted soft pink. I even had my own pillow. "It's getting late, and I know you're tired. Here's a teddy bear, so you won't be lonely."

All I could say was, "Wow!" From another room, the sound of Aunt Macel's voice almost convinced me that Mom had returned. Her sincere dark brown eyes reminded me of Mom. I could breathe freely again. The luminous oblong thing that had raced into the room each night had died. The loud noises had died.

The next morning I heard a warm, "Good morning Patty." Instead of oatmeal for breakfast, I had several choices. Although content, I seemed to be in a dark cloud where no one was allowed. I found it difficult to appreciate the changes.

A few weeks later the doctor told Aunt Macel, "Patty's examination revealed no physical problems, but she has encountered severe emotional stress. With your tender loving care, she'll be fine." She didn't mention the persistent wet sheets.

Will I ever see my family again?" I asked my new mom. "Is Daddy coming back?"

"I can't answer your questions now, but maybe we'll know later. Your dad works at a shipyard in Delaware."

Uncle Roy was short, small, and somewhat reserved. During World War I, he suffered from mustard-gas damage to his lungs. Aunt Macel helped supplement the small government pension by working as a nurse at the local hospital. She packed a delicious snack, coloring books, puzzles, and picked me up after school. "Stay in the car, Patty," she warned. Time usually passed quickly. The warm breeze sometimes whispered me to sleep. She never knew about my wandering up and down Hill Street. I thoroughly enjoyed the sound of autumn leaves crushing under my feet. I returned to the car just before her shift was over.

After a few months Daddy and Ailene appeared. We hugged. Between sniffing tears I said, "Didn't think I'd ever see you again. I've missed you so much. Can't believe you're here."

Daddy cuddled me in his arms. "Sorry I stayed away so long." I wanted to ask if he would never leave again. But I didn't. Life is full of surprises, some good and some not so good. I found out that Daddy had instructed caregivers not to reveal our whereabouts. Ailene and Paul had been living with Mom's sister, only six miles away.

After dinner I heard Aunt Macel tell Daddy, "We love Patty. . . . Roy and I want to adopt her. What will you do with two small children and a job 300 miles away?"

"I can't give up my girls," he insisted. "I miss my family. I'll move back to West Virginia and take care of them." Instead of his disappearing act, Ailene and I rode with him to the log cabin in the hollow.

"I'm glad we're together again," Ailene said when we crawled into a featherbed. "Patty, promise me you won't leave again."

"We'll always be together," I told her.

Like a snowball going down the hill, my memories became bigger and more intense each time I moved into another place that I called home. Living in the country was pleasant, but everything had changed. The cathedral quietness seemed different now. We were a family of three, not eight. I trained my mind to isolate, collect, and hang onto the clearly visible details. "We're sitting on the same log where Mom almost touched a blacksnake sleeping in the sun. That was the day we picked jack-in-the-pulpit and lady-slipper flowers." I said.

Ailene awoke one morning with a temperature and sore throat. She spit blood. Daddy's words frightened me. "Those tonsils have to be removed."

She talked about her trip to the hospital. "The nurse took my clothes and gave me a hospital gown. I felt naked. Alone. Looking through the slats of a cold, steel baby bed, I felt like a scared caged animal." She remembered Daddy's kiss and the word beginning with an "S" above the big steel door leading to the operating room.

When we left the hospital I told Ailene, "We're going to Thelma's house. She's Daddy's girlfriend. Don't be too friendly. She probably wants to take Mom's place. No one will *ever* do that." The July sun was hot. Ailene was weak and thirsty, but she kept trudging on, for four miles. We finally arrived at a small brown house with ivy vines on the porch and birds chirping in the trees.

Thelma's mother had a thin reddish face with sharp features. She scooped Ailene's drooping body in her arms and carried her to a bedroom, fed her chipped ice, Popsicles, and finally solid food. Lying on the white sheets and fluffy pillows reminded Ailene of hearing someone talk about heaven.

Even though he was strong-willed, Daddy had a warm and loving personality. He was a farmer at heart. He turned and raked the sweet smelling earth, dark as roasted coffee beans. We were sustained by a garden that produced delicious vegetables, potatoes, beans, tomatoes, and celery. I felt close to the earth, almost an immersion as the soil caressed my bare feet. We planted peanuts along the sandy driveway. Daddy said that peanuts are not nuts at all. The shells are pods with seeds, the peanuts. The plants bear small yellow flowers that turn into stalks called pegs that grow down into the soil. The pods grow from the tips of the pegs. We dug up the plants, let them dry in the sun and removed the pods from the plants. Next we dried them, and spread them on a baking sheet. I disliked the smell emitting from the oven, but I loved sitting by the fire eating the crunchy morsels while Daddy told us about our family.

He said the year I was born, 1933, the Great Depression caused devastation to the coal mining area. During a coal strike, sometimes lasting a year, the family did farm work to get us through the depression. My brothers and sisters carried food five miles, stored the carrots and potatoes in the ground, as all farmers did then. Every Saturday they took chickens to the mining camps and company stores and sold tender, six-week-old pullets for twenty-five cents each. Daddy searched for steady employment. He moved the family many times.

Years ago a continental drift caused a cataclysmic upheaval and created the Appalachian Mountains. Streams started cutting their way back to the sea, and formed the hollows of what would become West Virginia. Families settled in this dark, cool hollow in 1812. For generations miners lived cheek-by-jowl with the coal industry.

Anyone who is familiar with the coal miners of yesteryear has got to have compassion because of the dangers and the way miners lived. Following tradition, beginning at age twelve, Daddy spent most of his life in a dungeon, sometimes crawling on his knees in water up to his waist. Water didn't freeze in the mines, but by the time he walked home he had to stand near the stove a few minutes and thaw the frozen work clothes. I still visualize a tired, sooty 5'7" frame, eyes accented by bituminous coal dust.

Mom packed Daddy's two-story round lunch pail with biscuits, jelly and butter, or leftovers from supper. The bottom half of the pail contained drinking water. I thought I was the only recipient of his left over lunch, but he made each child feel special. Gee said the one who met Daddy at the bend of the road was greeted with a smiling sooty face and penny candy from the company store. Most miners' children remember the same tradition.

My brothers' nightly routine involved removing the carbide lamp that attached to a clip on Daddy's black hardhat. They unscrewed the bottom half of the lamp and filled it with carbide. They filled the top half with water. Once inside the mines, a flip of the striker wheel caused drops of water to ignite the miners' only source of light. Daddy took Paul and Gee through the Brooklyn mines and explained his work.

In drift and slope mines, underground stables, 800 feet deep, became permanent homes for some of the mules that pulled coal cars. Blindness soon occurred. Blind mules were more valuable because the strong willpower had been broken. They instantly obeyed the Mule Skinner, as his commands prevented them from walking into the wall. The cost of a new mule was $10 to $15.

After reaching daylight, the mules ran full gait into the mule barn. Even the strong man had difficulty holding them back. When age or illness forced the mules to the outside, they wore shields made of gunnysacks to protect their eyes for a few days. Mules were fed, cared for and treated better than the miners. Mules were not over worked.

During his mining career, Daddy worked in drift mines, a hole in the side of a mountain that seemed to tunnel to the ends of the earth. He used dynamite to fracture the coal then shoveled the black gold into mining cars. Failure to clean up the area (unpaid labor) automatically resulted in firing. Even if the assignment took until 2 a.m., after a twelve-hour shift, the miner was expected to report the next morning as scheduled. (Loose coal prevented the bottom-cutting machine from undercutting [the kurf], prevented the clean-up procedure, and created bottom air space.)

The most dangerous "hot mines" contained methane gas. Canaries, with their more fragile respiratory systems, were placed in the mines to warn the workers of increasing levels of toxicity in the air.

In low-coal mines, the roof must be taken down or the floor lifted to make height. Ventilation demanded a high heading. As the floor crept upward a foot or more, men riding cars could be squeezed against the roof. Instead of worrying about slate falls, an experienced miner watched for conditions. Rats, some as large as cats, became the miners' best friend. During a strike or lay-off, rats replaced the miners' lunch scraps by eating leather gloves, shoelaces and each other.

One day a rat tugged at Daddy's shoelace and awakened him from an after-lunch nap. The foundation shook. He said, "I leaped aside as tons of coal dropped where I had been sitting. Coal jumped like gunshot, ten to twelve feet rib rolls from the ceiling above. Within the hour the bumps came closer, like claps of thunder. The miners ran to the tracks leading to the mouth of the work place. The mountain crumbled. The force of air rushed toward the miners and blew them toward the entrance of the mines." Many were injured but no one was killed.

Miners wore cloth hats until the passage of the Federal Bureau of Mines Safety Act required hard hats and steel-toed shoes. At the first Union meeting the president stood and shouted, "Men—we are going to instigate a strict, fast rule: You must wear hard hats."

The strong reply was, "You can't tell us what to do. We won't wear those uncomfortable turtle shells."

Another phase of Daddy's life involved shaft mines, sloping seventeen degrees and 1,200 feet. Miners, in a metal cage attached to a steel cable, were dropped by a steam engine into 800 feet of darkness, where the 57-degree temperature remained constant.

The miner shoveled coal into the mining car and hung a brass medallion, his "pit check" on the side of the car. The Weigh Boss and Check Weigher (a union, company representative) recorded the weight, agreed on the figure, and dropped the pit check in a box. The monthly checks reflected ninety cents per ton. Unfortunately, the dangerous, hard work sometimes went unpaid because "coal thieves" stole the medallions. Depending on his ability to overcome certain hardships, Daddy loaded a high average, twenty to forty tons daily.

Coal companies began topping off the hills, layering the dirt and rock into the hollows, and covering up the streams. This practice of extracting coal was called mountaintop removal or strip-mining. Where coal is under shallow cover, it is a cheaper method of operation than underground mining. The honeycombing procedure removed eighty percent of the coal, leaving enough to hold up the mountain. A state law required that they replace and re-seed the mountain, and return it to the original contour.

During mountaintop removal, coal is exposed as the tops of hills are removed; the earth is dumped in nearby valleys. At times, streams are buried in the process, leaving a flat or gently rolling landscape. Some towns were narrow, no more than 100 feet wide, more a cleft between mountains than a valley.

Never far from the mind of southern West Virginia's coal field residents, was the devastation of the 1972 flood in Buffalo Creek of Logan County. Early on a rainy February morning, a coal waste impoundment collapsed and sent a wall of water raging down the eighteen miles of Buffalo Creek Hollow. It wiped out eleven communities and killed 125 people.

Thanks in part to competition, and tougher clean-air rules, burning high-sulfur coal became unattractive. In the mid-nineties, Wyoming ranked first among the twenty-five coal-producing states with 5.7 million tons. Kentucky was second with 2.8 million tons, and West Virginia third with 2.7.

In the 90s, with a machine as large as a twelve-story office building, one man could move millions of cubic yards of rock and dirt, shaving off the top of a ridge to expose the coal. Mines that resemble moonscapes can cover up to five square miles. People nearby live with dust, noise, vibration, and sometimes damage from the frequent explosions. Homes are pelted with "fly-rock," debris from explosions at the mine. But mining in the modern world has to be this kind of mining.

Hard hats, steel-toed shoes and a logbook with Daddy's mining car tag number displayed at the Beckley Exhibition Mines brought tears and memories of the many hours he willingly spent providing for the household.

Working twelve hours daily, six days a week left little time for pleasure. Daddy welcomed autumn. And so did his hunting buddy. Some of my best memories are of cool October days.

The silent earth glowed in the early morning dawn, and the beauty of nature rewarded my soul. The fog burnt off as sunlight cut through towering hickory trees. Woodpeckers rattled the big oak trees' trunks. They reminded me of a jackhammer man banging concrete into bits.

I remember Daddy's first hunting trip with Rex, whose valor had a flaw. One glimpse at the gun caused his tail to tuck in and his head to drop. With a small amount of training, Rex wanted to flush out the grain-fattened birds. We saw them in all seasons, pecking their way across hayfields or exploding out of the underbrush as we walked through the woods. Brown-feathered missiles ejected through the tall fern under the nose of Rex's excitement that never waned. The fall migration began, and we stood transfixed when a flock of wild turkeys took to the air with the sound of shirts drying in the wind.

Sumacs, dappled with crimson hues and mustard-colored goldenrod, lined our acreage. But the squirrels soaked my brain. Acorns and hickory nuts continually fell upon dry leaves. The aggressive black squirrels scurried to hide them before snow covered their supply of food. A group of gray squirrels mingled in the tall hickory trees. Daddy stood with legs apart and took a deep breath. He aimed at his target, exhaled and pulled the trigger. The louder the noise the greater the attention from animals, from me and from the mountain echoes. The chattering critter dropped to the ground with a thud, gathered its composure and scampered up the tree again.

Daddy turned his head toward the tree and prepared to fire the 12-guage shot gun again, but I heard a different sound, the rustling of cloven hoofs. With thick vegetation our gaze was limited, but the buck, sporting a large rack, sprang into view and quickly moved on. I raised my voice, a definite mistake for great hunters. "What a sight!"

"Be very still. You seldom see only one."

"That's the tough part of hunting, being quiet. It's hard for an eight-year-old to be still, you know." I watched spiders mysteriously spin a web. The marvelous thing about spiders is the way they launch themselves into space on a slender, nearly invisible filament. Suddenly they fling a bridge over the chasm and walk across with perfect confidence. They admire the fine work while waiting to snare their prey.

We sat on a moss-covered log. Daddy smoothed his thick brown hair. "I miss your mom. So much has happened in the last two years." He wrapped short fingers around my cold hands. "Even though you started school late, the things you've plugged into will produce superior results some day."

"I promise to make you and Mom proud of me." Rex snuggled, smelled wet from the chase. I shoved him away, put my hand on the log, and discovered that a large bird had left his calling card. A slow-drifting feather fell into my lap. A souvenir!

The hunt ended with three squirrels meeting their doom. Daddy stuffed them in a big pocket on his vest. Home seemed to be a hundred miles away. He used a sharp knife, and made a horizontal cut on the poor creatures. He put one foot on the tail and gave several yanks. In a flash, like removing a sweater, the squirrels became naked from tail to head. He removed the offensive organs, severed the limbs and tossed them in a pan of water. The buttered results of the hunt sizzled in the frying pan. I dined on a peanut butter and jelly sandwich. Daddy lit a Lucky Strike cigarette and grinned with satisfaction.

The family pet and great hunter was only six when he refused to eat. He spewed white foam, became weak, helpless and hopeless. Daddy told Gee, "Rex has distemper, an incurable disease. You'll have to shoot him."

Gee found it difficult to obey, but he knew it had to be done. He knew that with Mom's terminal illness and work stoppages at the mines, Daddy had enough stress to deal with. Throughout the afternoon, a boy and a dog sat together under the vine-covered arbor in the back yard. Neither spoke. Rex communicated with his ears, eyes and tail. Gee felt that his dog never misunderstood him, and sometimes he communicated better with dogs than with people.

I was too young to remember, but Gee said he'd never forget. "I took the shotgun from the hook on the wall and said, 'C'mon Boy.' We walked past the creek and over the next hill. The birds and animals silenced. I wished I had a silencer on the gun, a protection from the mountain echo. I stopped and meditated.

"Rex somehow knew that this was an unusual day. He walked in circles the way he used to do when he forgot where he buried his bone. He ambled up to me. I patted his head. He trusted me. He looked at me with pitiful glazed eyes that reflected unspeakable sadness. His warm pink tongue licked my hand.

"I kept backing away from my pal so I could get a clean shot. I just couldn't go a second round. I shed a few farewell tears and tried to forget the next few moments. I had to end the agony. His trusted keeper betrayed him to his executioner. Gone was my constant companion. I encountered the Judas Iscariot kind of guilt."

After a long pause Gee added, "This was the second painful loss that I had to face. I thought about getting another dog, but couldn't expose myself to the danger of someday facing a similar heartache."

Perhaps Daddy's cigarettes and the cold creek that flowed nearby had something to do with the family's respiratory problems. He warned Ailene and me that bronchitis and the cold creek didn't go well together. One summer day we were kicking up our heels in the chilly water. "We're in trouble," I said. "Here comes Daddy with a switch in his hand. He's never spanked us before, but I think we're in trouble now."

He tossed the small weed aside and snapped his fingers. "Come on girls, let's sit on the porch and harmonize." Daddy's instructions included soprano, alto and tenor parts. On Saturday nights, at the local saloon, we sang solo and duets. The patrons tossed a quarter for our favorite, "You Are My Sunshine." Daddy added his mellow tenor voice. His hazel-blue eyes twinkled; his thin face with sharp features radiated a friendly smile. "Memories keep people harmonizing long after the music is over," he said.

His sense of humor was finely honed like his understanding of life. Many times I heard him say, "Find something to laugh about. Life goes better if you look for humor. That's what got us through the difficult days of caring for six children." Remembering jokes, a moral obligation, and telling a joke successfully was an art because one must work to make them laughable. The tag lines of jokes were powerful expressions that we grasped early in life. He began sentences with, "Let me tell you."

Habitually, Daddy visited friends for a "drink or two." He came home late, if he came home at all. As darkness closed in, I remembered that our nearest neighbor was a mile away. I also remembered Gee's warning, "The nights in Brunk Hollow are so dark the cats run against each other."

Paul teased, "You'd better be careful when you're home alone. Bears come right up to the house and look in the windows. They're pawing for grubs and acorns. They're looking for two little girls. They're hungry. They love the taste of humans." I believed them, but didn't dare let Ailene know that I thought about the bears so I convinced myself that I wasn't afraid. It's hard to be brave if you don't know how long you have to stay that way, but I had to be my sister's protector.

One evening Daddy took us to visit Slim Stouvers. After waiting several hours, I declined Mrs. Stouvers' invitation to spend the night. I detested the drinking, smoking, and card-playing arguments. "No thank you. We'll sit and swing for a while." Chills raced through my body as I faced the fact that my dad had a drinking problem. Biting my lip to prevent free-flowing tears, I whispered to Ailene, "I hate being here. When the Mrs. isn't around, you must go inside and get our coats."

The moonlight accompanied our one-mile journey. "Now, don't worry about anything. We're alone but we're together. Daddy *will* come home, but until he does I'll take care of you." Once inside the dark and lonely log cabin, I shoved furniture against the door. Taking advantage of being on our own in our large playhouse, we pretended to be adults, drank canned milk, made gravy for breakfast, potatoes for our main meal. Every day we swept and mopped the floors, rearranged the furniture, and took our dolls for a walk. I thought about Rex and longed to feel his protection. Though he used to rush forward and roar out a challenge, he was a helpful companion. He used to take charge when Daddy was gone.

The fourth morning, as we practiced long jumps from the flat chicken house roof, Uncle Gil, Daddy's younger bachelor brother, came up the driveway. "You're coming to live at your grandma's house. Aunt Margaret [Daddy's sister] and I will take care of you," he said in a firm voice.

"Oh, that's okay. We're doing fine here. Daddy will come back any day now."

"Listen to me, girl. Your daddy won't be back. If the government finds two small children living alone, they'll take you to a foster home."

I tried to push aside the horror of living with strangers. "Daddy won't leave us here forever. He'll be back. Everything will be all right. I've heard about foster homes. Please let us stay here."

Uncle Gil shook his head. "I won't force you to go," he said as he slammed the truck door and drove away.

I tried to find the humor Daddy talked about, but I found none. Uncle Gil was dead serious. I asked Ailene, "Would we be better off living at Aunt Margaret's with almost strangers, or in a foster home?" She clasped her hand over her mouth, raised her brows, but said nothing. "No matter what happens, I'll take care of you." I climbed to the top of the woodpile and kicked the kindling to see how far it rolled. "Wish we could climb aboard a butterfly and wing our way out of this world and into another," I told Ailene. Clutching her rubber doll, she scrambled onto a log that rolled forward. She plunged to the ground. I jumped to my feet and retrieved her. "You need to be more careful," I warned. "Let's go inside."

We shared one potato, the end of our food supply. As darkness hung in the air, I mentally prepared to endure another lonely, frightening night. Juggling my short legs over the side of the bed. *Now what?* I wondered. *What will tomorrow bring? Wish I could hear Mom's whistling teakettle and taste her delicious lemon tea.*

The next morning Uncle Gil and Aunt Hannah came. She opened her purse and showed us a *Raleigh Register* newspaper clipping: photographs of a man on a stretcher, a hit-and-run accident. The intoxicated man was slightly injured, treated in the emergency room, and transferred to the Raleigh County Jail.

Reality intruded. That man was Daddy. We had no choice but to leave our log cabin home and hang onto the memories. We took a stuffed animal, tattered clothing, and broken hearts.

Another Home

The dusky-yellow frame house on the mountain belonged to Grandma and Grandpa Brunk. My sisters loved Grandpa, a short jolly person who enjoyed playing hide-and-seek with children. The townspeople referred to Grandma and Grandpa as Mr. and Mrs. Tom Thumb. I never knew Grandpa because he had a fatal heart attack two weeks prior to my birth. That same week Grandma had a nervous breakdown.

Daddy's sister, Aunt Margaret, was happily married to Paris Shepherd. But happiness was short lived. One day as he walked to the grocery store, a car struck him from behind, broke his neck and whirled his body several hundred feet. The drunk driver escaped the police and never faced punishment. Aunt Margaret heard the crash and rushed to his side. For seventeen years she cared for her paralyzed husband. When he died she returned to the home place to help Uncle Gil care for Grandma.

Everyone called the place Aunt Margaret's house. The street had no name. The house, on a dead-end road, had no numbers, and an unusual characteristic. On the right, a door led to the living room. The locked door on the left was Uncle Gil's room. A pine board porch stretched across the front.

The living room contained three rocking chairs, one for Grandma and the other two for family or company. A table near the front door held an old-fashioned radio that emitted the deep voice of Lowell Thomas and war news, but no sound of music. An oak table near Grandma and Aunt Margaret's shared double bed held a Tiffany-style lamp with blue and pink roses and gold edging.

All too soon, dark gray layers of clouds blotted out the sun and converged at the point of horizon. Flying V's of geese gave late evening cries. Shadows of darkness turned the dim surroundings into a sullen, unconscious gray. My family seldom went to Grandma's house, so we weren't familiar with the people or the surroundings. At five years old, Ailene was almost my height. "I want my mommy!" she cried. I held her on my lap and attempted to rock away the tears. Her feet dangled, and her frayed blue blanket moved back and forth with a swish-smock, swish-smock, on the linoleum floor.

"Honey, I miss Mom too. My heart tells me that she's happy in heaven. Everything is going to be all right." In a corner of the living room, a twin-sized bed with round metal bars on the head and foot, a pillow, one sheet, and a blanket accommodated our situation by forcing us to cling to each other. I gave her a hug, and doled out butterfly kisses with my long lashes. She giggled and I tucked her in. "Go to sleep, and maybe tomorrow Wilma and Yvonne will come."

The full moon cast shadows through the shades that didn't quite fit the windows. During the sleepless night, I surveyed my surroundings. Electricity traveled through black wires, stretched up the walls and across the ceiling. A pull string and a single light bulb hung in the center of each room. Behind the dining room door was a dresser and built-in wardrobe made of cherry wood, storage for clothing, linens, and Grandma's supply of Teaberry gum. On the east wall beside our bed, another window presented a three-mile view of the morning sun, rolling hills, and the smokehouse with a cellar underneath.

We had one storybook. Every night Ailene wanted to hear "The Three Bears." Every night I rubbed her tiny arms and played a guessing game, drawing the alphabet on her back. If I forgot, she reminded me, "We didn't share a butterfly kiss yet."

Every day Grandma sat in her rocker knitting rectangles,

unraveling her work and starting over again. She was an over-weight semi-invalid with crinkly, cornflower blue eyes and baggy skin. Someone had to clutch on to her hand and guide her to the dining room table. She pressed her heavy arms on my undersized shoulders. I helped her onto the wooden potty chair, to bed at night and back to the rocking chair in the morning.

We weren't allowed in Uncle Gil's room, but I'm a curious creature. I found a key under the mantle clock, opened the door and peeked in. Amazement overwhelmed me. My breathing stopped. Two girlie pictures with blushes on faces and lipstick on smiles hung above two full-sized beds. "He must have been fifty when he was born because he was an old man the first day I met him. He's too old for girls pictures," I said aloud.

Above the fireplace that he seldom used, hung a picture of a black horse. An empty barrel-top trunk covered with a tapestry from India sat near a door that led to the front porch. A library table held old vases, shotgun shells, and the contents of his pockets. His clothes hung on long nails. Off-white curtains covered the windows that stayed dirty until the spring thaw.

A six-foot oak table with curved legs and tall, uncomfortable chairs graced the dining room. I always wondered what secrets were tucked away in the locked rolled-top trunk hidden behind the door. A wood corner cabinet with glass doors displayed Grandma's favorite glassware. "I adore this bowl with a ballerina on it. Will you give it to me someday?" I asked.

"Oh, no. That goes with the house," Grandma replied. Sometimes I volunteered to set the table. On adventurous days I placed the ballerina bowl and stemware where I always sat.

Grandma had a photographic memory. "How old are you?" she asked on one of her better days. Before I could answer, she said, "Let me think about it a minute." She recalled dates by tapping on her chair with her fat forefinger. "You'll be eight years old this June, the twenty third." Although she remembered dates, each year her birthday rolled around she announced that she was a year younger.

The Warm Morning cook stove had a wide pipe extending through the ceiling. When Aunt Margaret cooked, her humming reminded me of primitive repetitive musical instruments. A wood cabinet with a gray marble counter held kitchen supplies. We had a sink, but no running water. A five-foot long table covered with flowered oilcloth, served as a place to wash, rinse, and drain dishes. A year before we left, someone gave us a refrigerator. We could have Jell-O in the summertime!

The screened-in back porch had an abundant supply of dead flies and various junk, but it offered a full view of the rolling hills. This was an excellent place of solitude, a place to shed pity-party tears, a place to surrender my disturbing thoughts. The concrete felt cool on my bare feet.

My sisters and their husbands lived three miles away, and next door to each other. Wilma had a newborn, a girl named Joy and Yvonne a boy, Ronald, born one month apart. We yearned to see more of them, but Aunt Margaret didn't encourage visits. When they came, she displayed a distant look in her eyes and an uncaring tone in her voice. She was afraid my sisters would steal us.

Let me tell you about Aunt Margaret. She was fond of black cherry ice cream with crunchy pecans. She said, "I'm slightly heavy and a little bit short. Four-feet-eleven and one-half inch tall. And proud of it." Her favorite words were, "pshaw," and "pert-near."

She sniffled and sneezed, and felt it unfair that fate had dealt her a handicap. In the fight to survive asthma, every day she opened a metal can and scattered some kind of strange black powder on the lid then lit a match. She held the can three or four inches away from her mouth and breathed the smoke. The house became spooky, especially on a cloudy day. Due to my aunt's allergies, only green pull shades graced the windows that turned sunshine into cloudy shadows. She used to say, "Company's coming. Hang the lace curtains. We'll take them down after they leave."

She told me, "After my husband died I had nothing to live

for. I came back home to take care of your Grandma. I've spent my life caring for others." I knew from her impatience and lack of dealing with children, that she resented two youngsters invading her life. She kept reminding her mother, "As soon as you die, I'll leave this place."

"How can you be so cruel?" I asked. "If I had a mother I'd be nice to her."

Several times a year a dump truck loaded with coal labored up the hill, made deep tracks in the yard, and stopped beside the smokehouse. The truck bed raised and coal slid downward, forming a pyramid. Black dust covered the grass.

At the age of eight, I received my first "hard labor" assignment. Aunt Margaret had a well thought-out plan. "Carry two scuttles of coal, morning and night, and set them on the hearth. The two fireplaces serve as our heating system. I'll tell you the other rules later." She positioned herself at the window to observe. "Now, if you dilly-dally, I'll deal with you later."

"What's dilly-dallying?" Ailene asked as we marched toward the big black mountain of coal.

"From the nasty look on her face she means that we will do what she says or else."

"Or else what?"

"Maybe it means no supper, but she wants us to get the job done without fooling around." I filled the man-sized shovel and dumped the coal into the bucket. "Look. Here's the situation. This shovel is too heavy, even when it's empty, but somehow I'll get the coal in the bucket. I don't want Aunt Margaret mad at us."

"What do you want me to do? She won't like me standing here doing nothing."

"You're only six. You shouldn't have to work. Just stand there and keep me company. On second thought, don't stand there. Move back. This black dust settles on my clothes and face. I have to hold my breath, 'cause breathing fresh air seems a better choice." Morning and night we carried two half-filled scuttles each.

That summer our well went dry, and we received a bigger assignment. "Several times daily, you must draw from the neighbor's supply. You can carry a two-gallon water pail in each hand." By the time we arrived home the pails that dragged the ground were about half full.

Every day brought more tasks. "I'm supposed to take care of you," I told Ailene as we crawled into bed. I couldn't hold back tears. "Here I am feeling sorry for myself. I'll feel better tomorrow." I whispered. "Even on a good day it's easy to notice the truth of the matter. Uncle Gil and Aunt Margaret hate us."

"Oh, Patty, don't say that."

"I'm sorry. Why am I telling you these things?"

"Well, you have to tell somebody. There's nobody else to tell."

"They have discovered that we're willing workers. What other choice do we have?"

"None. I guess."

"We're cheap labor. They want us to stay here forever and help with Grandma, who doesn't even care if we live or die."

"Oh come on now. It'll get better."

"You're right. It has to get better. I'm sleepy now. Love you."

Each night I fell into bed exhausted from strenuous work and the stress of feeling unwanted. The damp sheets and soggy bedding problem returned. I thought of Aunt Bela and the ping-pong paddle. I sleepwalked, awakening in various parts of the house like someone brought back from cardiac arrest.

Each morning I stood surrounded by poverty. I gazed in silence at my sweet sister. I wanted to pull the cover over my head and never wake up. A pattern of self-doubt brought mental pain. One morning as we dressed for school I told Ailene, "I'm sick and tired of wearing the same darn clothes."

"Me too," she said as she tied her shoes.

Comparison with other eight-year-olds became the root of inferiority. My self-image was shaped by how I stacked up against my peers. Evaluating myself critically, it seemed that other students had more to offer than I did. I envied the better looking, more athletic and smarter girls. I didn't measure up to my own expectations. Aunt Margaret's wall calendar portrayed childhood. Every page depicted an outdoor family scene: swimming, yard games, picnics. You could look at them and feel the water splashing in your face, taste the shortcake, smell the watermelon, and hear the hotdogs sizzling on the grill.

I don't want to recall some things, but I must. I can still hear Aunt Margaret's advice. "Peel those potatoes thin. Rinse the soap powder out of that box. Waste not, want not. Who do you think we are, the Rockefellers?"

In true form, without the alcohol that consumed his thoughts and life itself, Uncle Gil had the capability to love and sometimes laugh. He worked in the coal mines, a job that required courage and skill. He wore a gray felt fedora hat. He snacked on cornbread crumbled in a glass of buttermilk. No one was surprised to see him cry after returning from an overnight binge.

One Saturday night Daddy made a surprise visit. But he didn't choose to sit by the fire and visit with his two daughters. He and Uncle Gil ate a sandwich and left. "I know where they're going," Aunt Margaret said. "Alcohol is worse than ice on the mountain."

Late that night I heard voices in the kitchen. The stale odor of tobacco and slurred speech resulting from too much alcohol, gave me a sick feeling. The loud argument between Daddy and his brother seemed to last for hours. Uncle Gil lashed out. "You don't realize what I'm going through, having to deal with two temperamental, lazy girls all the time."

"And you don't understand that I want my children, but have no way to care for them."

"I just had a pain in my stomach," I whispered to Ailene.

"Indigestion?"

"Don't know. I heard a noise. Something hit the wall." Ailene screamed and the arguments ceased. I finally drifted off to sleep, assuming that Daddy would spend the night and I would see him again at breakfast.

As sunlight spread golden rays, and the coffeepot churned away on the wood-burning cook stove, I realized that Daddy had left in the nighttime Appalachian fog. I thought the argument was my fault.

It was a cloudless Saturday morning. Aunt Margaret shoved me into the pantry. "My asthma is getting worse. I can no longer use the flour to make biscuits. And bread costs ten cents a loaf." She took the big wooden bowl from the shelf. "From now on, you have a new job."

"Oh no, I hate putting my hands in that goop."

"You'll get used to it. First, you put flour up to about here."

"There must be twenty cups of flour in this bowl. Goodness, do you plan to invite the whole town to breakfast?"

"No, silly, you only use the middle of the bowl. Put in a chunk of lard and crunch it with your fingertips. Pretend you're making mud pies. Add a pinch of salt and soda. And be sure to mix it. Now, put some buttermilk in the middle of the bowl and fluff it with both hands."

"Can't I use a spoon?"

"Oh no. Spoons don't work well. Hands were made before spoons. Now, put flour on the board and dump the mixture in the middle. Knead it just a little."

"I don't need it; you need it."

"The word is spelled KNEAD, not NEED. Roll the dough to about ¾ inch thick. Use this glass to shape the biscuits. Grease them on both sides and put them in this pan. Always use the same pan because it makes good biscuits."

"Great." I said. "I'll let the pan do the biscuits." She laughed and pretended to throw flour in my face. I jumped about four feet. "You'll have to write it down for me. I can't remember all that stuff."

"Writing takes too much time. You'll learn. Eventually. Remember, toasting the bread to a golden brown is the test of the bread's true character," she said.

The next morning Ailene tried to cut my masterpiece. "Don't feed this bread to the animals. It'll break their teeth." I hung my head. *I'm a failure. I'll never be a good cook. I don't want to anyway. But tomorrow I'll show them a thing or two.*

Each batch tasted better. The compliments almost changed my mind about becoming a cook. "My biscuits have character and firm texture. They're crisp on the outside, yet tender inside, with generous pockets to take in all the melting butter." I baked raisin swirls that filled the kitchen with the smell of cinnamon.

Our nearest and dearest neighbor, Ray and Ardith Thompson, became our lighthouse, a harbor in life's storms. At seven years old, Ailene quoted Scriptures that were hidden in her heart, Scripture taught in Sunday school by Mr. Thompson. Their two oldest sons, Conway, and David were involved in sports. I called Tommy "the baby" even after he started school. He grinned and never seemed to object. He probably hated me. The others didn't matter, but I wanted his brother to notice.

"Dennis, will you be my best friend? Just until fifth grade?" I asked one day on the way home from school.

"I dunno. Guess I could kind of look out for you now and then," he said with a sheepish grin. Dennis became a true friend, my only real friend.

Walking home from school the next day, a heavy-set bully tripped me and uttered fighting words. "I saw your dad and mom coming out of the saloon last week, drunker than drunk. You'll be akin to her when you grow up."

"You're a dork. That was *not* my mom. She's in heaven. The person you saw was my dad's girlfriend. And you're right. She does drink a lot. But I won't do that. And don't you ever talk bad about my family," I yelled.

My favorite feed sack book bag happened to be loaded with some rocks I found along the railroad track. I grabbed a handful, poised my geography book across the troublemaker's backside. I peppered him with both weapons. "Keep talking and you won't grow up. If I can't beat you now, I'll get you later," I said. Dennis shoved him aside. My right-hand punch caught the intimidator off balance and he rolled down the hill. Reminded me of tumbleweeds whirling in the wind. The crowd of students burst out laughing. Dennis had replaced my brothers' protection.

Jackie, Ailene's age and her first love, usually flashed a broad smile when Ailene was near, but today, instead of smiling, he joined in the fight. "Hey, dude. I'm still mad at you over yesterday's lies you told about me. It's time to settle the score," he said as he landed another punch.

Jackie fought many neighborhood and school battles on Ailene's behalf. "He's my hero," she bragged.

Except during a rainy season, our well was bone dry and we drew water from the Thompson's well. Sometimes we set the galvanized buckets in the shade and took a spin around the house on Jackie and Dennis' scooter. As we grew older they introduced us to the bicycle. In the winter, we rode their sleds as much as they used them. I'll never forget the day Dennis got a new Radio Flyer sled. He gave me his old one. A new Cadillac wouldn't have thrilled my heart more.

Mrs. Thompson, a slender lady with light brown hair, cut long near her face and short in the back, provided more than water. She had a heart of gold, grinned a lot, and shared her homemade cookies and fruit. She always took time to chat, often reminding me that I was too skinny. I was determined to be a detective, then a reporter, and finally a famous author. I looked into ballet dancing, but she said I wasn't tall enough. My mind and emotions engaged in slices of beauty and minute details. I told her about my wonderful mud pies. "I make them on Thursdays so they will be dry by Saturday playtime. I carve dragons, roads, bridges and buildings."

This would make wonderful mud pies, I thought while retrieving a muffin tin from Mrs. Thompson's garbage can. I tucked it under one arm while carrying the usual two buckets of water. I wondered if the bruise I encountered from the weight was worth beautiful mud pies. Aunt Margaret quickly noticed my new cookware. "Where did you get a muffin tin?"

"Uh, Ardith gave it to me."

"Who? Where are your manners? You will call her Mrs. Thompson."

"Uh, Mrs. Thompson gave it to me. I mean – it was in her garbage can."

"Don't you know that is STEALING?"

"That's wild accusations! It is NOT stealing, she threw it away."

"Don't get sassy with me, young lady!"

"I'm NOT getting sassy, I'm telling the truth."

"I don't believe you. Go cut a switch because you've got a big one coming!"

"I WON'T get your switches."

"You'll be sorry, if you don't, 'cause I'll get a bigger one."

I was determined she would not whip me THIS time. "I didn't do anything wrong. I don't care if you bring in a WHOLE TREE," I yelled. The branch compared to a whole tree. Aunt Margaret swished her weapon through the air. I jumped, but so did the sharp hickory switch. She began wheezing, due to an asthmatic condition, and finally gave up the struggle. I felt sorry for her, until I felt warm blood ooze from my spindly legs.

She breathed heavily. "Now—you must—apologize for—for stealing."

I gathered enough courage to knock on Mrs. Thompson's door. She saw the humble look on my face. Her mouth drooped. "What's wrong, Patty?"

"I came to say I'm sorry that I'm a bad girl and I stole the muffin tin from your garbage can and I really and truly want to apologize," I mumbled.

"Honey, you haven't done anything wrong. But if it makes auntie happy, tell her I forgive you," She slipped a large Snickers candy bar into my pocket."

[Years later Ailene told Ray and Ardith, "I want to thank you for making our childhood years more pleasant. I'll always have fond memories of your family. "You'll never know how your support helped the "two little Brunk girls" cope with life," Ray passed away, and seven years later Ardith died. At the funeral the boys introduced their families and thanked Ailene for paying her respects. Jackie, Dennis and Tommy, who looked small for their age, stood over six feet tall.]

Maybe the streak of devilment that I possessed was due to curiosity and finding out how far I could go without getting my butt beat. It was summer vacation time, a time to let the daredevil feeling run wild. Pearl, our neighbor, was very black, of medium height, a large behind, and surprisingly long arms. She wore clean cotton housedresses. Pearl always acted timid, glanced downward as she talked. At an early age I determined that black families had to overcome severe and unfair obstacles. They came to the back door of a white family's house, rode in a separate part of the passenger train, sat upstairs in the movie theater and in the back of the bus. They attended separate schools and churches.

Pearl adopted her alcoholic daughter's two sons. Junior and Ty were full of adventurous ideas. Junior said, "We don't have a daddy." I knew enough to wonder how that could be true. I welcomed new playmates, although I preferred girls for pals. A large grove of shrubs separated our houses. Junior suggested that we go behind the barn and get the rusty rain barrel, crawl in and let Ty push us down the hill. (The one who stayed in the barrel until it stopped rolling was the brave one of the bunch.)

Ailene and Junior crawled in the barrel. As it rolled down the hill I saw a bushy head of black hair, mixed with golden blond curls. After a safe landing, they said it was my turn. That dizzy, frightening antic convinced me that Ty and Junior could show me up any day of the week. I didn't want to be the brave one in the bunch.

When Aunt Margaret had asthma attacks, Pearl just happened by. When we picked beans, canned beans, or peeled apples, Pearl came to work and chat. At mealtime Aunt Margaret invited her to join us. "No ma'am, thank you," she replied. I wondered why she refused to sit at our table because she had such a kindred spirit. But her heritage of feeling "less than" prevented her from accepting our hospitality. Her heart indicated that she was "more than" many people I knew.

I was nine, and all I knew about electricity was I had to replace the bulb that dangled from the cord in the kitchen ceiling with an adapter so I could attach the black washer cord. The teacher (and the whole town) knew that Aunt Margaret made me skip school every Monday because Monday was washday. I invited schoolmates who hated Mondays to join my weekly endurance, but parents frowned on the idea. The teachers usually made allowance for Monday homework assignments.

I'm not sure which I dreaded most, the washer or the wringer, but the shock I received when putting my hands in the old Maytag was no fun. I squirmed and screamed, "Arrgghh, I hate this washer. It's too energetic. And the wringer eats buttons and fingers."

Aunt Margaret twisted a swatch of gray hair into a bun, stuck hairpins every few inches, and placed her hands on her hips. "You have a real good imagination, Patty. Nothing is wrong with that washer. I've used it for years. You're just too lazy to work. Now hurry, and don't scream. It hurts Grandma's ears and makes her nervous."

"Sure does make her nervous. Life itself makes her nervous. And she's no fun either."

"Well, let me tell you something. I've taken care of Mama for years. When she takes her last breath, I'm gonna leave. Fly away, off this hill. I'm sick of being tied down."

"Don't let her hear you. Those aren't kind words. Mom told me to always be kind. But I don't know if I can obey that rule my whole life. Aunt Margaret, will Mom know if I disobey? In heaven, does she know if I'm good or bad?"

"Oh, hush, child. You ramble on and on. I don't know the answers to your many questions. They're too deep. Your mom was a smart lady. Quit chattering! Go get more water from Mrs. Thompson's well. Don't stay all day. And then bring in wood so we can heat the water for the next load of laundry."

The chugging washer whirled towels and bedclothes in the soapy Rinso-White water. A pillowcase filled with air. I punched it down and whispered, "She's full of air, too." I stared out the window, into a gray-white cloud with clearly defined edges shaped like a woman's face. I wondered if Mom knew that I longed for her comforting arms and the smell of her Ponds lotion. "Life has no comfort," I muttered.

I thought about the night I heard strange sounds outside. I opened the heavy screen door. "Oh look," I said. Ailene jumped with delight as a cold, drenched kitten pounced inside.

Aunt Margaret's small withered face seemed to enlarge. She screamed, "Scat! You beggar! Don't ever feed a stray cat, cause she'll never go back home, and we'll be stuck with another mouth to feed."

"How do you know it's a she?' I questioned.

She grinned. "Oh, I'm just guessing."

The stray cat became my best friend, and brought joy into my life. Aunt Margaret said I was cat batty. Every evening Paws enjoyed the remains of my dinner. Patting her tummy initiated loud purrs. Paws was no trouble. She was a capable mouser, an outdoor cat that occasionally decided to move into the house. I looked forward to Paws' hearty meow as she came trotting toward my chair. She avoided Aunt Margaret, but when five fluffy kittens came along, even Aunt Margaret grew to tolerate them.

But happiness didn't last. On Saturday Uncle Gil gathered Paws and her family into a gunnysack and headed down the road. I knew their destination. Paint Creek rose up to meet them and licked its chops. I yearned for a story with a happy-ever-after ending. *I reckon I don't have time to play kitten questions or paw at the loose ends of life.* I blinked away warm tears.

On Monday everyone in town heard my screams. The old Maytag washer was at it again. Putting my hands into the water caused an electrifying, tingling, sensation. "I've had it! Wake

Uncle Gil and tell him I'm quitting this job." No one had to wake him. He stumbled across the room and leaned on the door. I'd never seen him in pajamas.

He smoothed a hand over his tangled hair. "You're mighty loud, girl. Don't you know you're standing barefoot in water and that's why you're getting shocks from the washer? Don't splash water on the floor. And get some shoes on!" At least my uncle had the ability to frustrate someone other than himself.

"Rough night, huh? Better go back to bed. It's only ten o'clock. Too early for you." He muttered nonsense. That night I wrote in my diary: *It's always risky to go out on a limb and predict, but if that washer doesn't die, somebody is going to. All because of washday, blue Monday.*

The next morning I retrieved my worn out shoes from the back porch, found the scissors and cut new cardboard insoles, just like I had done for several weeks. I hung around the post office resembling someone on the Wanted posters. I waited for a letter and money from Daddy, but walked away empty handed. Words, in liquid form, came from my eyes. The trees began chasing me. The sun was too bright. My hopes vanished.

On Friday, as I mulled a new idea, the post office visit made my day. I zipped the envelope open. A twenty-dollar bill floated to the floor. Reading the few scribbled words caused joy that lasted sixty seconds. HELLO TO MY BEAUTIFUL DAUGHTERS. I'M DOING FINE. I MISS YOU AND HOPE YOU ARE OKAY. MAYBE I CAN COME TO SEE YOU NEXT SPRING. LOVE YOU, DADDY. "Short and sweet! Hope *you* are happy," I said out loud.

I showed the letter and money to Aunt Margaret. "Sure is nice that Sid could read my mind. The horse has been out of food for two days. The chickens haven't eaten for four days."

It was Ailene's turn to get new shoes, but she would have to cram her feet into the old ones for a little longer. I laced up my Cat's Paw half soles. "I love the smell of new leather. Aunt Margaret, my 'scat cat' you tried to chase away is famous. Paws' picture is on the bottom of lots of shoes. Famous cat!"

Born to Learn

*A*ilene is the baby of the family. I'm a middle child in the birth order, between the crown princess and snookems. Middle children are nice people, thinking people. My language teacher insisted on correct pronunciation and inflections. I made my share of mistakes, but I drilled my little sis on the proper use of words. I couldn't tolerate "ain't," "seen" for "saw," "done" for "did." She thought I was being a smarty pants, but I told her that someday she would thank me.

She also thanked me for suggesting a perfect place of solitude. Underneath a stand of oak trees behind the house the grass was head high and green as an Irish dream. We stamped the thick grass flat and rolled around on it long enough to create a four-walled house that became a quiet cathedral. Our blue jeans quickly soaked with morning dew. We shared our secret place with ants and a few buggy critters. Mocking birds generally minded their own business, but their territorial nature kept them from a peaceful existence. They attacked other birds, and became their deadliest enemy. Because they're not highly intelligent, they attack their own reflection. Right before our eyes, a shining hubcap resulted in a dead mockingbird.

Lying on our backs, we watched continents of clouds pass along the ceiling of our room. Looking for shapes in clouds, two questions popped into my head: Why do so many clouds create an image of Daddy? And why, if clouds are just water vapor, do they have such carved edges? I learned that what I saw was cumulus clouds, a bubble of rising, turbulent, moist air. The vapor condenses into a visible cloud when the bubble of moist air reaches a higher, colder level. The thermal is cooled to the temperature of the surrounding air, the whole thing gets fuzzy and, as Aunt Margaret says, "It peters out." Then it resembles Daddy again, and you're on to the next cloud.

Ailene sat on a log, the long eyelashes drawing shadows over her cheeks, her upper lip strained. "I still miss Mom. What would she want us to do?"

"Oh, I don't know. Guess I've got plenty of time to decide."

What do you want to be when you get big?"

I thought for a minute. Evening whippoorwills provided an answer. " I bubble with dreams. I want to live a thousand years. If I could enjoy the music that throbs in my soul, then I could finish my dreaming. I think Mom wants our dreams to come true. She wants us to follow our heart."

Summer brought the same dumb chores we had tackled last year. After spending hours picking bushels of green beans, we spent hours stringing, breaking, washing and stuffing them into the sterilized Mason jars. This year brought a bright spot along with all the work. Aunt Margaret said, "Girls, go get some cinder blocks and build a fire pit." I remembered watching Uncle Gil start the fire last year so I knew just what to do. My construction job looked quite praiseworthy. The pleased look on Aunt Margaret's face led me to believe that she thought the same, but she was careful to hold back a compliment. She gave the next set of orders. "Now, get lots of wood from the shed, get rainwater out of the barrel, and fill that wash tub. Put the jars of beans in the tub. Put towels around them so they won't break. Here." She placed a box of wood matches in my hand, and headed for the two-holer.

I stared at the box for a second or two. *She really trusts me. She handed me a whole box of matches. I've always wondered how it would feel to become a firebug.* Ailene was getting pretty good at reading my mind. "Don't get any ideas, big sis. You'll really get licked if you light anything except the paper and wood."

"How dare you think I could do anything wrong?" I reached into the tub and splashed a handful of water on her. She retaliated. Soon we were having a lot of fun. Until Aunt Margaret noticed. I saw the poplar switch before I saw her. Then I felt it. Ten lashes.

I finished crying, lit a match and tossed it in the fire pit. Within minutes the oak and wild plum wood crackled. The ambers spread out into shades of violet and tangerine. For three hours we stoked the wood fire and watched the beans become a faded green color. After the jars cooled, we carried them to the fruit cellar, placed them in neat rows next to sacks of potatoes and carrots, and hurried into the shady front yard to play paper dolls.

That summer it rained for several days. Muddy water rolled down the mountain and into Paint Creek. The next week as the sun began to set through a dozen willow trees, I realized that we had sat near the river bank for two hours watching objects float by: pine crates, banana boxes from Canterbury store, a sawhorse, twenty feet of garden hose, and several plastic plates. I wondered who wore the brown leather boots that floated past. I found a perfectly fine pair of dancing shoes and retrieved them with a stick.

When I got home I cleaned the mud with perfectly fine rainwater and wore them on opening night; the night I became Doris Day, and later, Debbie Reynolds, my favorite actress. The street light near our house on the hill shined as bright as Broadway. A tin cup became my microphone. Our stage, a discarded wooden truck bed, was enhanced by roaring applaud to Ailene's announcement, "Ladies and Gentlemen, please welcome the famous Patty." I sang for the whole world to hear. For me that was a dozen square miles and 2,000 people. My sister and I made wonderful music together. Our desire for music and education intensified.

After only ninety-four days of summer, another school year began. Teachers have a tremendous responsibility. They're the decisive element in the classroom. Their personal touch sets the daily mood. My third grade teacher, a first cousin, caused a tornado in my life. She knew that the daily chores allowed very little time for play and that recess was the highlight of my day.

Rain had soaked the huge pile of sand near a storage area that housed landscape equipment. "This sand is soggy, perfect for making castles." I told a classmate. Plastic cups, sardine cans and a rusty lunch pail became houses, garages and tall buildings. Creating the stunning artistry was foremost in my mind.

"Hey, the bell is ringing," my friend said.

"Oh, I hear it. It always rings twice. Let's make just one more."

We dashed into the classroom filled with students sitting quietly in their seats. The teacher's face was grim. She waved a ruler through the air. "Patty, I've told you a hundred times that you can't be your own boss and stay on the playground until you're ready to come to class." Beads of sweat popped out on her forehead as she whipped my dirty hand with the ruler. "Maybe *this* will teach you a lesson."

I felt disappointed, desperate, and wanted to become invisible. I was in trouble and couldn't have recess for a year, well, actually for two days. I sat at my desk and stared out the window. I remembered that Mom said you shouldn't hate people. You can prefer to dislike their behavior. Forget that! I wondered where the peace and joy was, the joy I saw in the other students my age. The duplicate in the mirror confirmed my lack of satisfaction. I longed for Miss Akers, an instrument of inspiration instead of torture, who brought more joy than misery.

A month later I found a note in my sock drawer. It read: I'M BEGINNING TO HATE SCHOOL! IT'S JUST NOT FAIR THAT I GOT SPANKED AND MY FRIEND ESCAPED PUNISHMENT. LIFE IS LIKE A SICKENING CARNIVAL RIDE. BUT I GUESS YOU HAVE TO HANG ON TILL IT'S OVER.

Years later my sister-in-law, Evon Aliff, and I discussed third grade. "Do you remember who your friend was?" I confessed that I had forgotten.

She smiled. "I always wondered why you were spanked and I was spared."

Teachers are the gateway to our future. They can humiliate or humor, hurt or heal. Their response decides whether a crisis will be escalated and a child humanized or dehumanized. They possess a tremendous power to make a child's life miserable or joyous. Life would have been more pleasant if teachers had sensed my inner feelings.

In third grade I suffered from distressing humility. The educational system called it the "Palmer Writing Method." I called it "the devil's torturing device" for children who weren't brought into the world with fingers that accurately formed "round and round circles, and push-pull marks" on the lined page.

My teacher, a thin, tall old maid (probably twenty-five) sailed up and down the row of seats. She scared the daylights out of me. Her rubber heels prevented guessing when she would peer over my head to see if I rolled my right forearm and held the pencil just so. It didn't matter to me if I made perfect circles and push-pulls without a line misplaced. But a good word regarding my performance of the unusual ritual was of utmost importance.

In spite of the fact that I cried into my pillow at night when I didn't receive that meager assurance, I must admit that something resulted from the bitter fear of failure and the desire to die from it. During my school days I developed commendable handwriting skills. I loved the smoothness of white lined paper and the smell of wood shavings that radiated from the sharpener. For as long as I can remember, Aunt Margaret talked about my undignified walk. If my pencil lead broke, I became agitated. I was forced to write with the lead crunched between two fingers. I refused to walk across the room to the sharpener.

Most of the students had two parents and a normal family. I

yearned to be normal, and imagined that my art teacher detested me because I lived with an elderly aunt, uncle and grandmother. She had pineapple blond hair that spiked into a grave personality. She took a quick look at my bird sketches, slashed red marks over the page, and in her whiny, nasal voice, the whole class heard, "This is not long enough. This is too long. Try again. And do a better job this time."

"But I don't have time to get it right."

She said, "The person who is good at making excuses is seldom talented for anything else." My love for art quickly diminished. I realized that some people were not tested at all and some were tested all the time.

Let me tell you about Valentine's Day. We decorated the classroom windows with cardboard hearts and cupids. The teacher placed cookies on lace napkins and cups of Kool-Aid at each desk. She opened the big valentine box, called out names, and students went up front to gather their treasures.

"Didn't I get anything?" I asked.

"Sorry, maybe your name wasn't on the list," Miss Holmes replied. Patty had no treasures because the kids must have remembered that last year, Patty had no cards to send.

That night I told Ailene, "I'm bone-weary of being embarrassed in school, being stuck in a nightmare, unable to wake up."

In health class I was not above a creative stretching of the truth to get out of uncomfortable situations. The teacher asked what we had for breakfast that morning. Embarrassed about having the usual bowl of oatmeal, I made up a list of luxurious foods, a breakfast suitable for rich kids. "I had the basic six: toast, eggs, sausage, bacon, orange juice and a tall glass of milk," I said.

At recess, sitting on the bleachers watching the band practice, my desire to participate was so great that when the brass horns wagged from side to side and the symbols crashed, my heart banged my chest. I became the bandleader, standing tall and commanding perfection. They played a song that reminded me of a book I saw in the library, "Much Ado About Nothing." I decided I wouldn't read that book. You can't do anything with nothing.

Summer went to sleep and the autumn air began to bite, like the taste of cider going hard. On Halloween night, I "borrowed" Uncle Gil's big shirt, used makeup and coal on my face, and became a hobo. In a disguise, I could forget myself and pretend I was someone else. I visited all the fun booths because the workers gave me extra treats from the fishpond.

In November a guest speaker came to our class to speak about the first Thanksgiving. She had a kind, well-scrubbed face, and seemed illuminated by a mystical serenity. At times, she folded her smooth hands in front of the lectern. She talked, in a direct voice, about the pilgrims' Christian roots and their expressions of faith. "Those early settlers thanked God. Our coins proclaim, 'In God We Trust.' The Pledge of Allegiance declares that we are 'One nation, under God.' The Declaration of Independence asserts that 'We are endowed by the Creator' with certain unalienable rights, and that the oath of office for the presidency ends with the phrase, 'So help me God.' Truth prevails."

I decided that if truth prevails, I should peal away the layers of past regrets and change my desperate anxiety. The word "impossible" took on a new meaning. Every time I heard the word it bothered me. It began to sound absolutely wrong. I launched a battle against the word, and determined to study with every ounce of my being. Math, my most difficult subject, took on a new meaning. That year, my friend, Jimmy, and I won most of the spelling bees. In gym class, country music blared from the overhead speakers. Instead of feeling that I was a square peg that didn't fit, I grabbed a partner. "Hold on, Jimmy. You're in for a new education."

He half-smiled, backed away and raised both arms, palms outward. "Uh, I never did this." I pulled him to the center of the dance floor. The teacher announced various moves. At first, Jimmy was poker-faced. By the end of the Virginia reel, he displayed a sunny glow that harmonized with the golden hair. I went home with my head still twirling. The tunes kept me going all week.

I participated in science projects. My teacher said that planets run around and around in circles and we say they're orbiting. People that do the same thing are called crazy. I learned that you get positive reaction from humor.

Fall flowers gave way to ice crystals. Snowflakes fell for many days, perfect preparation for winter fun, narrow escapes and challenges from neighborhood boys. The day Edward Helm attempted sliding down a steep gravel road near the Church of God he slid under a passing car, and slammed into the building. Edward was out cold. The driver panicked. Kids gathered around. The evening prayer group asked for healing. Edward suffered a concussion, but a short time later he was back on the slope, tempting fate. If Edward survived, I could too. The Thompson boys' Radio Flyer always brought me through.

Like the "Jack and Jill" story, I went, and Ailene came tumbling after. She took my dare to attempt something new. "Ride down the steep part of the mountain, but curve to the left when you get near the end." She poised the sled on her right side and gave a run. Her belly met the sled and the shining runners took off. Her first mistake was taking the dare. The second one was she turned right and smashed into the fence. The crash forced snow upward and reminded me of Old Faithful.

I rushed to her side, collected the bundle of snow pants, heavy coat and petite blond girl into my arms. Tears surged. "Oh, my arm hurts. Why did you ask me to do that? It's all your fault." Her voice sank into a whisper, a defeated sob. I held her for a long moment and sheltered her face from the wind. Guilt engulfed me. "I'm sorry, sweetie. You'll be okay. I promise."

Dr. Hitchman restored the arm that was fractured in two places. I went to Canterbury's store, bought some soul-restoring chocolate doughnuts, gave her first choice, along with a warning. "I hope you won't have any more mishaps. At least until summer."

Winter lasted forever, but finally a clump of tulips bloomed through the edge of a dwindling snow bank. New grass stretched green face through the brown sod. Tender leaves danced upon the trees to the energy of the wind. Coats gave way to sweaters; gloves joined rubber galoshes in the closet.

Physical Education included softball. The teacher chose two of the biggest guys to be team captain, who chose himself to be pitcher. One by one team members were chosen. I often dreamed that the first name called would be "Patty!" Never happened. Some of the fifth grade girls went into spasmodic flinching fits when a ball was thrown their way. They were real sissies, but sissies were chosen for the team. I wasn't popular. My name was usually mentioned last. On Friday, the last game of the season the teacher said, "We can't start the game till someone chooses Patty."

My friend Leona was friendly, wore cute clothes, a lovely smile that showed her perfect white teeth. One fateful spring day I stepped up to home plate. The pitcher put the ball in the perfect spot. I hit a fly ball and headed for first. Leona stood next in line. She forgot about my terrible habit of slinging the bat. Well, you guessed it. The bat met with Leona's mouth. She screamed and fell to the ground. The teacher scurried for ice and a wet towel. Leona wiped her face. "I guess I'm okay." She opened her hand and showed a front tooth.

I bit a thumbnail. My hands shook. I wanted to die. "I'm really sorry." That night I dreamed the tooth grew back in place. None of that dream stuff happened. I told Ailene, "Most childhood dreams can no more come true than cows can oink."

The next morning Leona was leaning against my locker. She hugged me and said, "Don't worry Patty. You didn't mean to hurt me." I decided that perhaps life does have something to offer.

May Day was special because each grade competed for the grand prize, the most colorful, best organized May Pole dance.

Students held onto a crepe paper streamer that dangled from the flower-wreathed flagpole. The guys formed a small circle. The girls circled around them. As we swayed, square dance style, to the fast country music, we intertwined the streamers wrapping them around the pole.

I envied the girls whose pastel dresses with "broom stick" skirts showed frilly petticoats as they danced. I needed a tall, pulled-together look, a fresh, natural look, maybe a flirty, flared skirt, but my crisp Sunday-best feed sack skirt displayed purple and pale yellow flowers. The boys wore white shirts.

Making and giving May baskets was an annual rite of spring. We spent hours decorating a shoebox with curly strips of crepe paper. At dusk Ailene sneaked up to Pearl's house, knocked on the door, placed the box on the narrow step and joined me behind the bushes. We waited to see what would happen.

Pearl opened the door and saw the box filled with Aunt Margaret's homemade oatmeal cookies. "Goodness sakes," she yelled. Feeling obligated to search the dark yard to find the conspirators, she peeped behind the lilac bush and recognized Ailene's golden hair. Reaching both hands into the air, she hunched her heavy torso in a downward position and said, "Come here, you sweet babies. Gimme a big squeeze. You sure brighten up the world of des ole lady."

We became acquainted with the joy of sharing, and the sweet response from that friendly gesture changed my feelings in a positive way. Something inside me seemed to say, "Just hang on. I'm going to do new things in your life, Patty. Important things."

Realizing that living in the past takes precious time away from the present, I resolved that next year would be better, and my attitude would be lighter. When Aunt Margaret helped me study for a test, my answers added a slight spark in her dull life. She thought my mind had taken a permanent vacation.

Q: What is the spinal column?

A: A long bunch of bones. The head sits on the top, and you sit on the bottom.

Q: What is the Alimentary Canal and how does blood flow?

A: Blood circulates through the body by flowing down one leg and up the other.

Q: What is the main cause of dust?

A: Janitors.

Aunt Margaret poured a cup of hot water, reached across the table to select an herbal tea bag, and started reading a library book I brought home. The delicious aroma, genteel and comforting, seemed a perfect way to spend an evening. "What is a census taker?" she asked.

"It's a man who goes from house to house increasing the population. I got an A on my essay. Aren't you proud of me?"

She grinned, closed the book, and threw the paper on the table. "Let's call it a night."

At school the next day I wrote and read an essay titled: GIRLS ARE BETTER THAN BOYS. Girls don't pick their noses. Girls chew with their mouths shut. Girls don't smell bad. Girls don't let stinkers as much as boys.

The view of Pax Elementary School was a straight line from our house, but fifteen minutes away. The town was located in the valley below. Each day two little girls rushed down one hill and up the other. We took the eighty-eight concrete steps two at a time.

I opened the classroom door with a whoosh. Gasping for air, I stumbled into the room. I hated being late. Everyone stared at me. "So, Patty," Mrs. Hasbrook said, "You decided to come to class after all." She knew why I was late. The chores took too long.

I took my seat and mumbled, "Um—I—I– I mean—I got lost. Then I got wet under the drinking fountain." I didn't mention that the other reason was going to the bathroom and becoming trapped in my pants by a faulty zipper.

"I'll overlook tardiness this time. I've selected a part for you in the operetta." She read the appropriately selected cutting words, "I'm so sorry I was tardy, but the clock was slow. If you will forgive me teacher, I will love you so." The class laughed. I hung my head. Refusal meant a failing grade.

The kids teased me about the word *love*. "The teacher in the play is my first cousin," I said. "I'm supposed to love my cousin. Don't you agree?"

My first memory of stage fright was the day I tried to recite a poem. My mouth opened and my throat constricted. The kids hooted and one boy yelled in a singsong voice, "Patty's a chicken head." I finished the five-line poem in tears. As I rushed to the bathroom to throw up I thought *I'd never, ever, do that again.*

On the way home from school I stopped at the post office. The postmaster shoved a blue envelope through the bronze mail slot. "Here, Patty. Looks like your dad is still alive." Even though the address didn't include my name, Daddy's handwriting begged for my attention. Ripping the envelope gave pleasure I hadn't felt in weeks. Reading the few lines that didn't indicate a visit ripped my heart for the umpteenth time. A twenty-dollar bill prompted visions of a pair of brown penny loafers from Canterbury's store. No more cutting cardboard insoles!

Resisting the temptation to shove the twenty in my jeans pocket, I handed the envelope to Aunt Margaret. "Nice," she said. "How'd he know we needed feed for the horse?"

"Feed for the horse? No way. I need *shoes*."

"So we all need things."

"I'm barefoot. My dad sent that money to Ailene and me."

"Is your name on it? Don't I get any pay for putting up with you? Huh? Is your name on the bill?"

I shrugged my shoulders and leaned on one hip. "Well, no, but –"

"Don't sass. If the horse doesn't eat, the field doesn't get plowed. If the field doesn't –"

"I know the rest. Shut up, Margaret!"

"That's it, you twerp. You sassy twerp." She reached for the fly swat.

I flew out the door. "Darn you all to –. I hate you." The peach tree, with heavy leaves and a limb that slanted into a seat, was a perfect spot to hide until suppertime.

As I cleared the table Aunt Margaret said, "Now you hurry to Canterbury's and have them deliver horse feed. Here's the twenty."

"*My* twenty," I said under my breath. I pressed the bill into neat folds and put it into my blouse pocket. During the one-mile trip, I muttered a few words that my Sunday school teacher wouldn't appreciate. "Daddy, if you only knew what my life is like. Sometimes I hate the world. Sometimes I hate you too." The words brought awareness that my heart was growing stone cold. I kept reaching into my pocket to feel the touch of money that soon would be gone.

Mr. Canterbury was putting the CLOSED sign on the door. "Ooh. I got here just in time," I said. "Aunt Margaret wants horse food delivered early tomorrow morning. Here's the—oh no. The money was right here in my pocket. Now it's gone." My body began to shake as tears clouded my vision.

"That's okay. I'll deliver the order and charge it to your uncle Gil."

"It's NOT okay. Nothing's okay. I can't go home. I can't face Aunt Margaret. Not this time."

Mr. Canterbury frowned, patted my head. "Honey, it's not the end of the world. I usually tell you to keep looking up, but on your way home, follow the same route and keep looking down. You'll find the money, especially if it was folded."

"I wish it were the end of the world," I muttered as I slammed the door.

When I got home the radio blasted a mid-week sermon from a singsong preacher. *I don't want to hear about how much God loves me, cause I know he doesn't. If he did he wouldn't let awful things happen to me.* "Hello dear," Aunt Margaret greeted me. After hearing the tale of woe she said, "I've lost things too. It's not the end of the world."

One Friday morning, on our way to Aunt Hannah's house, we had made our way through the railroad track shortcut, and now we had to traipse across a slippery log that extended over Paint Creek. Ailene dawdled behind. "Hurry, slowpoke."

"Look, Patty," she yelled. "Here comes a black horse. Running toward us!"

Three more giant brown horses rumbled across the meadow and headed in our direction. "Quick. Climb the apple tree," I shouted. Climbing trees, and racing to the top, was our favorite creative entertainment. Five limbs and we were half way up the tree.

The animals grazed for a few minutes. A train whistle blew and they went for greener pastures. I gave a long sigh of relief, jumped from the tree and landed in a sand pile. But Ailene wasn't so lucky. She and the dead limb she was standing on came tumbling to the ground. She landed in a fresh cow pie and skidded into a wire fence. She hissed. Tears were streaming down her face. I helped her get to your feet. "Are you scared half to death or really injured?" She didn't answer. "Just hold on. We're almost to Aunt Hannah's."

Aunt Hannah's doors were locked. "Let's wade through the river and wash you off, stinky."

"Don't call me stinky. I couldn't help it."

During the long walk home, without taking the shortcut where the horses had headed, Ailene's right arm dangled and pained with each step. Aunt Margaret sputtered about the cost, but took her to see Dr. Hitchman. "A sprain is worse than a break," he said. "Aspirin should help."

After three days of constant pain, Uncle Gil drove Ailene to the Beckley Hospital. He complained for thirty miles about spending extra gas money. The doctor set the arm, applied a cast and a white muslin sling. The pain continued and a week later another X-ray revealed that the arm had been broken previously, and set crooked. The specialist re-broke the arm and applied a new cast. Within a few weeks Ailene's face was alight with anticipation. "Look, I can hold an apple and it doesn't hurt."

One week before Christmas I met Dr. Hitchman on my way to the post office to get three-cent stamps. "Is my favorite blond girl all right now?" he asked. *Wish I had blond hair. Maybe I'd get more attention.* I said Ailene was doing fine. "Give this to her for being a good patient." (He gave all the children a quarter at Christmas time.) "Did I give you a quarter yet?"

I glanced across the narrow street. His office roof became a Snickers chocolate coating. The twinkling lights became caramel-covered peanuts. My mouth was moist with the thoughts. "Yes, you did," I said as the caramel and chocolate melted.

"Here, have another one. It won't break me." I wouldn't have been happier if he had handed me the gold watch chain that glistened from his plaid vest pocket.

I buttoned my haughty green hand-me-down coat and ran to the store. "I need one loaf of Sunbeam bread, Mr. Canterbury. I'm in a real hurry today." I tossed ten cents on the counter. "Skaters are gliding across frozen Paint Creek into their own world. It's a world of delight."

My friend Illia, a twelve-year-old orphan from Russia, was an excellent skater who had been adopted by an American couple. She said, "In Russia, we learn to skate at the age of three. It's never too late for you to learn." Illia wore bright red leggings, a white hat and matching mittens, both decorated with pointy evergreen trees. A green sweater with sparkles and snowmen made a cheery scene. She was comfortable on the white skates, but the sharp, glistening blades taunted me. Skating has drama, excitement and surprise.

Illia's tight ponytail bobbed as she skated with a vengeance. I held my breath as she displayed confidence and prepared for a jump. It broke my heart to see her hit a rut and fall apart on the ice. Red-faced skaters came to investigate. I crushed the soft bread while running to assist. "I hope you're not hurt. I have just a few minutes to watch." Illia reached for my hand, flashed a big smile and within a short time began whirling with precision. She spiraled across the ice and turned into a beaming ballerina. I endorsed the troublesome task of following the preacher's advice. "Thou shall not covet. Don't be envious of others." I wanted a taste of Illia's skill. I didn't have skates, but I encouraged my friend. "Always keep your dream alive. You'll go far someday."

I learned to listen very carefully when an intimate voice within me suggests something I may not understand at the time. Perhaps intuition was my protective shield. One night as we went to bed I told Ailene, "I'm going to move our bed away from the wall. That heavy picture hanging over our head could fall and break your arm again." A few hours later the picture crashed to the floor. Grandma snored till breakfast time.

Grandma loved sugar-cinnamon Cheerios, and hot biscuits with lots of fresh golden-rod yellow butter supplied by Aunt Hannah. I refused to destroy the flower petal imprint in the center of the molded circle, so I scooped the edge. At every meal Grandma had a big glass of rich milk. I grumbled, "After toting the gallon jugs three miles, Aunt Margaret limits us to one-half cup on cereal. Unfair!" Sometimes resentment and the temptation to steal from her supply overpowered me. Stealing was against the rules.

I discovered an antidote for guilt feelings. Volunteering. Someone had to cut meat into bite-size pieces so Grandma wouldn't choke. She needed help bathing, putting on the dark cotton stockings and button shoes. Probably soon she would need diapers. I didn't plan to feel *that* guilty. At mealtime, I observed Grandma's sour facial expressions across my Shredded Wheat and from behind my Nancy Drew. Grandma's face had forgotten what happiness meant. I couldn't figure out why she suffered from shrinking heart syndrome. Why she was so cynical. Why she wasn't wired for joy and expressing affection. Grandma gave only one clue that she cared. After a thrashing she doled out a stick of Teaberry gum. The day I was nine, she shared two pieces of her gum.

Most of the soap and cereal companies included gifts in their packaged products. The Quaker Oats Company initiated a new marketing plan. We had accumulated five white cereal bowls. I opened the box that completed the set. The bowl slid out of my hand, crashed to the floor, and splattered into tiny pieces. The smashing sound woke Grandma from her nap.

"Look what you did. Why are you so clumsy?" Aunt Margaret yelled. She rushed to the back porch to get a weapon she had cut from the orchard that morning. I bit a thumbnail until it bled, and thought of Daddy who was never unkind. He had been gone six months. *Why doesn't he realize that I need him this very minute?* "I'll teach you to be careful," Aunt Margaret said as she lashed my legs.

"Please don't switch me!" I begged. "I'm sorry. I didn't mean to drop the dish. I'll eat lots of oats so we can get another one." As she thrashed with the keen tree branch, my bare feet danced around in the glass. I slipped, fell on the kitchen floor and struggled to pull myself up. "Are you trying to kill me?" I screamed.

Ailene's outcry caused Grandma to yell, "Stop that." My aunt ignored her demands, and continued to beat my legs and back for at least an hour, or so it seemed. The protective role reversed that day. Ailene slung the oatmeal box, and its contents projected toward Aunt Margaret's feet, causing her to stumble.

Ailene helped me hobble through the back door. "Hurry. Aunt Margaret is allergic to hay and she won't come to the barn." She opened the squeaky door and I collapsed onto a wooden barrel.

"Where are you going with that pitchfork?" I asked. She pierced the red flannel horse blanket that was hanging on the wall and pulled it down from the hook. She covered a bale of hay, and ordered me to rest. My eyes barely focused. My feet were swollen. Like a nurse in an emergency room, she alternated wiping my tears and picking glass out of my bloody feet.

She found an old blue sheet handing on a nail, (not exactly sterile) ripped it into strips, and bandaged both feet. "There. You'll feel better in no time," she said. I tried to force a smile, but I was afraid I might give myself a brain hemorrhage. I felt cursed. Happy birthday to me.

The next day I hobbled outside. Our pet pig Sally Jo grunted and pranced in the mud. I pulled up a rusty metal chair and started scratching her back with a stick. I remembered the day I couldn't resist the challenge of walking across the one-inch wood fence that surrounded the pen. Ailene had continually warned, "You're gonna fall some day."

"Nah, not me. I've done this a hundred times with great success." The words were barely out of my mouth when I slid into an extreme amount of mud and other gross stuff that I don't want to talk about. Today, I sat and told Sally Jo about the perils of childhood. Just as sure as football games last sixty minutes and each team uses eleven players at a time, I operated under some supernatural force that must have decided years ago to teach me a lesson. How else could I explain the misadventures? I usually had plenty of explaining to do. I couldn't get away with diddlysquat where Aunt Margaret was concerned.

My teacher asked Ailene why I wasn't in school. "Aunt Margaret told me to tell you that Patty sprained her ankle."

I could hardly wait for summer, to shed my shoes and run over the hills barefoot. But with the delight of feeling new grass between my toes came the pain of rusty nails piercing my feet. Once or twice each summer, Aunt Margaret crushed a handful of peach leaves, added salt, and administered her foolproof remedy.

I had my own remedy for boredom. Paint Creek was down the hill, on the other side of town. "Ailene, we swore to Aunt Margaret that we would stay away from the fast-moving creek, but let's put on an extra pair of shorts so we can have some fun."

"We'll get whipped for staying too long anyway," she reasoned. The shady, worn path full of mystery stories was so slanted that we clung to the shrubs to avoid tumbling into the water. We looked for treasures, but found cigarette butts and beer bottles, hints of forbidden activities. "Let's peel off a layer and take a dip," she said after removing a pair of shorts and handing them on a tree branch. "The mush between my toes is quite enjoyable, and guess what, Patty, dear. This is a great place for make-believe castles. Let's cover the stumps and pretend they're chairs and sofas." We believed in God because no one but nature could create such thick, luxurious green moss.

The next day I headed out to do Saturday morning errands. My honey-beige cat climbed on my shoulders. Flood waters overwhelmed Paint Creek. After all, ten minutes shouldn't upset the whole day so I perched on a rock and became mesmerized with the various objects floating past. Honey became mesmerized with a mouse and wound up high in a tree that hung over the creek. "Here Kitty, Kitty. C'mon Honey." I yelled. *I'm in deep trouble. I can't get the cat. I can't go home without him. Asking for help is out of the question because the whole town will know about it, including Aunt Margaret. I shouldn't be here anyway. I've got tons of work to do.*

Daddy would have called it Lady Luck, but I thought a divine plan was carried out that morning. Charlie, the smiling post office worker, ambled along the riverbank. Seeing my dilemma, he reached in his lunch sack, brought out a ring of bologna and waved it in the air. "Come here, Kitty," he called. Honey straddled the limb and eased down the tree. I grabbed his tail as he devoured the treat. Charlie grinned and said, "Have a great day. Don't tell Aunt Margaret. She'll give you another beating."

When we got home, Honey seethed in a mewing puddle of fur at the back door. He looked tired yet dignified, in that cat sort of way. Cat lovers know the look.

THE "GOOD OLD DAYS" of living in a house without running water or indoor plumbing were not good. Twice daily, we carried the water supply one-fourth mile. Mrs. Thompson's house was filled with interesting things to do. She encouraged us to have fun. The day we lost track of time, Ailene lifted the lowest strand of barbed wire and I scooted the water buckets under, then myself. I held the wire. She bent down. I yelled, "Hurry. Here comes Aunt Margaret carrying a long stick." Ailene moved too quickly this time. "Oh no. Part of your leg is left hanging on the fence." Aunt Margaret activated the switch, my sister bled and cried. I screamed, hoping Mrs. Thompson would hear. Aunt Margaret whipped both of us all the way home.

I ran to the orchard, got some peach leaves and scrunched them in a dish. I added several spoons of salt, and applied the "medicine" to the 8-inch jagged wound. An old washcloth became a make shift bandage. I handed Ailene a glass of iced tea with lots of sugar and gave her the cross-my-heart-and-hope to die whopper of a promise. "Someday this part of life will be over and you'll be happy again," I said.

"Is that happenable?" she asked.

"Sure, honey. Someday." The scar remained, but summer refused to last. The winter season brought up to fifteen inches of snow, and lots of extra work. After heating the water in a dented washtub, the old Maytag washer churned out the weekly laundry.

We shoveled a path to the clothesline. Before I could get the two large baskets of wet clothes hung, they froze board hard. I knew the rules: Clothing with holes, and underpants, were modestly strung between the shirts, hidden from view. Sheets were to be thrown over the line, but fastened by the edges. Socks must be hung in a group, by the toes. Towels marched along after washcloths. You must hang dungarees by the waist.

The unfortunate person who collected the stiffened items had to suffer from frozen hands. Clothespins had to be yanked from unyielding fabric. If the wind didn't dry them, I brought them in to the dining room, "stood" the slacks on the floor, and told Aunt Margaret, "We've got company." She didn't think my actions were funny. On Saturday we finished the job by washing sweaters by hand. The smell of wet wool saturated the house.

Thanksgiving Day should have meant turkey with drumsticks as big as my head, excellent food devoid of turnips, poke greens, cabbage, and squash. Something deep inside yearned for pumpkin pie and all the other favorites. I knew that today wasn't a normal day, but I might jinx the job if I came right out and asked about my suspicions, so I looked for the telltale clues. If Aunt Margaret fixed enough breakfast to last until suppertime. Uncle Gil went to the bathroom often. If he had only one cup of coffee it meant certain doom for our fatheaded pig. My thoughts were confirmed by Uncle Gil's announcement, "Get ready for the town's Thanksgiving Day hog killin.' " Horrible shock waves tore through my soul and ripped through my skin. Porko didn't know that yesterday he devoured his last meal.

For the next hour, several pigs squealed and gave their last grunt. The caustic sound echoed from the south, then the same morbid answer screeched from east and west. Helpers met at Uncle Charlie's house at the bottom of the hill. I sat in the rocker with a pillow over my ears. Aunt Margaret knew the procedure. "Uncle Gil stands about eight feet away, points his Remington and pulls the trigger. The men know just what to do." With curious uncertainty I strolled down the hill to investigate. Sure enough, Porko had sunk into eternity. Hog heaven.

With a hunting knife, Uncle Charlie, the throat-slitter, did his job. I let out a groaning sound. "Isn't it enough that you shot him? Why do you have to stab him too?" They tied a rope around the front feet and hung the limp body on a two-by-four scaffold. *I guess they wanted him to get some air.* The butcher knife glistened in the sun and the organs oozed as another opening split the torso like lightning in a storm.

A roaring fire heated water in the metal rain barrel. Four men hoisted the poor pig into the boiling water, and let him soak a few minutes. *I knew all along that pigs were messy.* With sharp knives, they scraped the stubby black hair, doused Porko into the boiling water and scraped some more. After baptizing him six times they cut him into sections and tossed him into round enamel pans.

Try walking into the kitchen and seeing hog brains in a stainless steel pan, and the feet saturated with vinegar. Aunt Margaret said, "Brains 'n' eggs make you smart, but sausage tastes better, so get that grinder going. That's your job." I held my nose in one hand and my retching stomach in the other. Aunt Margaret mixed a standard formula of borax, salt, and other spices for the sausage.

"Yesterday I loved sausage patties, but not any more. I'll *never* eat again."

Every ounce of Porko was used for something. Souse meat was a conglomeration of meat from heads, feet, and other animal parts that were boiled to a thick, soft mush, heavily spiced, and congealed into a loaf that could be sliced later. The men spiced up the salt for curing bacon and hams. We shoved pans of fat in the oven to render for cooking and frying. The house reeked. We saved some of the fat for making soap.

The liver, the official food of death, stained the sink a deep red. The bloody mess looked like an autopsy from last week's highway wreck. Aunt Margaret fried the organ to the consistency of shoe leather. The cover-up-the-smell-with-onions dish reminded me of an inflated tire. To top the meal, she boiled okra as a side dish, the "snot food" from the deep sea.

Next, they ground bologna from ears, snouts and lips or any unspecified section of the poor beast. Your taste buds must be sweating so I'll mention Uncle Gil's favorite, "hog head" cheese that resembled stained glass windows, and smelled the same as last week's chicken skins.

I opened the screen door to toss out Porko's blood, and hundreds of ants came marching Army-style toward the sink. "I thought you guys died in the winter. Where are you headed? Don't you smell that? You're crazy to come in here if you don't *have* to. The smell is horrible." I carefully stepped across the parade.

"What's this?" Ailene asked.

"I dunno. Reminds me of a balloon."

Aunt Margaret gave a deep belly laugh. "I know what it is. When I was a kid we used the bladder for a balloon. I'll show you girls something you've never seen before." She rinsed the organ several times and touched it to her lips.

"You're not going to—" Ailene gagged. I laughed. Aunt Margaret inflated the strongest, biggest balloon I've ever seen. She tied a string around the top and tossed it to Ailene.

"Best fun we've had all week," I admitted.

Looking back, I realize that eating fried eggs, a plate of sausage, biscuits made with lard and soaked in red-eye gravy killed those people of the "olden days." Sure enough they died at ninety-five.

It must have been ninety-five degrees the day my eight-year-old sister and I sat under the fruit trees and tossed yellow Delicious apple cores into the nearby chicken coop. A Rhode Island Red rooster quickly devoured each morsel. "It's not fair," Ailene said. "The tiny ones never get to eat. Why do they quarrel over their food?" We named all the chickens, but couldn't agree on a name for the largest rooster in the group, so she called him Peter Arnell Popeye Guy, but I preferred Big Red.

Big Red crowed and thrashed, and intended to use my legs for a pecking post. My revenge was poking sticks through the wire fence that rattled each time he retaliated. I suppose my constant teasing forced a decision to keep him fenced. He seemed to enjoy the fun and games. I kept him occupied while Ailene threw apples in the direction of the smaller chickens.

One day Big Red found a way to escape. I was sweeping the sidewalk and, without warning, he charged out of the chicken coop with the full-fledged bass and tenor of his great range. Surging from behind, he flapped his wings and jumped several inches off the ground. He raised first one leg then the other, discharged vicious squawks, and began piercing my legs with his three-inch spurs. Running barefoot across the damp morning grass, I lost my footing and landed on my back. Big Red gawked and crowed. I sputtered to life, retrieved the broom, and began swinging. "I'm not in the mood to deal with you," I yelled, following him in close pursuit.

About the third time around the house, I glanced up and saw Ailene and Aunt Margaret standing on the porch. Aunt Margaret, who had been Big Red's victim several times, laughed until her short, plump body shook. After two more jaunts, Big Red wavered and dropped to the ground. I whacked my downed pray with the broom. "I'll beat you so far into next week you'll have to look both ways for Sunday." Flinging the broom over my head, I announced to the onlookers, "I won!"

But Big Red wouldn't accept defeat. He shook his head, stood tall, groaned and began a counterattack. I dashed into the barn and found another broom. Big Red waited at the door. Breathless, as if my audience expected an encore, I poised the two brooms like a cymbal player in an orchestra pit, and waited for my cue. Big Red flapped his wings and did a dance as if he had scored a touchdown. "Big deal," I scoffed. Upon hearing my series of bangs and shrieks he ran headfirst into the heavy hardwood gate and collapsed. Silence. I had terrified him. I attained the same sense of gratification that the hens confirmed after laying an egg.

Thinking the chase had ended, I swaggered toward the kitchen door as Big Red strutted into view. I whirled around. "Hello, big boy. Are you ready for another round? On a shelf in the barn is some rat poison. Sir, where shall I serve your supper? Would a silver platter do?" I asked. "On second thought, I couldn't do that to you. What would I accomplish? We couldn't eat you. Tough meat. Aunt Margaret says we need a rooster in the crowd so we can have the best eggs." I couldn't figure out how he could produce good eggs. He didn't lay them. As usual, she agreed to answer my questions next year.

Big Red had always been my enemy, but he now pranced around, happy to see me. He cocked his head sideways and stared. I opened the chicken coop gate. He willingly entered and found comfort behind the smallest hen. Thrusting a golden beak through the fence, he fluffed his shiny scarlet tail feathers and submitted a scratchy, insecure crow. Oh well, the hens admire him. Guess he's not so terrible after all. Big Red never bothered me again.

Everyone should get acquainted with chickens. Getting to know and name chickens is excellent therapy. Chickens have fairly skillful moves when you chase them. The white Leghorns had the greatest speed, so we chased them often. I'll never forget the delicious taste of pullets, even though it became difficult to eat our pets. But we didn't simply sit down at the table and enjoy the meal.

My job, at the age of ten, was to cut off the head. Ailene stretched the neck across the chopping block, and I lifted the ax in the air. I got real near to God at the thoughts of accidentally cutting off my sister's hand. Sometimes I missed and cut the beak. Sometimes the half-headed animal ran around the yard with projecting neck bones and skin hanging. Visions of fried chicken, mashed potatoes and biscuits produced the desire to chase that sucker and finish the task.

If they lived long enough to produce, Ailene gathered the eggs. I chuckled as I witnessed her blond hair tossing in the wind and her small frame traipsing to the chicken house. In one hand she clutched a handkerchief to cover her mouth and nose. A wicker basket dangled from her arm. She shoved the hens aside, stole their award-winning labor, and brushed her shirt while making a quick exit. "What's the matter, sis? The lice love chickens better than you. Hey, I'll give you what's left of my candy if you'll help clean the hen house," I petitioned.

"I hate that job more than anything. In fact, your job offer crushes my desire for food," she said.

"You gobble up sweets, then want more. I save part of

mine. Don't be so delicate. The hen house contains black waste products. Stinks, but you won't die from it."

Almost every evening Ailene and I endured face slaps at the dinner table. Usually I instigated the punishment. Aunt Margaret considered the six o'clock news reporter, Peter Arnell, as a special dinner guest. I don't know why the wartime newscast was an invitation for amusement. Wartime was surely no laughing matter. Unknown to me, my brother was somewhere out there fighting for our country.

The World at War

*R*APID GROWTH of the federal government began in the thirties. President Franklin D. Roosevelt profoundly altered the basic philosophy of American government when he created the Work Progress Administration. This group built ten percent of new roads, new hospitals and schools, the Lincoln Tunnel between New York and New Jersey, and Boulder Dam in the Colorado River. The workers were delighted to be paid forty cents an hour. Newspapers repeatedly featured cartoons showing men leaning on shovels.

In the 1940s, an innocent time, bobby-pinned matrons in freshly ironed dresses stayed at home and cared for their kids. I didn't understand the political situation, but I remember adult conversations concerning the Japanese attack on Pearl Harbor, and President Roosevelt, who made the economic welfare of Americans a federal commitment. He created Social Security, Federal Emergency Relief, Unemployment Compensation, and Civilian Conservation Corps.

I remember the anxiety that World War II caused. Parents' uncertainties couldn't be hidden from their children. On December 7, 1941, the radio announced that the Japanese had bombed Pearl Harbor. The household became somber and quiet. Kids talked about what it could mean. We didn't understand, but we knew the horrible effects of war.

Our future depended on the young men and women who marched off to war. Some were seventeen years old when they came under the withering fire in an endless barrage of artillery shells, machine gun bullets, and poison gas. They walked into the face of death, because their country asked it of them.

The most terrible war in world history killed and maimed, and resulted in deprivation, danger and inconvenience. Women helped supplement the income by doing piecework, peddling eggs, doing laundry, selling snacks or lunches to CCC and WPA crews. During World War I and II the women were responsible for holding families together while men went to war. They kept the country going. Millions of women took to the role of shouldering heavy industrial jobs, working long shifts. At the end of the day, after their hot dirty tasks were done, they went home to care for their families. Aunt Hannah's daughter Chlora left her teaching job to join the Waves, served overseas with distinction alongside her male counterparts. These women made a difference.

The government gave coupons (that resembled monopoly money) to each family, rations for coffee, sugar, shoes and gasoline. Red and blue dime-sized tokens were given for change. White margarine, with a tube of yellow coloring, replaced butter. Coffee and booze lovers traded coupons to suit their desires, therefore, children had to put up with worn-out shoes. Black market items bought and sold resulted in death, injury, fist fights, and hurt feelings.

Nylons were unavailable. Parachutes were made of nylon. I remember feeling considerable patriotic pride the day our class field trip included carrying gunnysacks and collecting milkweed pods to be processed into parachute fabric.

During the war, the air raid alarm sounded, and noisy schoolmates suddenly silenced. We marched to the basement, lined up against the cinder block walls and folded our arms over our heads. Teachers stood in the center of the room, making sure we followed the rules.

After dark the siren on the police department roof blew a solid blast. Fear griped each heart. Was it real? Air raid wardens—wearing a white helmet, an armband, and carrying a flashlight and whistle—checked each house and warned, "The government has ordered a blackout. You must cover all windows with sheets or dark shades." Men were appointed to watch the skies and report to runners, teenagers who took messages from one post to another. Men were jailed for smoking on the street during a blackout. I recall hearing three short blasts announcing the end of a ninety-minute alert.

President Roosevelt prayed this prayer on National radio hookup on D-Day, June 6, 1944 as our allied forces hit the beachheads of France to begin a liberating sweep across Europe. "Almighty God, with Thy blessing we shall prevail over the unholy forces of our enemy. Help us to conquer the apostles of greed and racial arrogance. Lead us to the saving of our country. Thy will be done, Almighty God. Amen."

Ernie Pyle, a great war correspondent, described the scene in the June 16 column:

> I took a walk along the historic coast of Normandy in the country of France. It was a lovely day for strolling along the seashore. Men were sleeping on the sand, some of them sleeping forever. Men were floating in the water, but they didn't know they were in the water, for they were dead. The water was full of squishy jellyfish about the size of your hand. In the center each of them had a green design exactly like a four-leaf clover, the good-luck emblem. . . . Four-leaf clovers are supposed to be good-luck charms, but for the doughboys who perished on this blood-soaked beach of indescribable mayhem, D-Day was anything but lucky.

Six months later the sweep had stalled, bogged down by snow, cold, and Hitler's counteroffensive to try and save his Third Reich.

With the pride of lions, young men lied about their age, attempting to serve their country by enlisting in various branches of the service. In September 1944, my brother Gee was drafted into the Army. I hadn't seen him for months. I never had a chance to say goodbye. Everyone prayed for the war to end. I prayed that I would see my brother's smiling face again. He was stationed in Alabama, transferred to Luxembourg, traveling via the Queen Mary. He went to Scotland, then to France with the 89th Infantry Division. The US Third Army, under General George S. Patton stormed across France, cleared the Palatinate and reached Pilsen before being brought to a stop by the war's ending.

Patton was the most brilliant commander of mobile armored forces that the Allied armies produced during the Second World War. His abilities as a fighting soldier more than compensated for his shortcomings as a diplomat. The Third Army's aim was to be the striking force, and its movements were kept secret for a considerable period in order to confuse the Germans. Patton, accompanied by his bull-terrier attitude and recognizable to the press by his tall figure, fought a slow and expensive battle through the hedgerows. He took the country yard by yard.

When Patton's army slipped across the Rhine, it was the Holy Grail of the Allied advance. The soldiers spotted wrecked vehicles, empty life rafts, and soldiers' ration boxes floating in the water. The next morning Patton went to Oppenheim to inspect progress. After satisfying himself regarding the bridge and its defenses, he led his party across the bridge. Halfway over he stopped. "Time for a short halt." He unbuttoned his pants and urinated in the river. "I've been looking forward to this for a long time," he said as he walked across the Rhine and entered the heartland of Germany.

Parents, grandparents, and many family members secured freedom with their sacrifice and blood. They paid a price to defeat Nazi Germany, the Imperial Japanese, and Mussolini's Italy. Gee felt sorry for the families who lost their possessions when the troops invaded homes. They seized chickens and cooked them on a makeshift grill. Even with feathers intact, the gourmet meal was far better than K rations.

He took part in Germany's last stronghold, where they liberated the Brockenbach Concentration camp. The Battle of the Bulge, fought from December 16, 1944 through January 25, 1945, has been called America's greatest battle. It was fought during the bitter cold and snow of the heavily forested Ardennes area of eastern Belgium and northern Luxembourg.

Patton had an indisputable intellect for handling armor in mobile warfare, and this campaign gave him every opportunity to display it. He was politically naïve and no sort of strategist. These shortcomings were less obvious in France, and in some ways they were to his benefit. He failed to see the political and economic consequences, but he was no fool when it came to forecasting military possibilities. His foresight in this respect saved the Allied cause from near-disaster.

My brother heard General Patton say, "If we live through this one, be forever grateful that you have brought with you, one of life's greatest moments." Six hundred thousand American soldiers fought in this great battle with 81,000 casualties, including 19,000 killed. I appreciate and recognize the contributions they made to the freedom we enjoy.

The war brought songs of hope, "I'll be Seeing You," and thoughts of the war's end, "Roll Out the Barrel." A popular woman's song was "The Yanks Are Coming."

Deep in the heart of the story, President Roosevelt died while in office. Many of his followers were broken hearted. It seemed that Aunt Hannah cried buckets of tears when the radio interrupted her radio "soap" to announce the sad event. Pictures of the president, who from childhood polio was bound to his wheel chair, remained on Aunt Hannah's piano for many years, a reminder of her beloved political figure.

A message from President Harry S. Truman to the Japanese ordered them to flee their cities. He guaranteed that an atomic bomb campaign would wipe out the Japanese war industry, city by city. Defense employees had worked Christmas Day to produce a heat exchanger used in the bomb. The device, eight inches in diameter and ten feet long, weighed 800 pounds.

Radio broadcaster, Peter Arnell, has seen more combat than anyone in the American military. He covered war non-stop for more than thirty years. On August 6, 1945, he announced that the US had dropped an atomic bomb on Hiroshima, an area of 4.1 square miles, an important Japanese Army base. A university professor talked about how this kind of bomb could emit radiation. Not many listeners knew about radiation. They thought an atomic bomb was an explosion.

On August ninth the U.S. dropped another atomic bomb on Nagasaki, and five days later Japan announced surrender. Estimates put the casualties at 100,000 for the two explosions. The next day the Japanese offered to surrender if Emperor Hirohito was allowed to retain his rights as sovereign. The Big Four Allies agreed to surrender with the proviso that the supreme allied commander would govern Japan through the authority of the emperor.

Japan announced its surrender four days later. A wave of horn-honking automobiles and people crowded the streets of America. Showers of shredded papers rained on citizens who came out to join the revelry. The wild demonstration lasted for seven hours in some cities. Church bells rang for thirty minutes. Factories, stores, bars and service stations remained closed over the next two days in keeping with a holiday declared by Truman.

Cancellation of war contracts totaled $4 billion, threatening the jobs of five million munitions makers. By August twenty-third defense plant workers were laid off, gasoline rationing lifted, and a shortage resulted as motorists flocked to the pumps. Government controls were lifted on civilian items, food, wages and rail shipments.

The war ended. The government relaxed the voluntary censorship that had muzzled the press for nearly four years. It was revealed that, of thousands launched, 230 Japanese balloon bombs had reached the United States, without damage or injuries. On August twenty-ninth President Truman released the results of the investigations of the Japanese attack on Pearl

Harbor that brought America into the war.

The Army report held Chief of Staff George C. Marshall partially responsible. Rear Adm. Kimmel and Maj. Gen. Walter Short, and the Navy and Army commanders, were held mostly responsible for failure to adequately alert their commands for war. The Navy criticized Adm. Harold Stark, Chief of Naval operations. Kimmel and Short demanded public trials. Truman refused to order courts martial.

Terrible telegrams began with every family's worst nightmare. "The War Department regrets to inform you . . . " Before the fighting ended, 405,000 had given their lives for the cause.

Troop ships bound for the Far East headed for home, setting off celebrations on deck. People were jumping, dancing, yelling, and beating on washtubs, happy that the war was finally over. They had followed the war closely on radio and in newspapers, trying to guess what the next move of allied forces might be. A phrase, "some sunny day" from the song "We'll Meet Again" brought tears. It was a sunny day when the war was over.

On December 9, 1945, Patton set out on a day's duck-hunting expedition. He was involved in a traffic accident, suffered a broken neck, and died on December 21. Rumor has it that one of Patton's troop trucks caused the accident. He is buried with his Third Army soldiers in Luxembourg.

Gee's company returned to US soil in 1946. Some kissed the ground. We rejoiced when he came home, but my brother wore the history of the fight racket on his face. It was a face that launched a thousand flashbacks. It took mental adjustment, and years passed before he recapped the encounters.

The soldiers were eager to establish homes and families. More Americans got married that year than any twelve-month period before or since. Commitment and sacrifice characterized the forties. Their marriages weathered the sexual revolution of the sixties because they realized the meaning of "till death do us part." They were the "stick-to-it" generation.

I look back at the fifties, the shift away from traditional

values resulted in sexually-transmitted diseases, thirty million babies aborted, marriages in shambles, unsupervised children roaming our city streets.

Then came the sixties, with high employment, great economic growth. Everyone had a minimum standard of living, adequate diet, housing and health care. There was more aid to the poor, foreign aid, Medicare, affirmative action, school lunches, and projects to combat health problems. The sixties brought "flower children," "hippies," "street people," with revolutionary notions and complete rejection of what their parents stood for and fought to preserve.

The seventies were driven by the "me" generation. The National Congress formulated grants for town hall debates and bike paths. Small government grew large and large government grew larger.

Who would have believed that in 1996, lawmakers in twenty-two states would be trying to decide whether or not to recognize marriage between two or more men, or two or more women? We have drifted far from the world our forebears knew in 1946.

Weird World

*B*oth people and animals found a path that led to Aunt Margaret's house. I can't remember much about Naomi Evans, except that she needed a home. I think she was fifteen. She had a large round face, shoulder-length hair cut short above the ears, large limbs and round hips. Her wide gray eyes looked deep and distant. She enjoyed displaying power.

We were helping Aunt Margaret cook Sunday dinner. She sent me to the fruit cellar, an underground storage for vegetables and canned goods. I opened the door and smelled the moist clammy earth. I pushed away cobwebs and counted six brown spiders. *Did she want peaches? Green beans? Why can't I remember what I came for? Golly, if I take back the wrong thing I'll get a good whipping.*

Naomi opened the door. "What's taking so long?"

"I forgot what I came for—just can't remember."

Her wide hand began pounding my skinny behind. "Well, I'll help you remember."

"Stop it," I kept screaming during the butt beating.

She slapped my face. "You deserve it."

"I do not deserve it. I just can't remember. Is it a crime to forget?"

"You're too young to forget." I pushed past her heavy body and ran up the hill. She continued to spank my legs, quitting just in sight of the house. I never told anyone about the incident. No one cared anyway. I wondered if my aunt had ordered the whipping.

A few weeks later about midnight I heard Naomi and Aunt Margaret talking just above a whisper. Naomi said, "There's no doubt that I'm expecting a baby."

When I got up the next morning Naomi was gone. No one mentioned her name again. My twelve-year-old mind couldn't understand why Aunt Margaret sent her away. "I think she needs a home now more than she ever," I told Ailene. "Will Aunt Margaret decide to send us away?"

On Monday I came home from school and found a bulging suitcase by the front door. A muscular, tall man with freckles and dark red hair was sitting at the kitchen table. Aunt Margaret introduced him as Ed. No last name. I wondered where he came from. Does he have anything to do with Naomi's little bundle of joy?

Even though he helped with small jobs, didn't talk much, didn't eat much, something about the man made me suspicious. He wore a pinkie ring in the shape of a skull. I had no idea why he came. I determined to stay near my sister and protect her from him.

Two weeks later he left in the night. Aunt Margaret said he would never return. I wondered why everyone leaves in the middle of the night. He left a card on the table: AUNT MARGARET: YOU NEVER HAD CHILDREN, BUT YOU HAVE BEEN A MOTHER TO MANY. MAYBE I WILL STOP BY AGAIN NEXT MOTHER'S DAY.

Aunt Margaret used to say "Tradition says that on Mother's Day you should wear a white flower to church if your mother is not living. Go to the flower garden and pick a white carnation." I wanted to defeat the rule and wear a red rose. On Mother's Day I didn't want to sing or listen to the preacher. I was busy looking around for colorful flowers and envying the wearer.

Every spring, neighbors, aunts and cousins came to wallpaper Grandma's house. "Other than food, nothing compares to the smell of clean windows and fresh wallpaper. To get cheerful smells, we need to get rid of the frust." I said.

"What in the world is frust?" Ailene questioned.

"Don't you know, girl? It's the dirt that refuses to be swept onto a dustpan and keeps backing a person across the room until she gives up and sweeps it under the rug."

"That's interesting. Humbuggery is a better word," she said as she lifted one corner of the area rug and searched for evidence. We cleaned the carpets by carrying them outside, draping them over a clothesline, and flailing the dust and grit out of them with a wire carpet beater.

A boring springtime routine was planting corn. Uncle Gil and his horse Bayard took care of the ground preparation. Ailene and I walked up and down the rows, and placed four grains of corn about a foot apart. Corn grows in orderly rows, if it is planted straight. The smaller corn comes from unusually wet weather. If it didn't sprout, we replanted.

Uncle Gil said the corn should be knee high by the fourth of July. "I thought today was a holiday, a day to eat ice cream. Nobody works on a holiday. But here we are, working again. Does it ever end?" I asked.

"Patty, you're a pain in the butt," he answered.

"Maybe so. Takes one to know one," I quipped while scuffling my bare feet in the rough dirt, unaware of the pain it caused. I could have spread my heart on a highway, and waited for a big truck to run over it.

I told Ailene, "Uncle Gil couldn't stand the heat. Guess he went to wet his whistle. I don't think he'll be back. I'm tired of this job, and the simple solution is to lift that big rock, get rid of the corn, kick dirt over the rows and our job will be done. D-O-N-E."

"What makes you think this plan will work?

"You have to trust me. It *will* work." I lifted the rock, and she dumped our problem underneath.

As we headed home Ailene asked, "What's that sound in the tree?"

"Caterpillars. They make a crunching sound like the droppings of a thousand family members. I don't know if they're eating or getting rid of food. They gotta go too, you know.

Aunt Margaret says tent caterpillars will infest all the trees and strip the leaves before fall." Uncle Gil made torches out of rags and saturated them with gasoline. He swiped the head of a large wooden match against a rock. Before making contact with the torch I heard an angry outburst. An explosion? I jumped four feet. "Caterpillars won't crunch any more, but I'll bet the tree will die from the heat." The next spring we had an abundance of shade.

When we got home Aunt Margaret said, "You planted that corn in no time. Quick job. Here's a quarter for ice cream." We grinned, accepted the offer and headed for the store.

A few weeks later my uncle discovered that the rock was fertile enough to produce corn. I told Aunt Margaret, "Don't blame Ailene. It was *my* idea. Go ahead, beat *me*." The keen hickory switch caused oozing liquid to stain my dingy skirt.

One of our few pleasant childhood memories was the annual Sunday school picnic at Beaver Lake. It never rained on picnic day. Elder, Clint Lively took his open bed truck, capacity of four grandmas in chairs, and twenty children. The one-hour journey, with wind and bugs in our face, hair whirling around our heads, created utmost excitement.

A couple invited Ailene and me to take our first rowboat ride. Sun glistened on the bright blue water as we skimmed across the lake. I heard someone talk about seventh heaven. This must be it. We strolled on sandy beaches, a moving mirror at our feet. Aunt Margaret insisted that we wear a dress. "You have to dress for a church function." We held our flared skirts above our knees and waded out as far as possible. Most children take a day in the park for granted. I cherished the precious memories, swinging high, feeling the wind rumpling my hair, and indulging in an all-day picnic.

An hour after eating, Glen Krause's daughter Bernadine encouraged ten-year-old Ailene to wade into deep water. "I'm a skillful swimmer," she said. "I'll be your teacher." They both disappeared in the deep water. Bernadine popped her head up and yelled, "Help, I'm drowning." Ailene was thrashing around trying to stay above water. Her skirt floated like a parachute behind her. She grabbed the back of Bernadine's swimsuit. Mr. Thompson heard the yelling, jumped from his chair and raced to the lake. I thanked God for Mr. Thompson's quick actions.

"Girls, both of you are ready for swimming lessons." He was a first-class teacher.

Summer time wasn't a vacation, or a time to just sit around and listen to the Katydids argue, "Katy did, Katy didn't." The transparent apple tree produced enough fruit for the whole town. We dried them, fried them, canned them, another task that took lots of time. I tried to convince Aunt Margaret, "If you leave them on the tree long enough, they'll pick themselves!"

Once I remember getting the work done, and had nothing else to do but sit on the cool ground watching the sun put shadows on wrinkled jeans hanging on the line. "Ailene, do you know what a nuff is?"

"I've never heard of one. Why do you ask?"

"Aunt Margaret told me we had to pick berries tomorrow. I grumbled, slammed the back door and she said she had heard a nuff." Ailene gave hiccups of laughter.

Every August we went berry picking. Aunt Margaret said, "Look, if you want blackberry cobbler pies, get out and help." Aunt Margaret made the best pies in West Virginia. We could almost smell the aroma. The large ripe berries were in the back of the patch, protected by massive tangles of thorns and prickly leaves. Dressing for the job, jeans and long-sleeved shirts, didn't make for comfort in the ninety-degree weather. Ailene didn't complain.

The fear of snakes was part of our unwillingness. We came across a giant patch of blackberries, and in the center of my view, a black snake the size of my arm was curled ready for striking. I scampered away, screaming for Ailene to "Get the lead out." She stepped on a rock and twisted her ankle.

The bucket crashed to the ground. Blackberries scattered over the dry grass. Tears streamed from her sad eyes. "I picked some really large berries. Now look at them. Here I am crying again; and I don't have a hanky. I guess I should learn."

"Learn not to cry? Or learn to carry the proper equipment?"

"Both, I guess."

"Don't worry, Aunt Hannah's house is just around the bend. She'll help us pick more."

The smell of cinnamon met us at the door. "Here. Have a fried apple pie, just out of the oven. I'm tired. Can't do any more work today." She filled our buckets with big fresh-picked berries.

The three-mile walk home, carrying two pails of berries created hunger and thirst that gnawed like busy termites. Aunt Margaret had dinner ready. I attacked the meat loaf, bloodied it with ketchup, and wolfed it down. Our friend, Peewee, was about three feet tall. At mealtime she pressed up, almost bumped into the table. If food wasn't offered, she'd say, "Ooh, those biscuits look good. I haven't had gravy in a month of Sunday's. I haven't had fried chicken for a long time."

I dreaded hearing Aunt Margaret's cutting words. "Go home now." Peewee's mother died, and her father never cooked. She lived on popcorn. According to my health book Pee Wee was undernourished and my aunt didn't care.

I needed a lock pick set to gain entry into Aunt Margaret's mind, her way with words and her method of operation. If I could tap into experience, I would have killed her with kindness and compliments. She had no children, but she thought she knew all about discipline. I believe she used corporal punishment to teach us the ropes.

Life is a tough coach in the game of growing up, and attacks when you least expect it, slams you around and lands many body punches. With each switching, I picked myself up, dried my bleeding legs, but was no less prone to make the same mistakes that got me into trouble the first time. Surviving life's ups and downs resulted in a well-seasoned sense of what makes things work. My problem was a big mouth and the need to protect Ailene. Instead of seeing her get whipped, I admitted guilt and took the fall without feeling sorry for poor Patty.

Speaking of feeling sorry, winter wind caused chapped, leathery skin. At school, whenever possible, I kept my cracked, bleeding hands under the desk. At night I applied a thick layer of petroleum jelly. White cotton gloves prevented giving in to the itching. Before bedtime, Ailene and I sat in front of the fire, stared at the bright red coals and imagined a big house with our family inside. I built castles in various designs. The fire cracked for a while, and died down to a few embers. The black mantle clock struck ten. "Sweet dreams," I whispered. "Tomorrow is Saturday."

Saturday was bath day. After about thirty minutes in the galvanized tub, the embedded dirt under my fingernails was gone. My skin resembled Grandma's breakfast prunes. I was clean all over except for my hair. In the cold weather Aunt Margaret said that wet hair caused flu and croup. I hated my baby-fine hair, the short bangs, and the smelly, oily feeling. Common sense told me why I had few friends.

Sometimes, when ordered to just brush, I committed the sin of shampooing, and took chances at getting beaten. After all, it was Saturday night. A tablespoon of liquid from the Halo shampoo bottle that displayed a radiant girl on the label brought miraculous healing to a troubled soul.

My corkscrew curls carried a painful price. The ripping sound from a pile of rags in front of me interrupted *Inner Sanctum*. I divided my damp hair into sections, wound it around the 12-inch rag until it met the scalp, and tied a knot. My uncomfortable "wiener curls" caused a restless night, but the next morning they brought satisfaction that lasted until noon.

On Saturday nights Ailene and I sat on the floor in front of the large RCA radio and listened to our favorite shows, murder mysteries, *The Lux Radio* Theater. My imagination went wild. I remember the night the station cancelled *Mystery Theater* to talk about a Broadway show.

Rodgers and Hammerstein's beloved *Carousel* opened in 1945 and wove itself into the fabric of America. The story showed life's darker side of which I was fully aware. In the love story Billie Bigelow, a bash, handsome carnival worker charmed Julie Jordan, a shy naïve mill worker. They married, but their happiness ended. Billy lost his job, schemed and botched a robbery, and stabbed himself rather than be arrested. The story withstood the test of time, and has grown in popularity. I'll always remember the music. The hauntingly beautiful "You'll Never Walk Alone," gave me faith to believe that I was never alone, no matter what happened next.

"Sunday is the Lord's Day, the day of rest," our Sunday school teacher used to say. I've got news for *her*. There is no day of rest. The coal and water must be carried, floors mopped, meals cooked, and dishes done. Ailene and I sometimes argued over which jobs to do, but we agreed on one rule: no one will touch my sister. I'd crawl over hot coals to protect her.

I didn't object to working, but sometimes my legs and arms hurt. I objected to Aunt Margaret's proclamation, "Stop complaining. It's just growing pains. All children have them. Be thankful that you're alive." She was the biggest pain in my growth and I was quite thankful, especially in December.

We seldom had fresh fruit. When December rolled around I began praying for the citrus and nuts to arrive from Aunt Flossie who lived in Oregon. Two weeks before Christmas I began begging Uncle Gil for a tree. The only way to get one was to search for branches trimmed from other family's trees. Part of my decorations included black electrical tape stolen from Uncle Gil's room. I considered it an art to select the correct length and tape the branches to the tree trunk. For several hours, the one string of lights tested my patience, but they always worked. "It's the prettiest tree we've ever had," I convinced myself.

We didn't have a stocking to hang on the fireplace. On Christmas Eve we put a knit hat on the mantle and crawled into bed. *I must keep my promise to make Ailene's life pleasant. She'll fall asleep in ten minutes. I'll ease out of bed and fill each hat with ten nuts, one orange, one apple, and a candy* bar.

I'll act very surprised in the morning. She must not awake and catch me.

The year it happened, she pretended to be asleep, but I saw the gawking blue eyes. Disappointed that the Santa Clause game ended, I decided she was getting too old anyway. The next morning Ailene informed me that she didn't believe in Santa Claus. I said, "Well, send a letter to Mrs. Claus."

Each year I made a wish: *maybe, courteous of Christmas, a Santa will visit and bring a teddy bear.* I told Ailene, "Those sweet, cuddly toys make kids happy. Teddies are great listeners and they understand any language. They always keep secrets, and they make great pillow pals. And teddy bears are always punctual for parties. I never went to a party, but if I had a teddy maybe we'd both go." I read a book about teddy bears. The term "teddy" is associated with Teddy Roosevelt, who in 1902 refused to shoot a bear cub on a hunting trip. He adopted the bear as his symbol. Someone started producing stuffed animals called Teddy's Bear. They become known as teddies.

"Patty, how can we buy gifts without money?" Ailene asked.

"I guess the only way is to "borrow" from Aunt Margaret's coffee can. If we're careful, that is. Aunt Margaret says she won't put up with thieves, not even with one who steals for something to eat. She says that thieves who get caught must pay back seven times what was stolen and lose *everything they own*. Once she was standing near a window of her house and she saw some foolish young men dressed in black from head to foot. It was late in the evening, sometime after dark. They pried open the neighbor's front door."

Ailene loved stories. As I continued, her eyes widened. She chewed a fingernail. "They broke into the house and stole money. Like a fool on the way to be punished or a bird rushing into a trap, the thieves lost their lives. The police shot them! Dead! It's Christmas time. Maybe God won't punish us for stealing. Maybe I could get a job at Pettry's store, but he doesn't hire anyone my age. Just forget the whole thing. Or just trust your heart."

Ailene's mind was made up. Somehow she would buy something to place under our shabby tree. She conned Mrs. Thompson into washing the windows and sills. With fifty cents jingling in her pocket, we went to Pettry's store and selected a lapel pin. "Why are you buying a pin with the word *Mom* on it?" I asked. "You don't have a mom."

"I don't know why. Maybe if I give this to Aunt Margaret she will become a kind person like my mom. Besides, gold has a rich look." By February Ailene was still wondering why she bought the pin. "I'll always miss Mom."

Wilma and Yvonne brought the only gifts we received, except the year Daddy appeared at our door. He opened a big black suitcase. A doll with auburn hair for me and a blond one for Ailene was tucked in white tissue paper. "Babe" felt so real in my arms that I forgot for a moment that she was porcelain. She had tiny features: a button nose, soft folds of skin, baby fingers and newborn wrinkles. At nineteen inches, weighing four pounds, she was actually newborn size. "Christmas is too good to have just once a year," I said. We still have those beautiful babies.

When snow thawed and after a rain, streets in Pax turned from the thickest dust into the direst mud. The block-long district, referred to as "downtown," consisted of three grocery stores, a barbershop, two poolrooms, a gasoline station, theatre, bank, post office, the town hall, Dr. Hitchman's office, and several churches that struggled for the townspeople's attendance.

Many of the townspeople met for lunch at Brocks Restaurant, a place where the menu rarely changes, the pop comes in plastic cups and the waitress calls customers "Hon." A neighbor told me I was thin, like Mrs. Brock's soup and biscuit hamburgers. She charged fifty cents for ten "sliders."

Mr. Canterbury's store had wood floors that creaked as you walked. Customers who ran up a bill dropped by to pay at the end of the month. When children paid, Mr. Canterbury gave them a bag of hard candy. After school several students stopped by for pop and a candy bar. We dropped in to observe the grand times. One day I asked Ailene, "Do you think Uncle Gil checks items charged on his bill?"

"Well, uh, we could find out. I'm really thirsty."

"Me too. Hey, Mr. Canterbury, charge two pops on my uncle's bill."

"Comin' right up," he answered.

A few weeks later, the day I became convinced that my uncle hated me, I told Mr. Canterbury, "Give us two Cokes and two Snicker bars please. Put it on our bill."

"Righto," he said as he slid the candy on the counter and reached in the pop cooler. I don't know if Uncle Gil knowingly let us play the game, but we started taking the risk twice weekly. I figured we had a right to keep secrets. Aunt Margaret didn't tell anyone about her indulgence. About every six weeks, she ran out of Prince Albert tobacco for her corncob pipe. She went to her "bank," the fruit jar that was buried in the bottom drawer, made a withdrawal, and sent us to the store. We paid cash for the tobacco and charged the other items. We never tattled.

Local saloon owners grew wealthy catering to the desires of miners on their Saturday night payday. The local pub rocked all weekend. The free flowing liquor and unrestricted firearm regulations contributed to a general atmosphere of violence. At dawn the men finished their biscuit and honey, rolled a toothpick around in their mouth, and talked between drinks of hot, strong coffee.

You've heard of the "Upper Room." The upper room above Dr. Hitchman's office was anything but biblical. The chips began to fall at nine every Saturday night. The older residents claimed that Dr. Hitchman carried a Derringer, a small pistol of large caliber, for protection when he made house calls. He carried it on Saturday night to warn the round table participants that poker was serious business.

The story goes like this: The cards were dealt and the

stakes were high. Dr. Hitchman's friend, Chalmers, didn't do much work except the work of a busybody. He spread rumors that caused Dr. Hitchman's blood to boil. Hot enough to decide that tonight Chalmers would fold his cards for the last time. The doctor ambled over to the bar, downed a shot of whisky, and slammed the glass on the wood counter. He walked ten paces and reached into his hip pocket. He pointed the pistol at Chalmers like an accusing finger, fired one shot, and returned to his seat. After two more drinks, he scuttled over to the man slumped on the floor and said, "I now pronounce that you are—Chalmers, you are—dead."

The newspaper didn't report the account, but news traveled fast, even in my young world. No news traveled about a doctor being charged with murder. Pax was an easy-going, slow-growing, area. No one locked doors at night. You trusted everybody, knew everybody. Kids could go everywhere. Sunday morning on the way to church I saw one of Uncle Gil's poker pals standing at the cross road, gently swaying as the cars zipped by, oblivious to the blasting horns. His hands were shoved in his jacket pockets. With head bowed he was singing, "Show me the way to go home."

When I was a child, the peaks and valleys of people's lives fascinated me. I was blessed, or cursed with curiosity. Details of joyous moments as well as sad events produced abstract emotions, microscopic in focus, telescopic in intent. I took note of how people dressed, how they held their hands, whose shoes were brilliantly shined. I was the one who inched a bit closer to the dry intonations of the minister, to the papery rustle of leaves overhead.

I was intrigued with the mystery of my surroundings, the scent of the wood-burning stove, the lonesome sound of the mourning dove. The blue jay sounds an alarm, and sometimes adds bell-like notes. I enjoyed spring peepers. The swamp chorus of frogs' rasping calls reminded me of tines on a comb scraping a rough surface. My optimism grew. My childhood courage overcame weakness and the dread of dying, fear of the oblong that slid under the door at Aunt Bela's house.

One morning I dipped water from a rain barrel setting in the corner where two tin roofs of our frame house came together. We used the soft water for shampooing our hair and watering houseplants. "Ailene, come here," I yelled. "It rained animals. Where'd they come from? They swim and play. I think they're tadpoles, but maybe they're disease-causing organisms. I could go down in history with a great medical discovery."

I didn't have a microscope, so I found another form of investigating my surroundings. My brothers used to tie June bugs to a string attached to the clothesline. I tried to get Ailene interested in my challenging undertakings. "The more you collect, the more noise you enjoy," I told her. "My childhood is half over and I haven't learned all about tadpoles or June bugs. What luck."

The hot spot of my childhood was Saturday night at the movies. Often the manager nodded us in free, and we spent our quarter for a Coke. If other kids were standing nearby, we paid the fare and Mr. Skaggs gave us free popcorn. I won't forget the sticky suction sound from layers of candy, gum, and pop. For a quarter we got a couple of cartoons, a newsreel and cowboy shows.

The audience filed in and the bouncing ball on the screen directed us through several choruses. The lights went out. I curled up in the deep shadows and felt the place come alive with music. I was thrilled with the flickering of the larger-than-life images, and sat in amazement at the lavish, sweeping scenes. Somehow the dreams became reality that someday my world would burst into a great story to tell. Romance stories resulted in complex cruelties and twisted betrayals. Sometimes the "goodies" died and the "baddies" went merrily on their way.

I believe Daddy's humor came from his favorite actor Will Rogers, who was also America's favorite cowboy philosopher. Full of wit and wisdom, Rogers was a national icon with his newspaper column, movie career and radio show. Known for his homespun one-liners, he started lectures with, "All I know is what I read in the papers."

Will Rogers encouraged Gene Autry to try his luck in radio. He soon became a hit at a local station, landed a contract with Columbia Records in 1929, made 635 recordings, and sold more than 100 million records. He had the first certified gold record "That Silver-Haired Daddy of Mine." Gene Autry's music and movies captured all that was pure and inspiring about America's Old West. He loved his horse Champion, and always found time to pick up his guitar and sing his theme song, "Back in the Saddle Again." That song will always bring back warm memories.

Gene played the unchangeable character: a true-blue son of the west who always fought fair. His comic sidekicks set off the drama. He treated everyone with class; considered himself the baby-sitter for three generations of children who watched movies on Saturday afternoon. These were not just bang-bang, shoot 'em up westerns. He always wanted to put a moral in the story.

He left to serve in World War II, and Roy Rogers replaced him as Hollywood's top cowboy. Roy's wife Dale was Queen of the West. Roy and Dale influenced America's children in the 50s. They reinforced moral standards by planting seeds. The clothes were cowboy and cowgirl, including the hat. Those wonderful eyes always beamed.

Gene Autry returned to the screen and performed in ninety-one movies from the 1930s to the early 50s. He hung up his performing spurs in 1956, but continued to own four radio stations and several other properties. He had incredible business savvy, and ranked for many years on the Forbes magazine list of the 400 richest Americans. In 1995, the magazine estimated a net worth of $320 million. Hollywood's original singing cowboy died October 2, 1998, after a long illness. He was ninety-one. He and wife Jackie never had children. His death came three months after the industry bid happy trails to Roy

Rogers. We lost a piece of America when we lost two of my favorite cowboys in one year.

Fifty years ago I was held spellbound by the movie *The Marble Face*. The circular flashing lights and contraptions in the scene still vividly remain in my mind. The night Ailene and I watched scientists transform a screaming woman into stone we were too frightened to walk home in the dark. I came up with a plan. "You should walk backwards, I'll walk forward and we can see if anyone is following us. After a hundred steps, we'll change places." She thought it was a silly idea, but it worked.

Amazing Grace

J love the sound of church bells' peaceful notes that steal Sunday mornings. These perfect sounds create images of angel choirs. My memories of Sunday school are crystal clear. In the white clapboard church with a high steeple, I sat in the third pew near the window.

Part of the church was built on a rock, similar to Stone Mountain in Georgia. Aunt Hannah continually quoted Matthew 16:18. *Upon this rock I will build my church; and the gates of hell shall not prevail against it.* I thought a church must be built on a rock, or it wasn't biblical.

With a comforting stillness, Aunt Hannah stood before the Sunday school class. Her features were bunched together. She had a colorful farmer's complexion, age spots on her hands and long gray hair piled into a bun. She was amply proportioned, with a short torso, and fashion options that included "sack" dresses. Her favorite was a tan silk dress, a fringed shawl with brown braid trim and a pillbox hat the color of her dress.

In spite of the fact that I used any excuse to go somewhere, church appeared to be an upright place go. I learned a lot from Aunt Hannah. I thought Jesus' helpers were the twelve fossils, and Moses got the Ten Commandments on top of Mount Cyanide. I grew smarter by my next birthday.

I studied the apostle Paul's journeys and coveted his intellect and his way with words. Maybe it was because I adored my brother who had the same name, but Paul, whose name was changed from Saul to Paul, was my favorite biblical character. I dreamed that someday a handsome prince would come along and change my name.

Aunt Hannah gave silver stars for bringing a Bible and gold stars for getting the questions right. I worked for two years to get enough stars for a prize. The next year I discovered you could buy packets of stars at the grocery store.

The silence of musical instruments resulted in near perfect four-part harmony. Children were invited to join the large group of adults who took advantage of a six-week course ["shape" notes] offered by the Stamps-Baxter School of Music. In fourth grade, I could sing three of the four parts.

In the morning church service, I usually managed to sit next to Vean Larraty, a plump, buxom soprano whose voice injured my ears. She projected sound within a half-block radius. Just before the last series of a sermon concerning gossip, she swallowed a fly. She choked her way outside and never returned. The religious training left me momentarily. I laughed out loud and thought *it serves you right, big mouth.*

During a seven-day revival, the preacher talked about hell fire-and-brimstone, and how everyone should accept Jesus Christ as Lord. Ailene went to the front of the church, and talked to the preacher. She told me she had made the most important decision in her life. The next Sunday she and several others were baptized in Paint Creek. She told me I should do the same. "I have nasty thoughts about Mrs. Larraty, and other people," I said. "The preacher says that converts should never play cards, never have unpleasant thoughts, never tell lies or watch movies again. Those rules are tough to follow. I've got a lot of living to do. I will make that important decision later." Every time she said evening prayers I felt guilty.

On the way home from church one Sunday, I asked Aunt Hannah if we had any undivided attention. "The preacher wants all of it," I said. The preacher said I provided some of his best material.

I remember the Saturday Aunt Hannah asked me to help

prepare for the Ladies Aid Society meeting. After scrubbing until the house shined, she took a lace tablecloth from the bureau drawer and spread it on the huge oak dining room table. A tray, laid with spoons that winked and gleamed, fresh napkins and a plate of sunny lemon circles, a bowl of sugar and pitcher for milk, looked as fine as the Sunday communion setting. "Wow, fit for a king," I said. "Someday I'll have one of these fancy parties."

Our weekly jaunt to Aunt Hannah's house was four miles by hot country road. Ailene and I discovered a shorter route that allowed more time to play. "It's just a railroad track, just a short distance," we told Aunt Margaret.

The K. George and Ernest railroad [the KGE] was a spur line that connected to the Virginia line. Our neighbor, Mr. Thompson, and his crew of workers rode up and down the tracks in motorized handcars with yellow canopies. They called them "Gandy Dancers," and their mission was to maintain the tracks. I wondered why they chose this name. I didn't see how swinging spike hammers and lifting railroad ties resembled dancing.

The trains puffed dark gray smoke as they came barreling through town. The haughty strangers rushed into our hamlet, slowed around the bend and saluted the people with a piercing whistle and a clanging bell. We never failed to return the engineer's wave. The breeze that carried the smell of burning coal sprinkled black cinders in our hair and eyes, and choked our breathing.

The extremely narrow, raw cuts through rocky hills where the cockleburs scraped our pant legs, proved to be a challenging feat. When we heard the lonely sounding horns echo through the mountains as the train approached the cutaway, we attempted to reach the top of the hill before it rounded the curve. After taking only a few steps uphill, the sharp, flat rocks caused us to slide back down. Often, we barely made it to the top before the train arrived.

Once we arrived at Aunt Hannah's, her short stocky arms

folded about me. I felt the warmth of Mom's cuddly bosom that I longed for. "Nothing takes the place of your delicious chocolate dessert," I'd say as she placed a glass bowl of goodies on the table and poured a large glass of milk. Sometimes we had a choice of muffins or biscuits. Aunt Hannah says you should eat lots of green things. She offered a Popsicle. I ginned and took a green one. "Why don't they call this a Momsicle?"

Aunt Hannah loved showing off her garden of vegetables and sun-drenched spices. Flowers with glorious colors and magnificent details edged each plot of vegetables. She planted every vegetable available. "Look at these perfect rows. Don't you ever grow weeds, Aunt Hannah?"

"No. This is a magic garden. In this garden, I can tell time by looking at the sun."

"I can't make out the numbers," I teased.

I can still see her sitting on the screened-in back porch, a heavy-set farm widow, unbuttoning peas. I can almost taste the cream sauce, with small white onions covered with black pepper. Her big mixer whirled fluffy white mashed potatoes. She added salad dressing just for me. While she cooked I sat on the tall white stool telling jokes so I could hear her deep belly laugh. We made cookies, and she said to double the recipe. "But I can't get the oven to 750 degrees," I said.

She chuckled. "You can do anything if you really want to."

Aunt Hannah had a five-gallon stoneware churn covered with a loose lid that had a hole in the center. She filled it half full of milk and set it against the white enamel cook store. When the cream came to the top and the stove's heat curdled the milk, we churned it by moving a wooden dasher up and down while counting to 500. She skimmed the butter off, salted it, and pressed it into wooden molds.

We enjoyed big glasses of thick, creamy milk from the Guernsey. Aunt Hannah let me try to milk Bossy, but she wouldn't give a drop. Maybe she knew that I had no desire to be a farmer, I only wanted to use the products. "Your hands are not fat enough. Bossy gets used to the same person twice daily.

And she's the boss." I asked her if the cow laughed would milk come out of her nose.

On Sunday afternoons she sat in an overstuffed chair; her hanky placed on the great shelf of her bosom. She treated minor ailments by relying on her medical manual. For croup she put red flannel on my chest. The smell of mustard plaster gagged me. I believe it was the tender cuddles that made me feel better.

One day at the drug store I questioned, "Aunt Hannah, what do you do when it's half past summer and you're starting to fray around the edges?" She ignored me and continued looking for lotion to heal her dry hands. "My hair looks awful."

Aunt Hannah's daughter, Lorene, fulfilled a life-long dream and converted one of the bedrooms into the only beauty shop for miles around. I helped her wash the brushes and combs, and put them under the blue light in the sterilizing cabinet. She said, "Your hair will be easier to handle if I perm it. I'll sacrifice one of her beauty shop specials." She wrapped the wet shoulder-length hair in curlers, and placed a thick packet of foil-covered chemicals over each one. Next came the black cords connected to the machine above me. She clipped a cord to each curler and plugged the monster into the electrical outlet. I couldn't back out now. I was busy talking to my Heavenly Father, confessing each and every sin and wondering if I'd ever see daylight again.

Unlike capital punishment, no one witnessed the turn of the switch that initiated a hissing sound as the chemicals prepared to do their job. I was the one convicted to die. I knew I wasn't an angel, and I wasn't ready to die. I was thankful that Ailene missed out on my make-me-beautiful day. She would have suffered a stroke at the tender age of ten. I made it through the ordeal, but I traded straight hair for tress stress, tight curls, Little Orphan Annie style, only I wasn't a redhead.

It took weeks for the burn on my ear to heal. The preacher said my soul needed revival. So did my drab brittle hair. I prayed about my soul, but I still had a hair problem. I slathered mayonnaise through the strands followed by a hot, moist, lettuce-green towel.

My face felt dry from too much summer sun, so I doused a heavy coat of Vaseline to my face and hands. Aunt Hannah said that in 1859 workers in an oil field discovered this wonder jelly. They used it to soothe cuts and burns. They couldn't get along without it. Ailene saw my condition and rotated on her heels. "Golly, sis, you look and smell like a bologna sandwich. Makes me hungry. Isn't it supper time yet?"

"Don't laugh. Unless you want to turn into an ugly."

"Who's laughing? And what's an ugly?"

"It's the devil himself. A weird thing."

I rubbed my face with a towel and looked in the mirror. She laughed. "Was anyone else hurt in the accident?"

"Oh, Ailene. Too much is never enough. Don't worry. Maybe tomorrow I'll be good-looking and lovable like Aunt Hannah. For now let's go home. Supper will be ready."

UNCLE GIL FINISHED DESSERT, scooted his chair away from the table and tilted on the back legs. "Go feed the horse, Patty. I'm too tired."

"But I've never fed him. I haven't been around animals, except my Persian cat that you killed."

"Just give him one scoop of corn. Simple task."

It was a hot, humid day, the kind of day Uncle Gil moaned, "Hate them damn gnats."

Bayard's shining chestnut-brown hair was covered with the tiny black insects that dive-bombed his ears and eyes. He bobbed his head to shoo them away. *I wonder why they attack your eyes. Dumb things probably want to drink from them.* I went into the barn, found a can of spray and spewed a stinky mist on Bayard. "There. No more problems. Wish I could put away my fear of being trampled by your enormous body. I want to get better acquainted with you." I tossed a scoop of corn in the feeder and positioned myself on a bale of hay. He soon devoured every kernel. I offered a second helping and hurried inside to argue with my sister about who would wash dishes and who would dry.

As I cleaned the sink, the best part of the job because you're all done, my uncle came bursting through the kitchen door. "Hey. Why is the horse still eating? He should have finished long ago." I confessed to disobeying orders. The room became silent. Uncle Gil's voice frightened me. "Young horses must not overeat. Come with me to the barn." Even though Uncle Gil was furious and his face was fluorescent red, I can still see his slow, cow-tail gait as I trailed behind him. The pointy latch hook on the screen door dangled when I banged the door shut. The hinges cried.

The evening sun cascaded over the area as we walked into the barn. My uncle grabbed Bayard's bridle from a hook and stood stone still, like a man watching his blood being drawn into a syringe. "Don't you know ANYTHING? Why did you do this?" he shouted.

Shivers crept up my spine. I thought of the wicked witch going into meltdown. "Uh, I thought he was still hungry. He had pulled the plow for eight hours and fought the damn gnats, oops, sorry. I thought he deserved more, so I gave him another scoop of corn."

"Stupid! You've fed him too much. You don't listen. I told you to measure out ONE scoop." His nostrils vibrated, he shook the bridle in my face. The metal glistened. Reminded me of swords. "If he dies, I'll lash this bridle across your back. Get out of my sight. I'm sick of looking at you."

The dilemma took me by surprise. I stepped sideways to get a better look at his angry face. Gaining courage to speak, I straightened my knees, and when I realized I was still clutching a dishtowel under one arm I threw it on the ground. I stared at the bridle swaying before me. "Uh, uh—" I couldn't make a sound. I wanted Daddy or Mommy to lift me up and say it would be all right. My face felt like the mid-day sun.

Suddenly, something inside me stirred up moral fiber I

didn't know existed. I looked into his snapping eyes. "Excuse me, Mr. Brunk. I think you're acting like a mad man. In the first place, I did not ask to come here. And second, even if I said I was sorry you wouldn't forgive." I howled to the rafters, stamping my feet for emphasis. "No, Mr. Brunk, I will not allow you to whip me with a horse bridle. I will tell the world."

The face before me changed. The look of anger was replaced with a look of unbelief. I had caught him off guard. But I wasn't through. "And finally, Mr. Brunk, if you had lost your mother after knowing her seven short years, you'd know how I feel."

Even though his words pierced my heart, I heard more than verbal communication. I heard a yearning to dissolve obligations: providing for an elderly mother, a sister who choked and wheezed, and two nieces—his brother's responsibility—who had become a thorn in his side. Uncle Gil rubbed his chin, took the truck keys out of his pocket and headed down the driveway. I assume he needed a shot of whiskey at this point.

Tears that I had kept under arrest, slid down my cheeks. I retreated to the oak tree behind the barn. A curved limb resembling a chair became my thinking tree, a place of solitude. *First, he make me feel guilty for eating his food, and now he had the nerve to stand over me and threaten my life, all because I cared about his horse. My life is over. A bridle thrashing will be worse than all past punishments.* A yellow butterfly landed on my shoulder. "I'm *not* much to look at," I said aloud. "I'm not short, just height impaired. My sisters are beautiful. I won't have to worry about being attractive if the horse dies. Face and neck scars will go with me to the grave. They'll never be erased, nor will my hurt feelings. If I live through this bridle whip, I'll have to bridle my pride. Hey, Daddy where ARE you? I need some of your humor." I began praying, not for humor, not for me, but for Bayard.

The tree limb cracked, but I landed on my feet. I thought about answers and like Alice, arrived at my looking-glass destination by walking away, down the hill, over the fence, past

Thompson's house. Halfway between Pensin's and Lottie Hatfield's fence, my body thudded on the ground in a deep ravine. Ailene followed.

Night rolled down and the air chilled. We sat hidden in the ditch. "I'm freaking out," I admitted. "I can't go back and face Uncle Gil. It's getting so dark, I can't imagine tomorrow."

"I don't like dark. Wish we were somewhere else," Ailene said.

"I don't know where else to go. And I don't believe in wishes anymore," I told her. The mosquitoes punished our trespassing by lashing out. I heard a crackling sound in a brush pile on the other side of the ravine. Mrs. Thompson's dog Samson had decided to have some nighttime fun with a stray cat. "Guess we're lucky that a black cat didn't walk in front of us. That would *surely* mean bad luck."

The great horned owl, a silent night stalker who works the graveyard shift from the trees, broke the sound of loneliness. Ailene slumped into a fetal position. "The echo-man is teasing me again," she stammered. "If you could just forgive Uncle Gil, I'd feel—" She choked back sobs. "If you could forgive him, maybe he'll forgive me too."

"What did YOU do?

"I don't remember. You and I are always doing something wrong." Samson situated himself next to Ailene and placed his long nose in her lap. She caressed his ample supply of tangerine hair. "Maybe this will help." She rubbed her Jesus pin.

"Ailene, stay here with Samson. I need to check on Bayard. I'll be right back." As I trudged up the hill, I felt like a criminal attempting an escape. I wondered if a few pleasures would ever come into my life. Would I become an old lady living in a lonely cabin, or would I even *live* to be an old lady?

Aunt Margaret was standing at the front door. "Who are you looking for?" I asked with a disrespectful frown.

"If you don't come back, we're going to get the police after you."

"That would be fine," I muttered. The barn door was half

closed. Bayard was lying on the dirt floor, long strands of spittle swinging from his mouth. I gasped, shut the door and headed for the ravine. During the long night I cuddled Ailene in my arms. I thought about Brunk hollow and the dreams I had for the future. *I'm on the road to nowhere, and I can't go anywhere from nowhere.*

Before daylight arrived I slowly opened the screen door, and rejoiced that the back door wasn't locked. We stumbled through the dark kitchen and tiptoed to bed. Ailene's snoring droned me into a strange sleep and a strange dream. I knew strange backward and forward. In the dream I pushed my uncle off a cliff, but somehow we switched places and I was the one that was falling. While plunging downward I saw him stare at me with a hurt look. Kitchen noises, the rattle of pots and pans awoke me before I hit the ground. I turned over and drifted back to sleep.

Ailene tugged at my arms and patted my face. "Wake up, Patty. Wake up. It's morning. It's Saturday." Aunt Margaret was turning the clunky handle of the worn-out can opener that protruded from the wall. I awoke from the uneasy dreams, made a little wounded varmint noise under my breath and slowly dragged myself from the warm bed. After numerous cold stares during breakfast, I slipped outside, opened the barn door and was met with a warm, healthy "Naaay!"

Kidnapped

Whatever the weather, Ailene and I optimistically looked forward to Friday. The weekly grocery shopping included a fringe benefit. Wilma and Yvonne lived in a duplex two blocks from the Long Branch Company Store.

"Aunt Margaret has a bad cold," I said while skipping some of the railroad crossties. "She'll take a long nap, and since I feel especially brave today, we'll sneak in an extra long visit with our sisters."

"Let's run down the track, rush into the store and quickly get the stuff," Ailene said with a sprinkle of happiness.

I brushed the long hair from my eyes. "Sure, little sis. You talk about hurrying, but you never do. Aunt Margaret says you dawdle because you have short legs. She also says the early bird catches the worm if he hurries."

I loved Ailene's giggles. "But if you're a worm you're better off being late!"

"Hurry, girl."

"I am. I am. Haven't seen my sisters for a long, long time. Bet their babies are really big by now."

Customers, three-deep along the wood counter, chatted, blew cigarette and cigar smoke in my eyes as I impatiently waited. The clerk announced, "Who's next?"

I managed a compulsory smile. "I am. But can you please hurry? I have no time to waste." I called out the items from Aunt Margaret's list.

Wilma and Yvonne met us at the gate and set our purchases on the front porch. The smell of cinnamon rolls permeated the house. I ate three, and drank three glasses of milk. Laughter and playing with the babies—who were now walking—was a pleasant encouragement in my dull life.

After a glorious sixty-minute visit, I gathered a bag of foodstuff in each arm and wiped tears with my sleeve. "Saying goodbye is the worst part of the day. I hate going home." Wilma tried to force a smile. Yvonne frowned.

Ailene's bag ripped. Potatoes rolled on the porch and down the steps. Some of them looked moist. *Aunt Margaret will be very upset if I bring home rotten potatoes.* Yvonne put them in another bag. She tucked a few cookies into my pocket.

"Ailene, we've got to make up for lost time. We weren't supposed to come here. I hope Aunt Margaret won't know that we disobeyed. Again."

"These things are too heavy," she moaned.

"Just hang on. It's only three miles. You can do it."

"It's no fun at home!"

I opened the yard gate and stepped over the cracks in the sidewalk. Aunt Margaret was standing in the doorway. A summer wind blew the delicious scent of roses. I instantly re-membered that roses have thorns.

Aunt Margaret watched us put groceries away. "You know that you two have to get that garden weeded before dark."

"Yes, Ma'am, we know."

"Well, get your lazy butts out there."

I slumped on a kitchen chair. "Please let us rest. We just walked three miles."

"I'll give you five minutes."

"Are you sure you can spare five minutes?" I smirked.

In the half-acre garden plot, yesterday's rain had caused a larger than normal amount of weeds. "Tenacious weeds," I told Ailene.

"What's that mean?"

"That's a new word I learned in school. I hate pulling

weeds. I thought about this horrible job all night. Had night-mares, nightmares cause headaches, headaches because weeds that spread tenaciously. Ugly weeds rush to overtake vegetables."

"Don't know what you're talking about, Patty."

"Don't ever become a farmer. That's what I mean."

Once each summer we took turns visiting Wilma and Yvonne. During that precious week of happiness, at bedtime I didn't feel exhausted. Loving hands tucked me into soft blankets, and a gentle voice mentioned my name in prayer. Time quickly disappeared. The tradition ended due to unexpected problems.

Herb worked full time in the coal mines and spent evenings overhauling the car engine. He had agreed to take me back to Aunt Margaret's in seven days, but couldn't meet the deadline. As the old Ford chugged up the steep hill on a narrow, rough driveway, anxiety and dread overwhelmed me. Within minutes I'd be inside the little yellow house filled with discontent.

Aunt Margaret stood on the front porch with her short arms on her large hips. Most adults would have understood the situation, but not Aunt Margaret. Nooo. "You're two days late."

"Sorry about that," Herb answered. "But it couldn't be avoided."

"Why can't you cooperate? I took the girls when nobody wanted them."

"We appreciate what you've done," Wilma told her. "You know we always try to get the girls back on time. We've had a lot of car trouble."

"And you know I need their help," Aunt Margaret yelled in her usual gruff voice. "I sacrifice to let them spend a week with each of you. I will not permit them to go again."

"Do you really *mean* that?" Wilma asked.

Aunt Margaret kept shaking her head and forefinger. "Yes, indeed. I mean that."

"You won't get away with this," Herb warned. One week of happiness with siblings who replaced Mom had been taken away. The news devastated my sisters. That night I lay in bed forever. I wanted to disappear, to become a flower in the wallpaper.

On Saturday Wilma and Herb, Yvonne and Jerry came. Aunt Margaret didn't invite them in. We sat on the front steps. She parked herself nearby and listened to every word. She went inside when Grandma called her name. My sisters took advantage of the situation. Yvonne said, "Girls, Aunt Margaret won't allow us to see you again. We can't let this situation continue. You're treated worse than animals. We're taking you away from here."

Ailene's high voice ranged between a major second or a minor third, or somewhere in between. "Where are we going?"

Yvonne circled her arms around us and stood in a long silent clinch before speaking. "We have decided that you, Patty, will live with Wilma and Herb. Ailene, you will have a new home and a new life with Jerry and me. You will never have to return to this place."

"We must take you now, before something drastic happens," Wilma added. "At six o'clock tomorrow evening, we'll be waiting at the crossroad where the rocky road ends and the paved one begins."

Hallelujah thoughts entered my mind. *Yee-haw. I'll never have to plant corn as long as I live!* Ailene was doubtful. "I'll miss Grandma. We've been here longer than anywhere else. Five years at the same place, and we're together. I don't know if I can leave Aunt Margaret. She can't get along without us."

"But she has more faults than an earthquake zone. And the future looks–" I squeaked because my voice had gone someplace else in my body. "The future here looks foggy and dim. We have to leave." Ailene hung her head and exhaled to hold back tears. I turned out the light. "Don't cry, Honey. Everything will be fine. Tomorrow will be a long day so let's try to get some sleep. Do you know how much I love you?" She smiled and nodded.

I pondered the matter until the clock struck four. I was

afraid that somehow Aunt Margaret would read my mind. Realizing that living as though there is no tomorrow is a sure way to kill dreams, I had made the decision to look forward to tomorrow's arrival.

The next morning, I don't know if the dazzling haze I saw was due to the lack of sleep or the southern sun's shivery heat waves. Cracks were showing in the flowerbeds where the thirsty soil had lost its moisture. I found a broken vase in the garbage can, and filled it with water from the rain barrel. "I can't do for you what a gentle rain from heaven could, but you poor plants are crying for a drink. So here's a big one. Hope you make it. Hope I do too."

All day I concentrated on the job at hand, and pretended that everything was normal. Sweat stains saturated the under arms of my purple shirt. After finishing dinner dishes I took a sponge bath and put on a wrinkled cotton button-up. Finally, the clock was about to strike six, the evening sun and world news floated through the living room. The last thing I saw as we ebbed out the door was Aunt Margaret asleep on the couch. Grandma dozed in her rocker, opened one eye and drifted back to sleep. "See you later. Much later," I said. The guardian angel picture on the wall seemed to stare at me. I whispered, "I'm doing the right thing. Don't you think I'm doing the right thing?"

Ailene glanced over her shoulder. Tears showered her sad face. "I'm scared."

"Well so am I. But we have to obey our sisters. We can't let fear stop us," I said with more confidence than I had five minutes earlier. "Our best days are still in front of us." I whispered to myself over and over, "We're doing the right thing. My heart tells me that we're doing the right thing."

We tiptoed across the front porch, taking with us only the clothes we wore and the Christmas doll Daddy had given us. The three wooden steps creaked. The marigolds near the cracked sidewalk seemed to bid farewell. I pushed open the rusty gate. The hinges whined. I brushed the hair out of my eyes. "How do I look, sis?"

"Terrific," she answered.

Halfway down the hill I found myself wishing the world worked differently. Bitterness overwhelmed and took charge. "I *hate* that house. I *hate* this town. Hope I never set foot here again. Never. Neeev-errrr," I yelled. I imagine my words echoed back to the painted mountains in the distance. Two cars were waiting at the bottom of the hill. I felt a cleansing gratitude, a most remarkable peace. My new "sisters" ten-month-old Brenda, and Joy, almost three, were asleep in the back seat. With unwavering faith that I was about to enjoy a ride into another phase of life, I climbed into the front seat next to Wilma. Herb put the black Ford in gear and hurried away.

Ailene smiled with anticipation, jumped into the back seat of Yvonne and Jerry's blue DeSoto. As the car lunged forward, she welcomed hugs from her new "brother" and two younger "sisters." The horn honked three times, they waved and headed in the opposite direction.

Like baby chicks coming to roost, comfort surrounded me as we pulled into the driveway of the white company-owned house with black trim and a manicured yard. The large, shiny front porch floor was painted a light gray. I opened the gate and sniffed the delightful pink roses that covered a white trellis. Wilma and Herb's bright and airy home had lace curtains that fluttered in the breeze. Colorful mums in a charming pastel wicker basket and a crocheted doily covered the dining room table. "Let's have a cup of tea," Wilma said as the kettle whistled and water babbled to a full boil. She poured the fresh brew into flowered china cups. The first sip brought contentment that soothed the body and soul, and warmed my twelve-year-old heart.

Life was getting sweeter. My days were filled with music, laughter and children. But Wilma seemed strangely subdued and contemplative.

Shattered Dreams

*T*he first warning of what was soon to quicken a situation came three days later. On Friday, the thirteenth of September, the lovely music in Wilma's home crashed into a minor key. As Herb was leaving for work, the doorbell rang.

Uncle Gil waited in the car. Aunt Hannah stood on the front porch. Her crimson face looked firm and strained. Her words were sharp and hurried. "Margaret had a heart attack. She's upset because Patty and Ailene left. Their dad is back in town. He wants Patty to come with me. He wants both girls to help take care of Margaret. Poor Margaret is in a terrible shape."

Aunt Hannah, who had held me, caressed me, and gave my heart hope, brought news that we knew was untrue, devastating news. Wilma and Herb tried to reason with her. "Can't you make other arrangements? My sisters are young children."

"Margaret needs them. You can't stop this from happening."

"Patty is twelve. Ailene is almost ten. How can you expect them to care for a heart patient? You *can't do* this. They need a stable home life."

Aunt Hannah huffed, "The sheriff has signed papers. You can't fight city hall. I'll take Patty now or a patrol car will pick her up within the hour. Their dad and Ailene are waiting at Margaret's house."

Emotionally, I felt like the morning weather report: threatening storms, damaging winds. The distress in Wilma's voice was breaking my heart. Her words were merged with tears. "It looks as if we have no choice. Patty, I guess you should go with them. We'll work out something. Please don't worry."

I thought the war between living and dying had vanished, but while packing my skimpy possessions, a new conflict became apparent. Aunt Hannah pointed a finger at Wilma and shouted, "I hope your kids will be cursed! Something horrible will happen to them because you did this terrible deed." Her words frightened me. My expectations that cried out for help shattered against the backdrop of what might have been.

Wilma held me tight. "We'll get past this problem. I'll see you very soon." Aunt Hannah gave Wilma a mean frown, turned her nose up and shoved me in the back seat of the old Packard. I stared out the window, taking a final look at the house that brought a few days of happiness. Brenda and Joy wrapped their arms around Wilma's legs. Joy wiped tears. As the car turned onto the paved roadway I looked back to see their little arms waving. It seemed as if everything, the tree with enormous leaves that shaded the porch and the roses on the fencerow whispered a final goodbye. Only the humming engine broke the silence. It appeared that my life was held together with coat hangers and Band-Aids, the metal eroding and the plastic melting in the heat.

I greeted Aunt Margaret as eagerly as one welcomes a swarm of mosquitoes on a hot summer's night. Aunt Hannah said she had to go milk the cows. Ailene hugged and hung on to me for several minutes. Daddy sat quietly on the porch, Aunt Margaret paced back and forth. Her eyes glared, her face was purple with rage. "Don't you two know what you did to me?"

"No. What did we do to you?" I asked as we went inside.

"Well, you upset me terribly. You upset Grandma too. Where is your loyalty? We took you into our home. No one else wanted you. We took care of you until you were old enough to help us, old enough to pay us back, and now you want to desert us?"

I pursed my lips and fixed my eyes on Aunt Margaret.

"Well, slap my butt and call me Fannie. By the way, what did Dr. Hitchman say about your heart attack?"

"Oh, he says I'll recover in time."

The odor of cleaning products filled the room. The lid on an aluminum pot jiggled on the iron cook stove and emitted the smell of beef. Aunt Margaret's condition had not changed. I ran trembling fingers through my hair. "Uh, huh. You're tough." *Fool me once, shame on you. Fool me twice, shame on me. You won't fool me again.*

After Grandma and Aunt Margaret went to bed, Daddy sat at the kitchen table and talked about the situation. His face moved in stages from serene to assertive. "I think you both should stay here for a little while and see how your Aunt Margaret gets along. She doesn't look well. I need to talk to Sheriff Krause." My angry face reflected angry thoughts. *I'll bet hard cash that she's telling lies.* Ailene displayed a dozen shades of distress that turned into an unflinching stare.

Two days later Daddy told Ailene and me, "I agreed with Margaret until Wilma and Yvonne convinced me that my sister lied about the heart attack. I talked with Sheriff Krause. He said, 'I'm glad your girls kidnapped Patty and Ailene.' He said they made a wise decision." Daddy hesitated, bowed his head and wiped tears. "The sheriff told me that the whole town knew how my sister treated you. Said he would never permit his siblings to live in such conditions. Said he would have done the same thing."

"What happens now?" we asked in unison.

"Yvonne told me that she and your mom made a decision long ago. Yvonne should take Ailene. Wilma ought to have Patty. That's what they decided. I'll call Yvonne to say I'm sending you girls by train."

Ailene was apprehensive about leaving again. "What if Aunt Margaret is really sick?"

"She's not sick. She's pretending," Daddy said. "It's getting late. We'll talk tomorrow." Realizing that Daddy was carrying out Mom's wishes helped me to sleep through most of the night.

The next morning Ailene said, "But I'm not sure we're doing the right thing. I'll miss seeing Aunt Margaret."

I kicked the chair. "I'll miss her the way you miss rain on a picnic."

That evening Daddy told his sister he was taking Ailene and me to see a friend, but he headed for the train station. We went inside and sat on a long, dusty bench while he talked to the ticket agent.

A few minutes later an aggrieved father and two small children walked across the wood platform that creaked with each step. We waited under a dim light bulb. The tang of creosote drifted through the splintered ties. The train came into view, the engine light brightened, whistles wailed. The ground shook, steam poured from the smokestack. The locomotive panted and croaked to a halt. A man in a conductor's coat, shiny with age, stepped down. He placed a metal step on the ground, and several people climbed aboard. After a long embrace I whispered goodbye and moved slowly toward the train. Daddy said, "I love you, Patty."

"Love you too."

Ailene waved both hands and wiped tears with one of Mom's hankies. "I'll think of you every day."

I grabbed the iron handrail and hoisted myself onto the train platform. "Remember, sis, when we're apart we're still together."

The conductor called out, "All aboard!" A wisp of steam rolled past and the wheels repeated clunkety-clunk, clunkety-clunk. I clutched the back of the dark-green seat to steady myself. The train that would separate me from my darling sister gave a long jerk and a hasty chug. Soot powdered the windowsills. I looked out the back window and watched the depot recede. The lovely blond-haired girl in a blue dress faded into the shades of evening. A sharp whistle blended with the turbulence inside me. Through the smoky glass Daddy's cigarette glowed like a beacon. He leaned against the wall to wait for the next train that would take Ailene to her new family at Yvonne's house.

Wouldn't it be something if we could keep the ones we love? The leaves of life have neither emotions nor conflict. They fall, one by one.

A New Life

At midnight the train pulled into Prince Station. The conductor opened the steel door and stepped onto a wooden platform. "Let me help you down that big step." He wrapped a husky arm around my tiny waist. "God bless you, honey." The wind blew air funnels around corners of the train. The mountain breeze was more than fresh after the stuffy train ride. Wilma and Herb extended their arms and cradled me into their world.

After a restful sleep, I awoke to the smell of homemade donuts. Standing in the sunlight on Wilma's back porch, I watched swift hummingbirds pollinate the impatiens. Butterflies filled the air, wings like cathedral glass against the sun were gently riding a breeze, rising, descending and sipping hollyhocks transplanted from Mom's flower garden. An almost perfect peace rested over this household.

Over lunch the next week, Daddy told me, "Good luck has been with me lately. I know I made the right choice in having you leave Aunt Margaret's."

"Coming to Wilma's wasn't luck. It was providence."

I was twelve when my sister became my mom. My heart wouldn't let me forget Mom's hugs. That same feeling flowed like lava and covered my whole being when Wilma was near. She reminded me of Mom, the high cheekbones, dark brown naturally curly hair, and a radiant olive complexion that reflected a warm smile. Wilma had an inborn musical ability.

Light from a brass lamp shined on the piano music and guided her fingers. Music was a pleasant solution for problems of the past. Soothing sounds of the "Black Hawk Waltz" helped erase the instability of the last few years, surrounded me with tranquility and lulled me to sleep almost every night. Wilma and Herbert's love had set me free. At first I perceived myself as an intruder, but the family welcome was strong and genuine.

Even though we visited every two weeks, I missed Ailene's giggling, sharing secrets, and sleeping in a half-bed with arms wrapped tight around each other, like vines on a fence row. I wondered who would pick up Aunt Margaret's groceries. At Canterbury's store I always took a few minutes to gaze into the jewelry case. I imagined a diamond on each finger, glistening in the sunlight.

The love for my sister-mom shined brighter than any diamond. She meant more than a whole chest full of diamonds. Wilma's strong faith provided the moral compass for her family. She used ingenuity and sheer grit to help us survive, improvised in many ways to stretch meals, substituted things at hand for household items that would otherwise have to be purchased.

She created patterns from the Sears and Roebuck catalog and sewed most of our clothes. She always looked neat in hand-tailored dresses with lovely crocheted edging. She decorated the house for holidays, made peanut butter fudge and let us stir cocoa with candy canes. Her home cast an otherworldly glow in my life. I could drink milk whenever I was thirsty. In the summer, white sheets, crisp and tidy, hung on the clothesline and flapped in the wind. I remember quiet velvet-covered evenings on Wilma's porch that served as an outdoor living room area where we laughed, discussed politics, the war, movie stars we read about in magazines. A square table held pitchers of lemonade. Walkers passed by to exchange bits of neighborhood gossip.

I taught my new sisters to play house. We ran through fields of maiden grass, picked wild daisies and pulled the petals apart. "Here's how to tell if your boyfriend loves you. He loves me. He loves me not."

"I don't have a boyfriend," Joy said.

"You're only three. You don't need one. What you need is more doll clothes. Some day we'll have your mom teach us to sew."

"Me too," chimed one-year-old Brenda. In the evening children and grown ups gathered in our yard to play games such as Ante Over, Kick the Can and horseshoes. The Friday night card games and homemade donuts will long be remembered.

On Saturday nights our neighbor, Lucille Wood, invited friends in for popcorn and television. Loretta Young entered my life through a door depicted on a black-and-white television screen. Her beautiful dresses were statements of charm and grace. She viewed her craft and her stardom as vehicles to teach moral lessons. Loretta Young movies were geared to happy endings. She walked in beauty and elegance, had sparkling eyes and marvelous high cheekbones. We scheduled activities around Red Skelton, the antics of Clem Kadiddlehopper and Freddie the Freeloader. My "sisters" and I sacked out on the sofa. Sensational!

"I look forward to seventh grade," I told Wilma. "But I dread going to a new school. I'm shy about making friends, cause I'm afraid I'll sound dorky. I know I look dorky."

She shook her head. "Don't say that! You do not look or sound dorky. You're a bright girl. You just don't realize it at this point." She hesitated for a minute or two. "Honey, your ego is stark naked. Inferiority can crush an individual, or provide emotional energy that powers success and achievement. It depends on your reaction to stressful circumstances. Patty, I know Aunt Margaret didn't encourage you to succeed, but you *will* succeed."

"Sis, I'll tell you one of my stress stories. I remember the day Aunt Margaret sat on the porch visiting with Pearl. I searched through an old trunk and found vintage clothing, hats and letters tied with twine string. In the bottom was a smelly album, and on the first page, photos reminded me of picture day in grade school. On picture day, I told the teachers I didn't want to participate, that I had never seen a good picture of me, and that we couldn't afford to buy the pictures anyway. Each year I heard the same explanation. 'The company expects a few dollars to go astray. You may keep the pictures.'

"I couldn't bear to look at photos of myself. I glared at my second grade photo, the one where I tilted my head back like my neck wasn't strong enough to support my head. After I ripped the face, the hair, the neck, and crushed the glossy paper in my hand, I thought of Aunt Hannah's Sunday school class. I remembered the Scripture, *Love others as much as you love yourself.* That commandment was easy for me to follow. When you don't love yourself you don't have to love anyone else." Tears welled up in Wilma's eyes, but I couldn't stop chattering.

"In third grade my eyes were closed. My smile was too big. I tore that one into small strips. In fourth grade my hair looked greasy, stringy, my face looked sad. I used a pencil to destroy the face." I saw my own flaws too well and couldn't see the attributes that certainly must be there. Now I realize that our self-image often doesn't match what we see in the mirror, or what the camera sees.

After one month in school, and with my sister's continual reassurance, I resolved to turn my childhood endeavors into something positive. "Wilma, from this day forward I'll feed my faith and starve my doubts. I don't plan to become the most popular student in school, but I want to be an honorable student."

Miss Sims was a tall, skinny, fragile teacher who raked her nails across the blackboard—screeeeeek! The students soon recognized that the chalk in hand and her chair scooting across the room meant we should brace ourselves for the onslaught. I must admit that I enjoyed her method of teaching English and the singsong examples of grammar, using various verbs. Every day she went through the same ritual. "Today I see, yesterday I saw, many times I have seen. Today I go, yesterday I went, many times I have gone." Up to now, no one had provided identification of my compensatory skills, but at an early age I established my niche in music and writing.

A science project regarding farm life evoked childhood memories. I chose to write about a familiar subject. Eggs:

> You have to appreciate eggs. They're so egg-shaped. They're so functional and practical. Some are spherical. And having no corners makes for a stronger package and happier chickens. The hens like oval shapes that fit close together in nests, conserving space and heat. They're less likely to wander off that way. Sometimes they roll out of the nest, down a hill to who knows where. Sometimes they just roll around in a circle. They fit into egg cartons so nicely. Eggs are not gravity-fed; they're pushed through their mothers. Squeezed, actually. They start out soft. The back end has to get squeezed more than the front end or else the egg goes the wrong direction. You can decide which end of the egg leaves the chicken first.

"This is scientific," Mr. Foors said with a callous grin.

I didn't do well in math. Mr. Ryan said, "Diophantine equations don't lend themselves to simple solving techniques, but you'll enjoy them once you learn the process. Some Diophantine equations have no solutions. Some have an infinite number of solutions and others seem to be out-of-the-blue numbers." I squeezed by and found no enjoyment in this type of learning.

Music remained a passion. My Glee Club teacher placed a note in my music folder, an announcement from the principle's office: THE FAYETTEVILE COMMUNITY SCHOOL MUSIC DEPARTMENT INVITES YOUR PARTICIPATE IN THE STATE CHOIR FESTIVAL, REPRESENTING THE ALTO SECTION.

The director selected "His Truth is Marching On." I knew

the song and was ready, willing and honored, but formal attire was required. After weeks of fervently hoping that a miracle would happen I informed the teacher, "I've dreaded telling you this. My family can't come up with the money for a formal."

"I'm so sorry, Patty. This is a wonderful opportunity. But if it's any comfort, several other students have relinquished participation for the same reason. Loletta would be my next choice." Loletta was the oppressor that I had a fight with last summer. She bad-mouthed my dad. I absolutely hated Loletta who was too rich, and much too sure of herself. My source of self-esteem didn't come through the acceptance of other students. I found them to be notoriously fickle.

September meant new teachers, new binders, a new circle of friends, and a hot baseball team. I loved baseball. The junior class started a pool. I always bet on the Yankees. "Joltin Joe" DiMaggio was one of baseball's greatest players, an icon. He *was* baseball. The magnitude of the man was thrilling. I remember game six of the 1951 World Series, DiMaggio's final game. He gave up baseball for two years while serving his country.

My senior trip to Hawks Nest Park in the heart of the Appalachian Mountains was a big deal. First times are important and filled with quiet innocence. I didn't travel much and fifty miles up and down curvy roads caused a strange feeling in my stomach. But the panoramic view offered a cure. I'll always remember the magic of the evening when I "discovered" the ancient West Virginia river valley. The world seemed vast from the 1,400-foot overlook. High school sweethearts crept to the edge of the mountain and gazed at the view. Smoke curled over the winding emerald-green river. The Upper Kanawa Valley was filled with a campfire haze. Purple mountain ranges that reach for the sky featured dark lavender rhododendron, the state flower.

One of my classmates always seemed polite, although he was known to connive and finagle to get his way. He was pleasant enough, but I knew that if my life were a movie, this guy would be buried in the credits. At nightfall he took my hand as we walked along a poorly lit path. He displayed a convincing gaze. "Let's check out the overlook."

"Let's have a cup of hot chocolate," I said. Students and chaperones stood around the huge bonfire, roasted hotdogs and marshmallows. We drank Coke, and sang the songs that nobody officially taught us. We just learned them unconsciously, absorbed the tune and lyrics. About midnight, after helping with clean-up chores, I boarded the yellow school bus and headed home with new memories of the coal mining state's breathtaking natural beauty.

The next week Wilma and I went to the company store and selected a white chiffon dress for my baccalaureate, a navy blue suit, red shoes and matching purse for the graduation ceremony. I'll never forget the grins on the faces in the front row, especially Wilma, Herb, Joy, and Brenda, who had helped me feel that I was a worthy human being.

Two days later Herb told the New River Company store office clerk, "Patty is looking for a job."

"They posted an opening today. I'll recommend her." I went for an interview and began work the next week. The grocery department stocked baked and canned goods, cooking oil, soap, plastic storage bags, fishing tackle and work gloves. For sweet lovers there was a large wood-framed candy case with glass sides and top so the contents could be seen at eye level by small toddlers or looked down upon by taller teens. I used a long rod with a gripper end to pluck cereal boxes stored on the top shelf. A wavering hand brought tumbling boxes onto the clerk's head. The cereal selections, devoid of Sugar Smacks, Lucky Charms and granola, included many of today's selections.

WHEN COAL WAS KING, coal companies ran whole towns. They provided scrip to the miners who took an advance on their paychecks. Books in different denominations could be purchased from the office to provide another way of advancing money for shopping at the notorious company store. Scrip, the coin of the realm, known as stickers, flickers, or clackers, came in an assortment of brass, copper, or aluminum shapes. Owing your soul to the company store was not just a line from a song, but a reality. Many miners said, "I live from week to week and never get a paycheck."

Another declared, "With black lung, I won't live long enough to see my account recorded in any other color but red." The company store was reminiscent of a neighborhood family grocery. You walked up to the counter, told the clerk what you wanted, and she jotted items down on a small green and white order pad. She figured the total price, rang up the sale on a four-drawer cash register that clanged like a trolley. Instead of the familiar question "plastic or paper" we asked if the customer wanted a cardboard box or brown paper bag. Most chose boxes to use for firewood.

In the meat department stainless steel scales weighed the fresh meat that was displayed in sparkling white enamel showcases. The manager insisted that we give customer-friendly service. I did everything except pump gas. That was a man's job. Within a short time the manager promoted me to the dry goods department that stocked clothing, shoes, fabric and furniture. The job boosted my self-esteem.

Wilma and my younger "sisters" sometimes interrupted my hectic day. The boss told me to take an extra half-hour. I opened the cash drawer and retrieved my charge book. In the grocery department I put together a picnic lunch, a candy treat for the girls. We sat under a maple tree and drank Orange Crush pop.

Every weekend, co-workers Helen, Jean, Betty Jo, and I cruised country roads and went to drive-in movies. Our evening ended with ham and egg sandwiches at the Top Hat Drive Inn where carhops recognized our borrowed cars, rushed over to take our orders, and filled our frosty root beer mugs three times. We gave great tips. Betty Jo and I soon became tight-knit friends. The two of us, and our boyfriends shared great memories.

On Wednesday afternoons underneath the Cotton Hill Bridge, four sun worshipers stretched out on an enormous rock. We competed for the best tan, but the real competition was more interesting and most challenging. One by one my brave friends took hold of a thick 40-foot jute rope that had hung there for years. Leaning against the bridge pillars, you had to get a running start and swing out over the water far enough to propel back to the ledge. Failure to do so forced a decision to let go of the rope, dodge the jagged rock, and attempt to drop into the calm, lighter-colored, shallow area of the river.

Even though I'm an excellent swimmer and unafraid of water, I respect the New River whirlpools, river valleys and rapids. The same inner strength that helped me get to this point in life now provided the courage to grasp the rope and start the pendulum. Many have been killed or maimed by teasing their success skills. It was a breathtaking moment. I returned to the ledge without dropping into the deep, cold water below. Once was enough.

Every other weekend I borrowed Herb's Chevy that gave smooth, assuring power. The radio speakers provided front-row performance that blasted Hank Williams' country ballads. The "Fearsome Foursome" group introduced me to the Winston cigarette habit. If given permission to go twenty miles, I went thirty. I remember the Saturday night I ventured forty miles. After our sandwich and root beer I headed home.

Like a flashing neon sign, my brother-in-law "dad" stood on the porch with one leg propped on the railing, his head cradled in his left hand. "Ugh, oh! This is a sign of trouble," I said aloud. I parked the car and sauntered up the steps.

"Where did you go tonight?" he asked.

"Uh, Beckley area. I know I went too far. Sorry!"

"I asked that question to see if you'd lie. I'm glad you were truthful. I'm not worried about distance. Sherman and I were in town and saw my car pass by at a pretty good clip. Smoke rolled from the windows. I thought the car was on fire. Do you smoke?"

"Yes."

"Do you inhale?"

"Yes."

"I have the nasty smoking habit, but I wish you wouldn't get hooked. It's harmful to your health." He reached for the door and glanced back at me. His stiff jaw and firm voice relaxed. "Don't get me wrong. I'm pleased that you have nice friends, and fun times. You deserve some enjoyment. It's late. Goodnight."

A thrashing after challenging Aunt Margaret would have been easier to take. I crawled into bed, turned out the light, and dreamed that I refused Aunt Margaret's request for acquittal. I awoke with new strength of mind, a new perspective.

I can't forgive a situation. I don't need to understand in order to forgive. Aunt Margaret never asked for acquittal, but unknown to my repeat offender, the charge has been dismissed. The mountain of forgiveness is difficult to cross, but true forgiveness liberates. I have been liberated from the bondage of bitterness. I have runaway visions of things to come.

MY FUN WITH company store friends ended in October 1953. I've replayed the scene many times. Herb had finished his shift, showered and checked the information board. Large bold letters shouted the message NO WORK TOMORROW. The disappointing words greeted miners several times a month, resulting in only two or three day's pay per week.

A few miners moved to Michigan, the automotive capital. Herb accepted a friend's offer for temporary lodging, found a job, and every two weeks made the 900-mile trip south to see his family. At the Kelsey-Hayes Wheel Company, he met a guy who had a cottage for rent. Herb told him, "It's small, but the price is right. Next weekend I'll move the family north."

As our light gray Chevy—pulling a U-Haul trailer with a

142

few belongings—rolled across the mountain roads of West Virginia, we were excited about the prospects of seeing a different part of the country. Passing the high school where I graduated a year ago, I sang the fight song, "Ode to Fayetteville" and realized that half the class had already left the state. In some counties, old strip mines were hidden under the cosmetic efforts to reclaim the wasteland. The land was poor and kept farmers and miners poor. Adjacent to small churches were stone markers where parents, grandparents and relatives had returned to dust. High school football fields were covered with crab grass. Water towers were rusty. Unpainted barns leaned against trees.

The narrow two-lane roads circled around mountains where rocks dared the earth to leave; reminded me of spreading hawk wings. Rolling soybean fields stretched for miles then grew steeper as the foothills began. Within a few hours I would get my first glimpse of flat country. Driving north on US 61, I wondered how we would thrive on city life. Herb anticipated a seamless move, and determined to put thoughts of doubt behind him.

At three in the morning, after several hours of driving through wind and rain, an Ohio State police officer flashed his lights. Herb pulled onto the muddy shoulder of the narrow road. The officer, a stout man of about thirty with a moon-shaped but rather delicate face, shined a flashlight in the front and back seat. "Did you know your trailer lights are out, sir?" he wearily protested.

Herb was wearing the look of a man with great apprehensiveness, but more importantly, he displayed a look of stamina. He gave a despairing sigh. "Didn't know that. I checked them three hours ago."

The officer seemed to be speculating on our purpose. He gave Herb a chastising glare. "It's a wonder you didn't get rear-ended. Where are you headed?"

"Got a new job in Michigan. Got expectations of a new life for my family." Three-year old Joy and one-year-old Brenda were asleep. Herb opened the car door and stepped outside to talk to the officer. "What I didn't expect was a downpour."

The officer shook his head. "Everything in that trailer must be soaked. I sure feel sorry for you folks." Clothing, bedding and three mattresses were water logged, and so was Wilma's beloved friend, the Singer sewing machine with an oak cabinet. Joy and Brenda's carefully chosen toys were dripping.

"Dumb weather report said clear and dry throughout West Virginia and Ohio for the next three days. I didn't feel the need to invest in a tarp."

"I see your point. I have a large sheet of plastic and some rope in the trunk." The officer helped Herb rearrange items in the trailer and anchored the plastic with the rope. "There. That gives you protection. How long have you been on the road?"

"Nine hours. With this weather, we'll probably be *another* nine hours," Herb said as he took a flashlight and a roll of electrical tape out of the glove box. "I'll tape the flashlight to the bumper."

"That won't do," the officer said. "The light has to be red."

I reached for my purse. "No problem. I've got some red nail polish."

The officer held a flashlight for Herb. "Guess that will do the trick. You guys sure have determination. You'll make it to Michigan. I wish you God speed."

We had passed hurdle one. I shoved a wet stuffed elephant aside, and retrieved two small dolls. Darkness and the cold October night air brought an eerie feeling. Once we were on the road again, I held the dolls near the heater. When the girls awoke, they cuddled the babies in their tiny arms and fell asleep again.

Sunrise in the mountainous country was framed in pale peek-a-boo peach triangles, but the flat land sunrise was gray at first, then silver, then powder puff pink as the early rays unrolled before our eyes. An unobstructed presentation of beauty surrounded us and presented a mental picture I'll always remember. My mental picture of our new home included a house nestled in trees and shrubs, a porch, large windows and a spacious yard with flowering shrubs.

After viewing the legendary American countryside scenes: motels, truck stops, cafés, conversations regarding the Burma Shave signs and the humorous advice the company doled out, after taking much pleasure in the flat country, we arrived at our square-shaped white cottage with a small yard not worth mentioning. The owner, who lived next door, pushed aside the wood slats of her Venetian shades and watched us pull into the driveway. By now heavy rain gushed along the shoulders of the paved road that was about two feet from our front yard. "She must think the Beverly Hillbillies have arrived," I said.

Joy had a questionable look on her face. "Our name isn't Beverly." Joy was a patient child, content to wait for answers to her long line of questions.

"You know, the television family that came from California?" Wilma said.

"Nah. I didn't ever see them. Are they a nice family, like us, looking for a home?"

I honored her question with an exhausted laugh. "They say that hillbillies don't keep things in order, and don't care how their trailer is junked up when they move. Enough said about the subject. The Michiganders probably will *give us* that name."

After eighteen hours of sitting in the same position and the last three hours listening to the swish, swoop of the windshield wipers, I was ready to stand, walk or jog in the rain. When our new landlady came over and viewed the drenched mess, everything we owned, she brought extra clothing, blankets and sheets. She even offered to help unpack. We slept on the floor; had two blankets each. The girls used their dolls for a pillow.

The next morning bright sunshine broke through the dark clouds and glistened in beads of moisture that covered the lawn. The air was crisp and fresh. Even though we lacked basic conveniences, the prospect of a perfect day was expressed in the sound of birds chirping and shaking their wings in the dew-drenched grass. Three days of sunshine dried our belongings. Wilma cleaned and polished our humble abode, and made blue ruffled curtains that flapped in the northern breeze. This house was filled with love. This house was filled with possibility.

Like most coal miners with financial troubles and hearts worn thin, Helen, Lester, and a dozen families came to Michigan to find a new life. Instead of searching for work right away, I welcomed the idea of taking a two-week vacation getting acquainted with the Michigan winter wonderland. On Monday Lester's sister had a job interview. "Come along. I'll take you downtown. We can have lunch at the famous Homemade Cafeteria. You know I love to eat. They have the best southern cooking. I'm trying to get work at Michigan Bell Telephone Company. They need lots of people."

In the waiting room, the Employment Interviewer interrupted a story I was reading in *Seventeen Magazine*. "Would you consider working for a fine company?" I thought of Herb's job and the possibility of a layoff. *If opportunity knocks, I should answer.*

"Might as well try." She asked what department I preferred. I thought, *I'd like your job*, but I said, "Anything." The test was easy. She said she would call within two weeks.

Herb's job at Kelsey-Hayes appeared to be stable, but all too soon the haunting words appeared on the bulletin board: NOTICE OF TEMPORARY LAYOFF. He applied for a tire builder position at Goodyear Tire and Rubber Company. The interviewer frowned and pointed an arthritic finger. "It's the same story. Kelsey Hayes people come here, get trained, you hear the call and you're gone."

"If you'll take a chance on me, I'll sign a contract. I'll stay. My word is honorable." Herb started working the next week.

Two days later the Employment Office called and asked me to report to work as an operator at eight o'clock Monday. People from the north gave me a hearty welcome. On the other hand, I've had my share of put-downs since this southern bell came north. During break time and at lunch, co-workers asked

146

me to repeat myself. My accent was the brunt of jokes. Although my instructor seemed to enjoy the sweet tone, sometimes I felt misunderstood.

Sometimes I needed to talk and Wilma was a qualified listener. She had a way of raising my spirits. Listening binds up wounds and smoothes rough places. She said, "The mountains you crossed during childhood will slip away, and new memories will develop. There's nothing wrong with having an accent. As long as you use it in the south."

The southern accent can bring ostracism and feelings of inferiority. Even presidents have been ridiculed because of the Dixieland voice. I met a true friend my first week at MBT. Dorothy came from North Carolina, and she knows all about good accents. "You have a beautiful southern voice," she said. "Don't let it get you down. I lived through it."

I not only lived through it, but I handled the situation with pride. My silk-suited boss asked how I was getting along. "Don't worry, Mr. Dawe. I've learned to us the northern voice when saying 'nine' 'five' 'my' 'kind.' Not only that, I've learned Spanish with a southern drawl. Vamos, y'all!"

"Fine Job," the instructor said after three weeks training. I give credit to the Bell Company for what I am today. Management employees took a country girl and taught her how to tackle five activities simultaneously.

The red and white lights on each switchboard and in front of each position reminded me of a busy highway. I learned to navigate through heavy traffic. Twelve sets of cords connected operators, customers, emergencies, business places and lovers. Early one morning I answered an Inward Operator's request. I plugged the front cord into a connection marked PULASKI, properly grasped the ringer key between my thumb and forefinger and counted, "One thousand and, two thousand and."

A sharp voice coming through the headset caused my low blood pressure to shoot up to normal. "Pull-ask-eye!"

"Where in the…"

A voice growled, "Who's there?"

"Sorry, ma'am. I'm ringing Pulaski."

"You got her!"

Marge sat next to me bursting with laughter. "You've never met Mrs. Pulaski, the most influential lady in town?"

"Don't think so."

"Next Saturday night, my sister Esther and the MBT gang will take you for a spin; a night on the town, in the big city of Pulaski."

What a spin it was! Traveling west on M-60, we passed through Spring Arbor. "This is a college town, a religious town where you can't buy cigarettes or beer," Esther said. "It's been dry and smokeless for years. Remember hearing the operator at Concord answer, 'Kahn-Kurd'? Well here's her office. If you blink, you'll miss the town. Let's go in and say hello." We stopped to chat with the operator, a matronly individual that reminded me of a Hitchcock movie.

As we left I said in a sarcastic tone, "And they drilled me for six months about how to speak properly." My evening was already enlightening with meeting some of the tributary operators, but the best was yet to come.

The town of Pulaski has an interesting history. Since the early 1920s the small settlement jumped with three saloons and a dance hall. At that time only a dozen families lived in the area. Pulaski's one-room schoolhouse was similar to the one I attended. Residents traveled to Concord to find a food market and high school. They say the township's biggest moment came in 1906, when Buffalo Bill's presence drove many women into a tizzy, fainting spells and screams.

In 1923, Fay and Harriett Butler purchased a grocery business and turned the second floor into a lively dance hall. Every Saturday night for thirty-five years, the business attracted people from several counties. The center of Pulaski was bustling with nightlife. That night an irate wife entered, grabbed her husband by the hair and dragged him past a gigantic upright piano and through the dark oak swinging doors. His friends jeered as she yelled, "I'm takin' you home."

Dancing to the soft music brought back visions of Little Jimmy, my first dance partner in gym class. Our Saturday night spin to the site of the famed—some say notorious—Pulaski dances lasted until early Sunday morning. My partner walked me to Marge's car. "Thanks for the memories. Stick around. In a few hours, I'll take you to the church just down the street. They dance there too. They're a happy bunch."

My co-workers were not always happy. The biggest complaint about the work place was, "It's too cold. It's too hot." You wore summer clothes in winter and winter clothes in summer. Sitting at "the board" in summer was dreadful. Perspiration saturated your back and butt. Some passed out, were carried to the "quiet room" for rejuvenation. In July and August the iceman came every day at noon. He placed a large chunk of ice in washtubs and positioned a fan behind them. For every six people there was one "cooling system." We celebrated when air conditioning was installed.

A year later I moved up to Service Assistant. After years of Wilma calling the shots, I became her boss. She was a new recruit and I was careful not to be too demanding. As a supervisor I learned to accept losing friends who refused to adhere to company rules.

In the fall I began instructing new operators. Even though I loved teaching I found that older students had difficulty learning. The third year of employment, I was still a shy country girl. In a crowd of three, when I spoke I blushed. I told my boss, "I'd rather be lying in the casket than delivering the eulogy." I'll never forget my first attempt to stand before an audience and remain upright. My job as Employment Interviewer involved contacting schools to recruit employees. I rehearsed day and night and felt quite prepared. But it was a worst-case scenario. I was alone in the office that day; an interview lasted longer than I anticipated. After locking my desk, I hung a plastic clock on the door: RETURN AT 1:00 P.M.

Driving south on M-50 to Brooklyn High School, panic struck. In my haste I left the script on my desk. I'm half way there and fifteen minutes late leaving the office. "Got to wing it," I said aloud. And wing it I did. Being forced to rely on my memory proved to be advantageous. Stage fright, the most basic primitive fight-or-flight reaction, produced sweaty palms and a queasy stomach. The symptoms had been hot-wired into my body and soul, the fear of failure, and concern that the teenage audience would give me a cold shoulder. Fear struck. I struck back. The butterflies flew in formation.

Standing at the tall lectern in the auditorium, I grasped the waistband of my cherry red skirt and glanced at the English teacher. "Be careful what you say and how you say it, Patty dear," a small voice inside me cautioned. I felt threatened, but the adrenalin kicked in to help me survive. The voice added, "Defend yourself and fight. You know your subject."

I focused my eyes on the audience and took a deep breath to send more oxygen to the brain. I thought of the song, "I'm Special," and envisioned the listeners standing at the bathroom sink brushing their teeth. I pictured my English teacher's smile and praise for an essay I wrote. Whether or not the audience accepted me was their decision. By programming my nervous system I made things happen. "Wasn't it nice that I helped you skip class today?" The students applauded.

"Come back tomorrow," a student sitting in the front row yelled.

The next week the third level boss paid a visit. "Patty, you're doing a fine job. I've scheduled a public speaking course next week in Grand Rapids. You'll have a company car, hotel suite and expenses." On graduation day, with poise and self-assurance, I accepted a certificate.

The economy improved and the company hired more employees who were forced to tolerate the crowded workspace. Next came workstations, cubicles, and a perfect solution to over-crowding. The walls were low and workers could pop their heads over the dividers to look for someone or talk to their neighbor. The practice, called "prairie dogging," can drive workers with highly detailed jobs to the brink of distraction.

Figuring budget and doing payroll with people talking and telephones ringing was difficult and frustrating.

Endless rows of box-like workstations gave rise to the term "cube forms." Employees get the feeling they're stuck in a little box. I set up a politically correct prairie-dogging guide that added a little humor to an employee meeting.

It read: Before poking your head up to converse over the cubicle you should: burp or create another bodily sound to warn others that you are going to prairie dog.

Don't make eye contact with intervening cubicle occupant if you intend to prairie dog two or more cubicles down the row. Name the person to whom the message is addressed. Don't talk to the walls or say "hey you."

Never prairie dog during ten o'clock break or lunch hour. Never start conversation until you and the dog-ee are standing.

Never continue conversation if the neighbors snort, cough or pound pencils on the desk. Go elsewhere to talk.

Before deciding to prairie dog, make sure the boss is either on the golf course, (tell callers he's in an important meeting) or close his door. (Tell him there's a gas leak). Bosses aren't fond of bobbing heads. They want brain power.

Don't be a "sheep dog" or a "prairie pup." Sheep dogs are workers lazily hanging their arms over office panels. Pups are people too short to see and talk over cubicle walls. If you follow the rules, prairie dogging is an effective way to communicate.

My job as District Secretary brought new challenges every day. The other secretaries said, "You keep us laughing. When you're on vacation this place is too quiet. It's like a morgue." I arrived at the office early because the employees looked forward to a caffeine fix, the best part of waking up. If the coffee pot could talk, here's an example of how our conversation would go:

"Good morning, coffee pot."

"Good morning, Patty. Weak one. I'm empty as the desert bed. Get with it, dear slave. Fill me! I know how much you need a cup. You vowed to kick the habit. But you're *always* making promises you can't keep."

"I know that today's the day to kick the habit. I don't feel like playing games," I reply.

"It wasn't *my* decision, weak one. I *love* being your master."

I unlock my desk and catch sight of a cup displaying Wilma's artwork: green leaves, red cherries and PATTY'S POISON on the rim. My coffee cup screams for attention. I slam the drawer and sputter, "Shut up. You're making me moody." I fill the pot with water, measure the brown gold into the brew basket, and plug the cord in. The pot hums. "I'll ignore you. I will not listen to your plop, ploom, plop, ploom. Plop all you want, evil pot, but I'm *serious* this time!"

"Huh! I heard *tha*t before."

"Today, Mr. coffee pot, is the end of loving and wanting and yearning for you. I will forget you're here. What do you think of *that*?"

"Within ten minutes, you'll smell my aroma. You'll come to me and fill Patty's Poison to the brim with my hot, dark juice. You'll press your lips into my savoring brew and kiss me, just like you kiss Mel."

"No, no. You're dead wrong. Today will be different. I won't. Leave me alone!"

"You'll have a cup. Then another. Co-workers will arrive, and you'll have a social drink of me. If you don't, your caffeine nerves will be fragile and you'll have a lousy day."

"Cool it," I demand. "Leave me alone."

"Patty, my friend, this office crack *owns* you! You're addicted. I am only the usher."

"*I* control me!" I hiss. The fumes keep rising. I hear purring. Soothing purrs. Temptation soars. *The Bible says to run away from temptation. Going to the copy machine down the hall, won't help. I'd have to run back to my desk to answer a nagging telephone. I must get control.*

"It's impossible for you to run away or declare this office

as a caffeine-free, just-say-no-area. This whole building reeks of my aroma. Did you know that all fifteen departments in this company own my brother and sister pots? They come in all shapes and sizes. They make all kinds of sounds. They all do the same thing—support your habit."

"I told you to shut up. Can't you hear? I've grown into a full-fledged adult, a stronger individual."

"Last Friday you chose a special blend for the boss's birthday party. He doesn't *drink* coffee, but *you* wanted to celebrate. You never waste time, but honey, if you give me up, you'll have let someone else enjoy the gourmet selection you spent half your lunch hour choosing. You're a *loser*."

"Am not. I'm not a java junkie either. *You're* not the big guy here. I could hurl you out the window."

The pot whispers, "Come to me. I'm waiting for you. Take me to your tummy."

I stare out the window and try to relax. "Oh no," I say under my breath. "Here comes that serious sixth grade teacher to borrow a film. I vowed that someday I'd make Mrs. Snodgrass smile for the first time in her life. Today is the worst day of my life."

I forced a pleasant greeting and unlocked the filing cabinet. While locating a film for Mrs. Snodgrass, who was teaching about the Alaskan telephone cable project, a ceramic mug and Patty's Poison leaped into my hand. Just touching the cup brought contentment. "Mrs. Snodgrass, come with me to the brewing station."

"Told you," the pot murmured as I poured two cups of the evil stuff. The teacher sipped the hot beverage as we walked down the hall and found a comfortable chair near the door. Pressing Patty's Poison to my lips and sipping the mouth-watering brew was a delight. Wonderful. Scrumptious. Seventh heaven.

The pot chided," Don't feel defeated, my slave. I'll always love you."

"Miss Snodgrass," I said, "you teach science. Word has it

that you're a strict disciplinarian. I need your input on a master-slave story I'm writing. Could you come by tomorrow and enjoy a cup of my famous chocolate raspberry blend?"

She gave an award-winning smile. "I have a day off. I'll be there. I love teamwork."

Teaming up with Michiganders resulted in a fine blend. Even though it was difficult to leave the state where I was born—the state that brought memories, some good and some not so good—Jackson, Michigan is considered a land of opportunity: a blue-collar town known as a prison town, a flat land with lush green parks and many golf courses. They say that Jackson's only mountain is Mount Evergreen Cemetery. The "Parlour " serves the biggest and best ice cream sundae in the state. The "Dare to be Great" features eighteen scoops. The Jackson Community College planetarium offers a clear sky every night, a perfect time for a star party even in the middle of the day.

The October autumn announced the passage of time with gusts of wind and dips of mercury. The darkness that pushed in on our dinner hour insisted on being noticed. Mother Nature, that first year in Michigan, began its annual decline. Ice and snow crusted on leafless trees and froze the pond at Loomis Park near our house. I never had the opportunity to ice-skate, but I could fulfill my skating dream through my "sisters."

The current generation places trust in a wallet full of credit cards. I had some emergency tuck-away money; this was an emergency. I counted the bills and thought of Aunt Margaret's fruit jar that she kept buried in the clothes closet. In my mind's eye I can still see her making periodic withdrawals for her smoking pleasure. What would she think of non-personal dealings with plastic cards that talk to a computer that talks to the bank that talks to the company where you do business transactions? She'd say, "Well, auh declare if it isn't the new version of the fruit jar. No counting coins from one hand into the other. What's this world coming to?"

After trying on several pairs of used skates at Knibloe

Hardware, Brenda and Joy found the right fit. At Loomis Park we met new friends and agreed to keep in touch.

Life is filed with friends who really connect, especially my friends at the company store. For a year or two Betty Jo and I corresponded, but friendship gave way to distance. We became haphazard about keeping up a correspondence, with cards and visits lengthening into non-existent. Before long I met new friends. We like the same food, same music and activities. We even share the same political views. Those friends pop into each other's homes with the greeting, "Put the coffee on."

Falling in Love

*L*ife is like a staircase with each year taking me to a higher destination. Brief stages of male friendship suited me fine. Being cheated in the height department, I admired tall men, but the tall guys I knew were already taken. I dated a 6-foot 4-inch basketball player with a 7-foot ego and a peanut-sized brain. Friends insisted on playing cupid and arranged blind dates. My girlfriend and her fiancé set me up with an intelligent, handsome, charming individual who was great company. During dinner I asked what he did for a living. He said he was an undertaker. Up to now he seemed like a very nice guy. *I hate hearing those words. Hey, don't even think about touching me.* I couldn't wait for the night to end.

One year after I came to Michigan, Mel finished his tour of duty in the Air Force and came to visit Herb, his uncle. I knew Mel's family, and that he had recently divorced, had a six-year-old son, Richard, and a daughter Betty, almost three. Although I didn't realize it at the time, when this handsome, dark haired guy, 6'1" with a pleasant smile and a winning personality walked through the door, it must have been love at first sight. My girlfriend Marge met Mel on a Saturday, and on Sunday she called to invite him to a movie. She called several times, but Mel made excuses. "What boldness!" I told Wilma. "The *guy* should ask the *girl* out."

A special friendship developed between Mel and me. More than any other structure in Jackson, the Cascades Falls Park is a

156

monument of beauty and distinction, a source of fond memories of our dating days. During a visit to Barcelona, Spain William Sparks, saw a fountain that formed an idea. The cascades resulted from his dream to do something for the people of Jackson, and build an attraction that would provide visitors with a positive impression of the city.

History has it that the falls opened to a crowd of 25,000 people on May 9, 1932. At dusk, water splashes down concrete steps into reflecting pools. Powerful lights flash on and the colorful, fast changing spectacle draws gasps of admiration from viewers. Visitors from all points of the globe come to view the falls. The old electro-mechanical control system has been replaced with a computer system. Sound response programs were developed so that the cascades lights and fountains change patterns in direct response to pre-recorded or live music. Jackson's most famous land mark still stands proud and ready to serve the next generation of visitors. Romantic engagements and stories like ours continue to be written.

Mel and I roamed over the Cascades Park's four hundred acres of picnic areas and championship golf course. In winter we enjoyed toboggan slides and the ice skating pond. At the first hint of spring, we took snacks, soft drinks, and Mel's green wool Air Force blanket to the landscaped grounds. Between reading and resting under a huge spreading oak tree, we waxed the chartreuse green '50 Ford until it shined.

Another famous landmark was the reasonably priced Regent Café at the corner of Otsego and Courtland streets. The personnel manager who placed me at Michigan Bell said, "Here's complimentary coupons, an invitation to a restaurant owned by my husband's parents, a welcome to Michigan. The Regent is one of the most popular eating spots in Jackson since 1926." Even though people warned Angelo and Ira Johns that they shouldn't take chances, that the location was wrong, that people don't eat out often, the Regent was rated in the top fifty restaurants in the country. Angelo and Ira were always at the helm of the tightly run ship, a family of six, including spouses and children. John wore a suit and tie every day of his life. Ira wore a dress, and always had fresh flowers in her hair.

Shortly after I arrived in Michigan I met Helen, one of my favorite Regent Café waitresses who stayed with the restaurant from 1937 to 1955. She told me, "The boss is demanding, but tips are fabulous. We have to spend two years behind the counter before we're allowed to wait tables. Imagine being hired as a waitress at age fourteen, and being told to go out and buy a girdle. Imagine having the boss check your appearance, making sure your nylon seams were straight, that you wore a hairnet, and did not wear nail polish or lipstick."

Each shift included ten waitresses, three busboys, five cooks and four dishwashers. Imagine a restaurant so busy that sometimes an employee was assigned to hold the door for patrons who lined three deep down the street. They planned to indulge, selecting from a base menu of 100 items plus two hand-written pages listing daily specials; everything made fresh and handmade. Imagine canning 700 bushels of hot peppers to serve all year as a side dish or appetizer. The owner was also the full-time creative cook. The menu choices were: eggs, omelets, pancakes, soups, salads, fries, vegetables, sandwiches, chops, and my favorite, breaded veal cutlet with homemade rolls or garlic toast. Imagine being ushered into a cooler, choosing a cut of aged beef and telling the full-time butcher how you wanted it cooked. Thoughts of chocolate cream pie, fresh from a bakery on the second floor, still make my mouth water.

After a movie or banquet, and in the spring on prom night, a steady stream of couples in formal attire waited for a spot in the 170-seat all-night restaurant set with white linen tablecloth and napkins. Most dates with Mel ended at the Regent. Once after a Pink Ball, our group of twenty-three stopped for dinner. Angelo was a husky guy that towered over most basketball players. He loved to laugh and always found time to greet his guests. "I believe this is a fun-loving group," he said with hands on his hips and a grin on his face. "I feel lucky tonight.

I'll gamble double or nothing for each check." The waitress had given out ten tickets for couples that ordered dinners. One by one, the couples won the coin toss. The three singles paid for a sandwich and coffee. Angelo folded his arms. "Well, I win a few and I lose a few."

It was a sad day when the forty-year-old Regent became victim of urban renewal. At the huge farewell party, Mel and I witnessed bittersweet embraces, memories of late-night dates at the best hometown restaurant that will never be duplicated or replaced.

On Christmas Eve in front of bright lights and a Kodak 8mm movie camera, Mel put a Keepsake diamond on my finger. I wanted to share the happiness with Daddy, but he and Gee lived in Delaware and we seldom heard from them. When they finally made contact with family members, rather than sharing happiness, we learned that black lung caused from coal mining dust and Daddy's smoking habit had caught up with him.

He tolerated removal of a cancerous lung. Soon after recovery he continued to indulge in alcohol. A year later he endured a ten-hour brain cancer surgery. In December, fifteen years after Mom's death, we buried Daddy. He was fifty-eight. After the funeral Yvonne told me that as Mom approached her final days, Daddy's girlfriend, his saloon buddy, often sat in the hospital corridor while he visited Mom. "How could he? I asked. "I thought he adored her." Yvonne was certain that Daddy worshiped Mom, but couldn't cope with the terminal illness. I finally forgave Daddy. But I will never understand.

HAVING A COMPANION for life, along with comfort and security is a worthwhile goal for a marriage. Wedding plans progressed. Wilma designed and sewed my wedding dress, white satin, covered buttons, pointed sleeves, and Venetian lace. Joy and Brenda were eager to be bridesmaids.

On a windy March morning, Wilma called me at work.

"The school principal sent Brenda home with a high temperature. The doctor ordered tests for spinal meningitis." The next day a specialist transferred Brenda to University Hospital in Ann Arbor. Several doctors conferred and we received heartbreaking results. "We believe that encephalitis is caused from female mosquito bites. We lowered her temperature to 105 degrees. The outcome doesn't look hopeful. Research hasn't been done, and we have no medication for the condition." We stayed by her side for two days and nights. The doctor suggested that we go home.

Early the next morning we learned the devastating news. "If she had lived, she would have suffered severe brain damage." Wilma and Herb were overwhelmed with grief. They will never forget the ache in their hearts and the pain they felt. My mind returned to the day Aunt Hannah came to Wilma's house and wished that horrifying things would happen in Joy and Brenda's life. I was careful to keep the thoughts to myself. *I'll never forget that day. Aunt Hannah lied about Aunt Margaret's heart attack. Could she have cast a spell on Wilma's children?*

We knew that Brenda would want the wedding plans to be carried out. On June 6, 1959, in a Nazarene Church, Mel and I promised to love, honor and cherish until we parted in death.

Dorothy, the matron of honor, my first and best friend at the telephone company, had a small apartment in town. "Buying a house came at a perfect time," she said. "Apartments are hard to find. I could recommend you to the landlord. The rent is only $60 a month."

Sounded perfect. We loved the place. As the years went by, I found that love was perfect; love was enough. When I think of Mel, I think of abundant life that goes around like a carousel. If you're lucky you'll get the brass ring. I got the brass ring when I got Mel, for he wrapped me in his arms and drew me into his heart. Love will last until the game is called because of darkness. Memory will thrive beyond the last dance. Even if we do everything right, it still takes two to dance life's most radiant tango.

My boss invited friends to put on their dancing shoes and head to the nearest square dance hall where the beat is fast and the music is country. "Square dancing is friendship set to music," Irene said. "The greatest bunch of people you'll ever find." Women wore dresses puffed with cotton crinolines. Some of the talented seamstresses sewed matching outfits, $50 skirts, $25 blouses, and full, ruffled petticoats. They stitched up men's shirts for $50, half price. Men sported ornate bolo ties and leather boots.

Square dance moves are standardized across the country, making it easy for dancers to visit clubs in other states. The couples became a rainbow of bright colors sashaying across the wooden floor. They came to dos-a-dos the night away. The caller told dancers, "Do the right and left through, bow to your neighbor." I thought about Pax Elementary School gym where I first learned about exercise country style. My teacher announced that she would explain twenty-five moves. Advanced level dancers do 126 moves.

We left the hall and continued the party at Irene's house on beautiful Duncan Lake. She put a record on the machine and gave instructions for "The Texas Star." I believe that one included all 126 moves. After numerous attempts to accomplish perfection, someone in the set would make a wrong move. At four in the morning our husbands were still going strong, but I decided that aching feet didn't make for pleasant friendship. "The next time we meet, we'll pick up where we left off," I said. "Tomorrow night I'll anticipate a quiet evening playing cards with the Tingleys."

The stakes were high in the battle between the sexes. The pinochle score was tied at 455. The bidder wins. I gave a meld bid and Barbara progressively bid. Out of the blue, as if the score didn't matter, Harold said, "There's a television commercial about New York. I'd love to see the Big Apple, Times Square and night life."

"It's November, you'd freeze on the east coast. We've got a game to win. Let's talk later," I suggested as I placed eighty points on the table.

After the girls put another winner's circle around the calendar, Mel poured another cup of coffee. "We're used to cold weather. Michigan has snow and ice from October through March. Are you a patsy?"

"I came close to being one. I ended up a Patty. Barbara calls me Patty-Boobs, but not many call me Patsy."

The day we received airline tickets in the mail, Mel's dad had a fatal heart attack. We had just enough time to travel to West Virginia for the funeral. As we were leaving, Mel's mom said, "I suppose you feel that you should grieve instead of vacation, but your dad wouldn't want you to grieve." The words were welcome. In those days people thought you were disrespectful if you didn't spend a certain amount of grief time.

In the airport Barbara hugged her purse and chattered nonstop. She pulled me aside. "Don't tell anybody, but I'm scared to death."

"It's pretty easy to guess, when we see your trembling lips. Just kidding. Calm down. You'll live through it." High winds accompanied our jaunt to the plane setting on the paved runway that had a black patent-leathered look of freezing rain. I opened an umbrella to protect my new hair-do. The wind almost lifted me into the air. Mel came to the rescue. Barbara was now frantic. The American Airlines 747 looked considerably larger than she had imagined. "Don't know if I can get on that plane." Once in the air she began to relax, even looked out the window to view the vast snow-covered scene.

The vibrant, exhilarating city was alive with tourists and working people staying out late. "New Yawkers" are constantly exhausted from their late-night lifestyles. You couldn't walk ten feet without seeing Starbucks Coffee shops. They seem to own Manhattan.

Our days were filled with tourist attractions, window-shopping, sightseeing, street vendors selling hot dogs and hot pretzels. The nights were filled with theater productions, and gawking at Hollywood stars. At the Rainbow Room in the

RCA Building, Barbara and I mustered up enough courage to ask Liberace for his autograph. He gave the familiar pearly white smile and wrote: "Patty, you're a sweetie." That grand piano ring covered three fingers.

In November city crowds exist, but not too many chose taking a subway to Coney Island. Even with strong winds, Coney Island was enjoyable. When darkness moved in we headed down the boardwalk to wait for the subway. One dimly lit bulb hanging from the wooden ceiling cast eerie shadows on the wall. As our foursome stood in the middle of the boardwalk, three men in dark clothing and oversized raincoats walked between us. Maybe I watch too many crime stories on television, but in my mind I mulled over using either plan A, run like heck, or plan B, hope our brave husbands could handle the situation. The punks tipped their hats as they passed by.

Our next adventure was a ride through Central Park on a horse-drawn carriage. The driver provided a grimy blanket to protect our legs from the bitter cold. Being bitten by critters that we expected to crawl from beneath the blanket seemed a better choice than freezing.

The next morning Barbara and I boarded a taxi. "Saks Fifth Avenue," I told the driver. He took a tour of the city, dodged in and out of traffic and zipped across eight lanes of speeding vehicles. He dodged several pedestrians. I asked, "How many do you mow down in a day?"

He looked through the rear-view mirror, let go of the steering wheel and made a temple with his hands, as if praying. In foreign, eastern accent he said, "Oh, three or four. They know to get out of my way." He pulled to the curb, and before I had a chance to read the meter he flipped the lever and warned, "Be careful girls, swindlers are all over New York."

I glanced at the change left from the twenty I gave him. Barbara said, "That's right. I'll pay for the return trip."

"Hope he doesn't cheat *you* five dollars," I groaned.

At Saks we window-shopped and dreamed about being able to purchase gifts that were priced high above our budget. At

Tiffany's I admired a bracelet, diamonds edged in emeralds. A sales clerk handed me the $144,000 elegance. Ten security guards were posted throughout the store.

After lunch in a quaint French café, we returned to the hotel to dress for Radio City Music Hall, the luxurious theatre with hundreds of lights and a stage that seemed to stretch for miles. A giant Wurlitzer organ appeared from the sidewall and filled the room with cords that resonated in my ribs. We sat near the stage and watched dozens of high-kicking Rockettes' facial expressions, skin texture and beauty. Makeup used in the theatre and television covers a multitude of beauty sins, although the outstanding talent portrayed perfection.

Disney stores replaced 42nd Street sex shops and porn theaters. There's a whole different feel to the Big Apple, clean and safe. Times Square has been converted from X-rated Sin Central to PG-rated Family Friendly. The city has a new attitude. New Yorkers smile at tourists as they give directions that are usually wrong. I recommend getting a second opinion. A short time after we returned home, the Tingleys called. "Know what? We're going start a family. A New York baby."

On a regular basis, my co-workers asked the question, "Are you ever planning to have children? You've been married four years already."

Others said, "How sad not to have children to brighten parties, massage potato chips into the rug, track dirt on your light beige carpet, and paint the glass tables with jelly."

"I know it's sad to be childless," I said with a twisted smile. "We can stretch out at the swimming pools from north to south, suntan, and take a miserable cruise to the Caribbean. We're just lonesome fools with money to spend, time to enjoy each other. Sure is sad. But somehow we'll tolerate the Before Kids days."

In the cafeteria's gossip corner, a new employee complained about having seven kids. "They fight continually. Jack and I fight over discipline. But you don't have kids. You don't understand."

"No, guess I don't. I've seen couples with messy kitchens,

164

sticky floors. They wait for sitters who don't show. We don't fight over discipline. We fight over what restaurant to patronize."

"Count your blessings honey," she said. "I've rushed kids to the emergency room so often the doctors know me by name. If I could live life over –"

"Don't say that. You may have to eat your words," I warned. One employee had a baby at forty-three. "Andrew" is king of the hill. He is the most handsome child born. He'll be president some day. I decided that if I had children I wouldn't bore people with every accomplishment.

At this point in life, we're members of the childless couple class that never shares such growing experiences. Childless couples fill their lonely lives with the theater, golf and trips all over the country. What a shame! I hear of dads taking sons hunting. "I didn't mean to shoot you in the leg," the son says. I hear moms talk about their beautiful daughters eloping with the village idiot. My husband still looks boyish, unlined and rested. I'm still slim, well groomed and youthful.

Sometimes, in spite of myself, I'm in the middle of adventure. At two in the morning, the moon was bright and Mel snoozed in the passenger seat. The Oldsmobile, with lots of horsepower waiting to be used, was a pleasure to drive. The big problem on the Pennsylvania turnpike was dodging potholes that aren't repaired until they're large enough to swallow compact cars. After ten days on the road, I was impatient to get home, although thoughts of unpacking and getting back to the grind on Monday morning didn't seem all that exciting. Some say they work because they like the people. I work because I like the money.

Just past Erie the newly paved road and country tunes brought sweet relief. While harmonizing with Patsy Cline, I whizzed by several vehicles creeping along at fifty-five. "Sunday drivers," I said to the darkness. "Can't see any reason to go so slow." I pushed the gas petal to a pleasant speed of eighty and set the cruise control. After zooming past several vehicles,

I passed a dark blue Chevy, glanced back and noticed an oval inscription on the door: PENNSYLVANIA STATE POLICE. I slowed down by pressing the cruise button. *Maybe he'll think I'm in an emergency situation, or perhaps my husband's loud snoring distracted me.*

Flashing lights in the rearview mirror forced me to pull onto the rough shoulder. Mel leaned forward, his dark brown hair scrunched to one side. "What the heck?"

"Oh, just a problem with a guy wearing a wide-brimmed hat, a gun in his belt, and driving a shinny blue car."

"What's he stopping you for?"

"Don't know." The officer approached my car, my heart was pounding and at the tender age of twenty-nine my hair was turning gray. I finally found the button marked WINDOW. Mel remained silent, and offered nothing in my defense.

"In a hurry, huh? Let me see your license."

My hand shook as I shoved the license through the open window. "Uh, that stupid accelerator stuck, officer. We'll get it fixed when we get home." A voice inside me cautioned, "Be calm Patty. Don't get sassy."

The officer took my license to the patrol car. I sat and stewed. Mel searched the glove box for emergency cash. "The vacation was perfect up to now, my billfold proves it. Got any money?"

"A little. I have plastic."

"Plastic won't do this time, honey. Why did you speed any-way?"

Our first argument was developing. "You have the nerve to ask that? You should have stacked up a half-dozen tickets by now."

"We're not talking about me."

The officer informed us that the car wasn't registered in our name. "There must be a mistake," Mel said. "Here is the proof."

After a long telephone conversation the officer returned. "I'm sorry, but you'll have to see the judge. He lives up the road about two miles. You should drive, sir. Follow me." *How does he know that Mel is a licensed driver?*

Mel started the car. "Can't go very far before we reach empty."

"Didn't you hear him? He said it was two miles. We parked in front of a small ranch house with a dark green door. Two miles was long enough to calm my anxiety.

"The officer is on the telephone, checking to see if you have a record," Mel teased.

"How does he know that *you're* a licensed driver? I do have a record, lots of them." Mel's face took on a look of astonishment. He thought he knew all about me. "The records play Hank Thompson, Jim Reeves. Golly, I thought judges were rich. His house is like most houses, only physically challenged.

"Don't worry about the house. Worry about being a jail bird."

"You could bail us out by offering to paint the judge's house next summer."

"Shut up, silly girl."

"Can't you see I'm using psychology, trying to think of something other than the problem we're facing? I'll turn on my charm. I'll flash my beautiful brown eyes and he'll let us go." We followed the officer up the sidewalk. A German shepherd dashed from the garage. I almost fainted. The officer patted the dog's head and rang the bell.

Mrs. Judge, in a purple robe just like Pilate's, had gray hair hanging in her face. She opened the door and spoke hurriedly, "Jus a minit. He's comin'." The officer stepped inside. We followed.

Interesting, I thought. *Humm. This living room looks so normal. They're real people. Never in my life have I been in a judge's house. Never wanted to.* The room was dusty and dimly lit. A shabby red wool rug absorbed our footsteps. Heavy linen curtains, variegated dark gray and red, lapped across tall windows covered with wood Venetian shades. The musty smell made me sneeze.

Mrs. Judge was shapeless, shy. She left for a few minutes. The judge shuffled into the room. She handed him a cup of coffee. *Sure could use a taste of brew about now. What a hostess. She didn't even offer. My mouth is dry as a hayfield. My stomach churns.* Courage returned when I remembered reading a Jewish proverb that said, "He that can not endure the bad will not live to see the good."

The judge buttoned his robe—also purple like Pilate's. *Doesn't he have a comb? On second thought, I suppose at three in the morning no one cares about hair.* His shoulders were stooped, his pace slow. *He should have retired long ago.* He sat in a red and black flowered chair and leaned on the dark monstrous-sized desk with dragonheads carved on the corners. Folders and papers were stacked in boxes on the floor. He slowly sipped coffee, looked at the ticket, and stared at me. *Creditable eyesight for his age; no glasses. Wonder if he'll issue a punishment and say, "I wash my hands of this matter. I can't believe she's guilty of a crime."* He yawned and pointed a finger at me. His hands were wrinkled and broad as bricks.

My hands were sweating, my heart racing. I stretched my neck to read the ticket. The policeman must be moonlighting. He must also be a doctor. He can't write legibly. I must have a split personality. I had the nerve to ask, "What's this accusation?"

The judge stared at me with dark beady eyes, empty as the devil's soul. "Patricia Ann."

"Yes sir?"

In the state of Pennsylvania, you have been charged with speeding; eighty miles per hour in a fifty-five zone. How do you plead?"

"I was speeding."

"You have to say the word *guilty*. How do you plead?"

"Sir, uh, Your Honor. I was speeding."

"Are you guilty?" I hate the word guilty. I nodded my head. "All right, fork over eighty dollars—that includes court cost—

or spend a night in jail." My legs turned to jelly. I gave Mel a sick look and grabbed the dragonhead to steady myself. I'd even part with my Estee Lauder makeup if it would help the situation. I emptied the change from my purse. Sixteen quarters for the turnpike toll.

"Hold on please," Mel said as he went to the car to get an emergency twenty I had hidden in a curler bag. He emptied his billfold. I found a twenty stuffed under a credit card.

As the judge witnessed our scrambling for funds, he warned, "A lead foot can be dangerous. And costly."

I gave him a nervous, "Uh, huh. Yes, Your Honor."

I exchanged the money for a receipt. As we walked down the steps, Mrs. Judge waved and shut the door. I heard a dead bolt click and the porch light went out. Mel started the engine and we headed out of town. "Hope you're not hungry. We have $1.35 for a cup of coffee, and five hours to drive."

"Not hungry," I muttered. "Those dragonheads almost scared me to death."

Special Delivery

The doctor confirmed our suspicion that something new and exciting was about to happen. We rejoiced. No longer would I have to listen to my co-workers talk about the childless-couple syndrome. Someone at work said, "All the fun is going to be sucked out of your life. No longer will you have the pleasure of sleeping until noon every weekend."

A gal returning from leave of absence said, "Having a baby is frightening. Television distorts the picture. The woman's makeup never runs, she grunts and it's over."

I went on leave at six months. Marie, one of my co-workers who lived four blocks away, was on leave with her first child. Every morning we walked several blocks and discussed the mixture of anticipation and terror that we felt. We wondered what our swollen bodies would produce. We added defining characteristics to the visions of what our little bundles of endless possibilities might become. Marie's six-pound girl was born twelve days before I delivered. She labored several hours. Holding her baby made my wait even more difficult.

I describe childbirth as amazing. You check into your room, nurses prod, poke, take blood, and check vital signs every ten minutes. The pains come faster and sharper. You grit your teeth, squeeze your husband's hand until it turns white. They say some husbands faint. Fathers were not allowed to witness the transaction. The nurse told Mel, "Find a comfortable chair in the waiting room."

My ordeal lasted three hours. Seemed like a freight train rolled over me. At 2:18 a.m., on September 26, 1964, our first child came into the world. An instant love affair was born. After Dr. Filip finished his job, the nurse called Mel into the room. The first cry, and the first touch produced a proud-papa smile. "He's handsome," Mel said as he kissed me. "Good job mama." Mel had a lot in common with the doctor who took a camera from his bag and said, "Let's get the first shot of your beautiful family."

Gary Calvin took center stage in our household. I marveled at my baby's outgoing and radiant personality. I held him in my arms and whispered, "Do you have any idea how blessed I feel for having you in my life?" He kicked approval. Every day Marie and I pushed our blue strollers down Jackson Street, in rain, snow or sunshine.

Just before Gary's first birthday we bought a nearly new ranch style house in the country with an acre of land, a walkout basement and attached garage. Our "Mom and Dad landlords" said, "We knew the day would come. The news breaks our hearts. Guess we'll put the house up for sale. We can't think of someone else renting the upstairs, tearing up the place."

Although I appreciated the new house, the move itself was horrible. It was like going through childbirth only without the epidural. I told our friends, "Thoughts of moving still give me a headache. For seven years we had stashed items into every closet, every cranny; items we deemed too good to toss were stashed in the third floor spare room."

Moving forced a painful decision. Should we pack our new house with old junk? We moved on Labor Day weekend, with two extra days off work. No time to sort. Gary was at the crawling stage, the clinging stage. We carried boxes from the U-Haul truck. Gary followed close behind. By the time he caught up with us, we had set the boxes down and rushed to get another. After this scene was repeated several times, he sat on his little round butt and wailed a pitiful call. We located a box marked "Toys" and the three of us sprawled on the soft beige carpet for an hour. Everyone benefited from the rest.

We still have old junk plus a new junk collection. "I'll never, ever, move again," I said. So far I've kept my word.

At twelve months, Gary's vocabulary consisted of a dozen words, the most popular being doggie. We "inherited" a black Labrador retriever from one of Mel's co-workers. Gary called the dog Dodo. We told the vet that Dodo paid no attention to our commands and needed to enroll in obedience school. He scratched his head. "I wouldn't obey either, if someone called me Dodo."

When Gary was twenty months old, I was expecting another baby. Dodo kicked Leisa before she was born. Every time I ventured into the yard, he was by my side. Standing on his hind legs, he was my height. I gained sixteen pounds; he thought my large tummy was a punching bag and his job was to puncture. I fell several times, but knew that Gary adored the dog so I said nothing. One day Mel was mowing the lawn. He glanced across the yard as Dodo pushed me to the ground. Mel grabbed the collar, shoved him in the garage and shut the door. "That's the end of you, little doggie." He told Gary that his friend at work lived on a farm and wanted Dodo to live with him.

A month later at midnight I woke Mel and said, "Get dressed. It's time to go to the hospital."

"Why are you in such a hurry? I want to watch the late show. It took three hours the first time."

"No late show tonight dear. Believe me, it's time." He sauntered into the bathroom, shaved and took plenty of time combing his hair.

I woke Mel's mother, who had arrived the day before and hoped that her two-week stay wouldn't have to be extended due to a missed due date. (Both children arrived the day predicted.) I dressed, grabbed my purse and suitcase. Mel was still in the bathroom. "Hurry. Do *you* want to deliver this baby?" After the second terrific pain, Mel was careful to dodge potholes on Wildwood Street. The clock at the corner of Ganson

Street read 12:25. "Hurry. That was a biggie!"

The nurse brought a wheelchair to the hospital door and rushed me to the examining room. "No time to prep." She told Mel the familiar words, "There's a waiting room down the hall."

He had time to finish reading one page of the newspaper. At 1:25 a.m. on June 29, 1966, after three labor pains, our daughter Leisa Ann made a grand entrance. She gave that intense fuzzy newborn stare, and the same feeling of love happened again. Holding newborn babies, sweet and perfect beings with button noses, cherubic faces and angelic smiles, makes me shed tears of happiness. I forget the pain of childbirth, and gain a reward that squirms and finds my eyes before squalling.

A nurse peeked around the corner and announced," Mista Lively? Ya gotta fine baby girl." She handed him a round-faced, dark haired little bundle tucked in a pink blanket. His face beamed. With the first delivery I was a dragged out, dark circles under eyes, scared-to-death mother. With this event I teased, "See. I'm always right. Well most of the time. I told you to hurry." I may have hated him during the first labor and delivery.

Children are gifts from God. A precious time in our life came when their voices rang in the halls of our home. After the second baby came along, the house fell apart. The housework proved to be equally challenging. My BK (before kids) idea of "clean" didn't match my present status of mind. If you want a mental picture, imagine an earthquake. Plaster chipped by toy trucks, black tire marks and Crayola crayon roads leading down the hallway, dirty dishes growing monsters in the sink, beds unmade. The dryer spins constantly, churning out small overalls and flowered dresses. Mel came home and mentioned the mess. I suggested that he keep an extra wife inside a case and when an emergency such as this arises he should break the glass with a toy hammer.

I remember their first cold and being on constant runny-nose patrol. After using all the Kleenex tissues, I strapped a roll of toilet paper to my belt. The telephone bill was due so I hurried to the mailbox. A passing driver glared and ran out of the road. I returned to find a previously occupied rocking horse empty, and two squalling kids. Rocky's squeaking had sent baby number one to lullaby land, and he fell between Rocky and the wall. The noise had awakened baby number two, who went to the bathroom right in her pants. Should I solve this problem by employing a garden hose? After all it was a hot summer.

The terrible twos mean the age of "No!" He doesn't want to eat his breakfast. No, he doesn't want to play with the green dump truck. No, he doesn't want to share a toy. And she definitely doesn't want to go to bed. It's the tendency to spill, destroy, and get into everything. Any silence of thirty seconds throws adults into panic. One day I opened the bathroom door to find Gary covered with lipstick from his blond head down to the white rug on which he stood. On the wall was an artistic creation. Throughout the room was the aroma of Windsong perfume he had used to anoint his baby sister.

I attempt to do all the right things, prepare and eat organic food, and adhere to the basic food group idea. They say the key to a healthy heart is exercise. I used to wind down my twelve-hour day with a short walk. Among the benefits of walking is meeting a special friend.

My pregnant neighbor lived three houses away on the north side of the road. Janie was always busy hanging laundry on the line, washing windows, mowing grass and taking care of two active children. After dinner one evening I jogged past her house. She was watering her dark red roses. "I see you had your baby. Did you know we have a two-month old daughter?"

"Yes, my neighbor told me. I finally had mine, a boy named Jeff. Come in and see him."

I gazed into the crib that was dwarfed by the size of the handsome baby. "He's adorable. A football player."

"Felt like it too. He weighed over nine pounds." Janie was petite, about 5'2" looked very young, and must have tipped the scales at 105. We chatted as though we were old friends.

The next week she called. "Come up about noon and we'll have a BLT sandwich." We met often, shared recipes and home-made cookies. Several times a week we swam in her backyard pool. I had one semester of sewing, but with Janie's help I fashioned dresses, suits and matching bathing suits.

Frozen images are lined up in my mind: I watch our children's expressions waver between fear and delight as Daddy pitches them into the air. Toddlers can dismantle the peace and tranquility of a home, but there is a thrill with the unfolding of new words. We're walking along the street. Leisa reaches up as if Mel's arms are branches. "Daddy carry." She sits on his shoulders and grabs his ears. When angry she folds her arms in front. Her lips pout. If I rock her and Mel walks by she reaches out her arms and yells, "Daddy's girl."

At bedtime she picked two pals from the stuffed animal pile and wrapped her arms around them for the night. But not before those arms reached up and curled around Daddy. You didn't gently try to break her tight squeeze. She never wanted to let go. She was there for life. She knew what she wanted.

Balance is comparing value and relative importance. The challenge is the inherent tension between satisfying our own desires and fulfilling our obligation to others. I know about that. My life was my career, a singer and would-be writer. I believed that a feeling of success came from work, but I discovered I was wrong. I returned to work a week before my twelve-month leave expired. We found a reliable sitter who came every morning, a rare happening in most households. I told her, "I'm envious. You get to spend the day enjoying my new house, new furniture and precious children."

I found ten extra minutes that December, and used the time searching through last year's magazine for a "scratch" cake recipe. I set the oven at 350 degrees and read the directions. Here's an example of the next thirty minutes: I removed toys from the countertop, measured two cups flour, got the baking powder, removed Leisa's hands from flour, got baking powder, removed Gary's hands from flour, put flour, baking powder and salt into sifter, vacuumed mixture the kids spilled on floor, set sugar canister on counter, got an egg, answered the phone, separated egg, gave baby a glass of milk, helped Gary figure out how to hook up his John Deere tractor, greased pan, answered the doorbell, took ½ inch salt from greased pan, swept sugar from the floor, looked for kids, put mess in wastebasket, dishes into dishwasher, called the bakery, ordered a chocolate cake, took an aspirin and headed for the couch.

Gary often stood on the couch near the living room window and watched our neighbor buzz around the yard on his tractor. "There's Jay," he'd say.

Jay often shared his garden vegetables. One day he brought a bag of plump, red, Big Boy tomatoes. "I have a favor to ask of you." I thought *I'm so busy, what could he want? Maybe help with the garden. I need to somehow pay him back. If he asks me to plant corn, I'll refuse. I remember the planting corn days.* Before I could answer, he added, "Sunday is friends day at church. You and your family are invited."

"We'll see about it," I told him.

Several times that week Gary asked, "Going to church with Jay?" On Sunday Jay greeted us at the church door. Gary shook hands with several people. Beginning that day, church was important to him. The Scripture, *A little child shall lead them*, came to mind. The next week Pastor Berry came to visit. Mel and I rededicated our life to the Lord. The choir needed alto and bass singers for the Christmas drama. We added practice sessions to our busy schedule.

By the age of three Gary had ridden his squeaky rocking horse several hundred miles. I can still visualize standing at the kitchen sink washing dishes, thinking about all the work I had to do. The squeaking stopped and I glanced over my shoulder. Gary looked dreamy-eyed. He spoke in a quiet voice. "Mommy I love you so much my heart hurts." He rocked a few times, leaned his head on Rocky and fell asleep.

I carried my favorite little guy to bed and took a Bible from the shelf. I pulled up a chair and began reading words that I hadn't taken time to read all week. Some may think it's useless to read to a sleeping baby, but parents play a powerful role in preparing children for the world. Three-way communication is always useful.

We read and talked to the children at an early age. It was a time of excitement over puppies, holidays and stories. Leisa insisted upon stories nightly. "How about two tonight?"

"No, we don't have time."

"Okay, two tomorrow."

"Maybe."

"Are you sure?" Sometimes she sent the story in a direction all her own and nothing would deter her from a happy ending. Stories grew fewer over time. Leisa believed that the happy ending to a perfect day was playing with Krissy, who lived next door. They carried kitchen utensils, folding chairs and blankets into the back yard. "We're building a house. Our campground is the front yard." When they played dress-up Leisa valued her dad's approval. "Look at our expensive evening wear."

I called her for dinner. "Look at this *mess*! Put everything where it belongs. Now!" Mel reminded me that someday the dress-up parties, laughter and playhouses would be missing from the yard.

The first day at school she was afraid she wouldn't fit in. She came home saying, "Today was nice. I think I'll go back tomorrow."

I had a mental picture of a guardian angel above each family member as they left the house. I waved and said, "Have a good day. All of you." When Mel left for work, Leisa and her brother stood at the large living room window and waved. Sometimes he found a note in his pocket, "I miss you." The children ran to the door to meet him at the end of the day. Leisa leaped into his arms with an unbridled laugh.

The holiday season was an excuse to shop with Janie. Our children were the same age, and even though their wish list looked like a carbon copy, Janie and I never bought the same games and toys.

On Christmas Eve Santa and Mrs. Clause were busy putting doll furniture and boy toys together. I heard a giggle and discovered two little sleepyheads sitting on the third step. "We woke up early," five-year-old Leisa said. "Is it still the night before Christmas?"

"Yes, it is," I answered firmly. "And if you and Gary don't get to bed Santa will forget to come here." They scurried off before noticing that someone drank the milk and ate the cookies they left on the hearth.

The next morning they surveyed the presents and goodies in their stockings. Leisa said, "Mommy, Santa has wrapping paper just like ours." The year she was seven the turning-point Christmas, she admitted, "Daddy it was you. They told me at school that it was you. I just had to find out. I knew last year but kept it a secret."

"Christmas is real. It's not about Santa. It's the love in your heart," Mel told her.

I'll never forget our children's first plane ride. Six-year-old Gary asked, "Will an Army plane shoot us down?"

At Disney World, after waiting in line an hour for their favorite ride, a thunderstorm forced all attractions to close. Within a few minutes Leisa looked into the sky. "Mom, there's a double rainbow."

Traveling by car challenged my patience. Passing a Volkswagen gave an excuse slap the nearby sibling and yell, "Slug bug, no rebounds."

Mel explained Leisa's announcement, "He's *looking* at me" by assuring her that Gary looks because he finds her attractive.

Every evening after dinner, the dreaded words, "piano practice," sent Leisa into orbit. I dished out a nickel for each song she played, if I could recognize the tune. When extra coaching was necessary, I upped the ante to a candy bar. "Chocolate calms my nerves," she said with a gleam in her eye.

"This is an important conversation," I told her. "You're in

third grade, you wanted lessons and we have a teacher, so you're going to give it a try. You have to practice in order to play well."

"Are you preaching?" she asked. "So what if everyone else is better than me." Then she shot one of those sidelong quizzical looks. "Why bother?" The sassy answers resulted in grounding for three days.

She agreed to wear the blue dress I bought for her first recital. She stepped onto the platform, glanced at the audience and sat down. Long blond curls hung to her waist. The only flaw was timing as she turned the page. After two years I couldn't handle being a piano nag so I gave up. There must be a special award for parents who accomplish success during the music lesson era.

That fall the Dixie Melody Boys came to our church to do an evening concert. The harmony struck a cord in me. My simple wish and prayer that night was to sing in a group. At the end of the service, Mary Shinabery and Vicky Gorsuch asked me to form a trio. We called our group The Gospel Lights. We performed with The Dixie Melody Boys and several well-known singers. Gary and Leisa accepted the love and forgiveness that we sang about. On a Sunday morning they were baptized. They loved communicating with God and with His people.

Communication during shopping is a shocking activity. My daughter had a vision of what her wardrobe should be. The top had to be white. It had to have a pink ribbon. She wanted a solid color dress, bright colors, preferably pink. "I hate blue," she said firmly. "You always want blue to match my eyes." We trekked to many stores before finding a dress that fit her requirements and my budget. She inspected herself in the mirror. "It's perfect, Mom."

There's the saga of the winter coat. She wants to be tall like her brother, but every fall I pray that she won't have to select a new coat. "That's perfect," I'd say.

She said in her best eye-rolling tone, "Mom, do you know

everything?"

"Of course I do. I'm your mother."

She disagrees with my decisions; I coax her into a compromise. "Your dad would really like this one. When they outgrow clothes—Leisa wore them three times longer than slender-built Gary—I price them for a garage sale, and pieces of myself go with them.

I remember witnessing the cooperation children demonstrate when playing hide and seek with Mom. "Okay," announces Leisa. "She's not in here. Let's split up. Gary, you go that way. I'll check down the hall." Finding me brings a moment of excitement, victory dances and screams of joy.

Gary, the man of action, says, "Let's do it again." Ten minutes of special playtime before bed is wildly inaccurate. Time stretches to thirty minutes.

There were pillow fights, pajama parties, lost teeth and brother battles. Leisa did her share of brother bashing. On primary election day I made an educational endeavor, took her with me and explained the voting procedure. "Can I vote my brother out of the family so I can be an only child?" she asked. "Or you could get me a sister."

"You don't want to be an only child," I said. "I loved having a younger sister. When we were kids, snowstorms were blessings. On Saturday evenings Ailene and I felt a celebration coming on. My job, as the big sister and instigator of trouble, was to sneak into the pantry, steal vanilla, sugar, a large bowl, Pet evaporated milk and a can opener. The product of our undertaking was one of the necessary basic food groups, snow ice cream."

Now that I'm a mother, I've grown up and become capable of making important decisions. I find that ice cream isn't a treat to have only on the fourth of July, but it's necessary to make life complete. The desire to make homemade ice cream still lingers. I found, on sale, a hand-cranked freezer just like the folks used in the olden days. I cooked the mixture using a dozen eggs, whole milk, sugar, a liberal dollop of vanilla, and let it cool overnight.

I poured the rich mixture into the metal freezer container. Mel packed ice around it and added course salt. "Let's help turn the crank so we get that old fashioned feeling people used to get," I announced. Fifteen minutes later the kids were bored, I answered the telephone, and Mel sat under the maple tree, all alone, cranking the handle. The wooden freezer wept with melted ice. I failed to read the directions that suggested waiting an hour or so for the contents to finish hardening.

Mel removed the lid. Ice cream dripped from the dasher. We waited to lick it clean. He lifted the inside container and poured the contents into drinking glasses. "This is the best $15 milkshake I've ever had," he said with a grin. The ice cream maker ended up in a garage sale and netted $3. In the future I'll bring ice cream home from the supermarket. I've never outgrown my need for calcium.

Nor have I outgrown the need to exercise. Taking a credit hour for golf lessons is an attractive way to get the job done. I learned that with golf, progress comes before perfection. The first night we learned basic etiquette, rules and logic. The second time out, the class came face to face with a small ocean that we had to cross before advancing to the fourth hole. "Pretend you're on dry land," Professor Bockwitz said. "Believe in your ability to reach the flag."

Like the little train trying to chug up the hill, I whispered under my breath, "I think I can. I think I can." I poised my three-wood, checked my stance, breathed a prayer and shot the ball over the water. The other students forgot about "The Little Engine That Could" story. I made it on the first try. I loved the game and the scenery at Whiffletree, the same golf course where Gary began his golf career.

Memories made on golf courses can either last forever or disappear quickly. The next week, Janie and I attempted the back nine at Cascades Golf Course, where you cross the same dogleg of lakes three times. Feeling gloriously confident, I gripped it and ripped it. Six balls landed in the water. Janie put in five. Determination and aggravation set in. With the tenacity of dandelions, I used every ball in my bag, stole Janie's supply, and landed in the water. The sun faded and darkness drew near. It was time to face defeat.

Remember Moses and the Israelites? I carried the ball across, over dry land, and finished the game. On my thirteenth shot, I landed the ball in the rocks. It ricocheted into a bunker. I blasted it out and three-putted for a twelve "Let's have a turtle sundae at the Parlour," I suggested. True friendship just seems to work out that way.

Cautious Optimism

"The doctor wants to see you in his office right away," the nurse said when I answered the telephone.

"What's wrong?"

"I can't discuss it. You'll have to talk to the doctor."

"Marsha. I can't stand this. What is going on?"

"Can you leave work and come in now?"

The five-mile drive seemed like thirty. I told Dr. Filip, "I had the feeling that something was wrong. I called your office last week and the nurse said, 'The paps test was completely negative.' "

"I'm sorry. She read the wrong chart. But only two weeks have passed. You had a negative report eleven months ago. The test indicates suspicious cells. We'll do a conization and go from there."

The biopsy revealed Class III cancer cells. Dr Filip said, "We'll wait eight weeks for this surgery to heal, then we'll do a hysterectomy." Eight weeks seemed like eternity, time enough for the cells to spread.

In May 1969, at the age of thirty-six I faced a situation that Mom had encountered at thirty-eight. Would the outcome be the same? Would I leave my husband and two children at the young age of three and five years old?

As the nurse wheeled me down the long hallway and into a cold, sterile-smelling surgical unit, I could still feel Mel's tender kiss—he was chewing Juicy Fruit gum—and hear his words of reassurance. With a twinkle in his eye he said if I would make dinner tonight he would do the dishes.

I'll always remember the bright lights and a hard, stainless steel table. The anesthesiologist explained his job. The nurse recorded vital information. Dr. Filip squeezed my hand. "I thought I'd be taking more babies out of this uterus instead of removing it. Don't worry, honey. I'll take care of you." He kissed me on the cheek. "Even though you don't realize it now, everything happens for the best." As the words faded, I drifted into a pleasant sleep. After three hours I was in the recovery room and vital signs were normal.

That afternoon, divine intention seemed to be the reason why a nurse friend from West Virginia was scheduled to work in the recovery room. (Her husband had helped Herb get a start in Michigan.) Eloise Pennington, a beautiful angel with a smiling face, took care of my needs. I overheard her conversation with another nurse. "I'm going to lunch. Watch Patty carefully. She seems to be hemorrhaging." She returned an hour later and told me that Dr. Filip had failed to tie up a blood vessel.

Within three hours, just after Mel returned to work, the nurse wheeled me into the surgical room. Dr. Filip was leaning against the wall. He had already scrubbed and his arms were folded. He didn't speak. *What's happening? Why doesn't my friendly doctor talk to me? I've known him for years.* My feelings were hurt. My heart ached. I wondered if I could endure another surgery.

My condition was carefully monitored. For several days I could barely manage to sit up. When I came home six days later, I was too weak to open a pop can. I realized that life is not a smooth pond upon which we gaze. When life snorts whitewater rapids, we have to breaststroke wildly and swim to shore. With my siblings giving undying support, and Mel as a constant companion, I made it through those difficult times. The malignancy was confined to the uterus. I won the battle. Life with my family has taught me that the only balance worth worrying about is the balance between our investment in the material world and our investment in our spiritual and emotional health.

After six weeks I returned to work. I had missed the friendship, and compliments on a job well done. I loved the secretarial position. Being productive and creative satisfied my deeper need. God is the most important component of a well-lived life, and gives meaning by teaching the values of cooperation and compassion. I had a plan for tomorrow. Sometimes, however, plans go astray.

A year later on September 14, 1970, at five o'clock, I shoved unfinished work into the desk drawer. With purse in one hand and shopping bags in the other, I hurried down the steps. Mel waited in our new white Oldsmobile. I climbed into the seat beside him and held up a pink sweater. "Mary Lou and I went bargain hunting on our lunch hour."

About four miles from home, we approached an intersection. On my right a rusty blue Chevy with several children inside waited at the stop sign. I noticed the wheels rolling forward, and thought the driver was preparing for a quick start after we passed by. We had the right-of-way, but that was minor consolation for what happened.

The Chevy pulled in front of us. Metal screamed. The impact propelled the vehicle into a ditch. My head broke the windshield. I blinked through warm liquid. The dashboard and blue nylon seats were splattered with blood. When I saw glass covering my lap, I realized that I, a staunch seatbelt advocate, had sacrificed safety to show off my new clothes.

Mel's firm grip had bent the steering wheel. His forehead was lacerated by the garage door opener clipped to the visor. Believing that our injuries were secondary, his voice shifted from disdain to quiet courage. "Two young boys are lying on the pavement at the crest of the hill. I'll go alert traffic."

A co-worker traveling behind us stopped to offer help. "Oh, Donna, the taste is awful. Maybe I have internal injuries. My face must be a mess." She told me not to worry about my face.

Hoping to lessen the bleeding, Mel helped me into a prone

position. My right foot dangled and bones surfaced. Donna gasped. Through the open door, a gentle rain soothed my face. An unfamiliar male voice swept me away from panic and into calmness. "Don't worry. You're going to be fine. Help is on the way."

Mel asked if I was in pain. "No, just the pain of the unknown. What about the others?"

"Three children and the driver are injured. Here comes the rescue squad. Get this. The driver informed the police that her children told her that traffic had cleared."

The genteel voice spoke again. "You've got to believe that you will be all right. Just relax. Everyone is okay, including you. Keep your eyes closed and listen carefully." I heard a robin sing. I felt a shield of protection.

Constant reassurance from Mel, Donna, and the mysterious voice convinced me to remain calm. "I can't see anything," I murmured.

"Everything is fine. Just transform your thoughts and emotions into pleasant thoughts. God bless you," the vigilant communicator answered.

A rescue squad transported the children. Mel rode in the ambulance's passenger seat. Lying on a hard cot, I peered tensely through the side window. The train station and several business places seemed to whiz by. I groaned. "Please tell the driver to slow down. I don't want another accident."

"Don't worry. He's being careful," Mel said. A paramedic applied more bandages to my face, and said my dark brown hair had turned crimson. On the gurney next to me, the tall blond who had caused the mishap was crying and moaning. Suddenly I felt a supernatural presence and forgiveness.

Hospital personnel whisked patients into various rooms. The emergency room clamor and rattling of equipment seemed deafening. Chair legs scraped the tile floor as relatives came and went. While waiting for X-ray results, the technician picked shards of glass from my eyelashes and hair. Meanwhile, traumatism, the killer of a lot of people involved in accidents, became my enemy. My body shook. The mattress felt like ice, the sheet a layer of snow. Warm blankets gave comfort. The doctor's words gave security. "I know this hurts. I have to remove all the glass." *He's using a wire brush on my face.*

Mel called Janie. She picked up Gary and Leisa from the day sitter and gave them a comfortable explanation.

At nine o'clock as they wheeled me into a six-bed ward, Pastor Berry and his wife arrived. The milk and crackers I had just eaten resulted in losing the lot! I ached with embarrassment—white blotches on Mrs. Berry's black raincoat.

Medication had been delayed until the doctor evaluated my condition. The prognosis: critical, a compound femur fracture, more than seventeen fractures in the "crushed-like-a-lightbulb" ankle. Unknown to me, Mel paced the floor with the agony of knowing that I might never walk again or run and play with our children.

By now unbearable pain surged. Morphine brought temporary relief. Mel went home to explain the circumstances to six-year-old Gary, and Leisa, four years old. He called our relatives and word spread quickly: "They may have to *amputate*." Dozens of prayer chains developed throughout the United States. Even with pain injections, all night I heard creaky carts in the hallway.

Strange uncontrollable flashbacks filled my thoughts. I remembered the doctor's statement. "A seatbelt would have prevented your head from crashing into the windshield and the foot from absorbing 500 pounds of pressure."

The thought of death never entered my mind until a roommate's visitor asked, "Could I pray for you?" I nodded. He petitioned, "Lord, bless this dear lady. Heal her body." I cringed upon hearing the words: "If you decide to take her to heaven, please care for her family."

Thirty-seven is too young to die. I longed to hear the comforting voice I'd heard earlier. I thought about last Sunday's sermon: "Angels are created spiritual beings, with the power to become visible in the semblance of human form. They care for believers." I had faith in God and knew He believers." I had faith in God and knew He worked in mysterious ways, but I never thought about angels on earth.

The next morning after three hours of surgery, the doctor told Mel, "Look at these X-rays. It's a miracle. I inserted two 4-inch screws and two 2-inch pins to hold the bones together. She will walk with a limp, but we saved the foot."

When the children saw my hip cast, wheel chair and bandaged face, Leisa cried, backed away and refused my hugs. Gary questioned every detail and understood my dilemma.

Bright flowers caught the sun streaming through the window. Donna brought a sunshine basket filled with thirty gifts, and instructions to open one each day. "Will you answer the same question I asked Mel? Who was the man talking to me the day of the accident?"

Her firm reply was the same as Mel's. "I stayed until the ambulance came. I never saw anyone except Mel and the emergency personnel."

After therapy and fifteen days in the hospital, I came home. The estimated disability time was one year, the insurance company totaled our car, and Mel took advantage of a perfect opportunity. He bought the truck he had always wanted. The children looked forward to "trucking with Daddy."

During my recuperation Janie appeared at the back door once a week. "You need to rest. I'll take the kids for a few hours." I was in a cast for nine months, followed by learning to walk without assistance, learning to accept limping. Gary and Leisa played "hide Mommy's crutches" game. If I failed to guess, I lost. But I didn't lose. I gained renewed faith, and extra time with my children. I discovered that someone always watches over me.

My guardian angel works overtime. Nine months later, the week I returned to work, I fell down the back stairs. A neighbor, Arlene, drove me to the emergency room. "Just bruises, no broken bones, but you must take three days off work," the doctor said. I assured the boss that I would stay out of trouble and be a loyal, reliable employee.

I welcomed summer, but I'd had enough of hot afternoons and muggy evenings. The fall season announced an assortment of sounds: the drone of distant chain saws, tractors clanking, choppers mowing ranks of corn that smells like a compost heap. In the fall nature demands that we take notice. Road rage gives way to Sunday drives. Color tours on back roads seem more important than the destination. The outside of the refrigerator door fills up with fall schedules, rehearsals and sports. Walt Disney lunch boxes are piling onto school buses. We march to a man-made tune, following a calendar dictated by the school year. School began in late August.

Bell employees were granted another holiday that year, Columbus Day. I told Mel about the long list of things I wanted to accomplish. Nothing slipped by Leisa. Her brain continually turns. "You have a free day with nothing to do? Can Gary and I skip school? Just today. We love being with our mommy," she begged.

Gary was in sixth grade and he was ready for a day off. At ten I was mopping the kitchen floor. The telephone rang. "Hi, Mom. This is Gary. Will you come and get me? I have a splitting headache."

"I guess I could. But you'll have to stay in your room all day. Headaches need lots of rest."

"Oh." Silence.

"Maybe you could stay at school until lunch time. If eating doesn't help, call me."

"Okay, Mom."

That evening I asked, "Do you feel better? You didn't call back."

"I feel better. You didn't believe I had a headache, did you?"

"Yes, son, I believed you. But I realize that today was a perfect day to have a headache."

Gary loved baseball; the unhurried game from America's rural past. The Little League games, where parents insist that they call the game much better than the umpire, will forever remain in my mind. Because of baseball, we met Chuck Orr the assistant coach and his wife Jeanette. We immediately became best friends. Mel missed one of Gary's games; the night of his first home run. His birthday present that year was a trip to Tiger Stadium.

He emerged from a catwalk beneath the stands, and for a moment stood transfixed, awestruck with the eye-catching playing field and emerald carpet. The game wasn't the World Series. It just seemed like it. That night, September 17, 1977, I became a loyal Detroit Tiger fan. Dick Tidrow of the Yankees pitched the ball and Jason Thompson cleared the roof with a homerun and victory. Ernie Harwell became the play-by-play announcer for the Tigers in 1960. In 2002, at the age of eighty-one he announced that this would be his final season.

I thought about my first visit to the glorious playground at the corner of Michigan and Trumbull. My thoughts returned to high school, the baseball pool and my belief that the Yankees would win the pennant that year. I enjoyed the prestige as well as the pot of money. That was a lifetime ago.

Football is at the bottom of my sports recommendation. I don't understand the strategy of defensive back, punt returner, running back, wide receiver, streaks, stats and stuff. My curious, want-to-know-something-about-everything personality is a pain in the petute. No matte how many times I try to grasp the concept of "downs" I just don't get it. Players have four tries to do something with the ball. I think they call it "yards." If they do the wrong thing they get penalized. Sometimes the team gets three points instead of one, or six.

Nonetheless, Friday nights found the Cornstubbles, Orrs and Livelys sitting on the Western High School bleachers. Sometimes all six, dressed in snowmobile suits, huddled under Mel's golf umbrella and sipped coffee from a Coleman thermos. Our sons covered the field as their dads covered the coaching job from the bleacher. The moms chatted, occasionally yelled with the cheerleaders, clapped when our team got a touchdown.

190

I played basketball in high school, loved the sport but hated being forced into guard position because of my height. Wrangling my way around the tall players and blocking passes made my heart proud. Gary was a do-it-by-the-rules basketball player. He stuck to two-handed jumps, set shots and left-handed lay-ups. He set a few school records during his career. One night the score was tied with one minute left on the clock. Gary roared down the court to a breakaway, rose as high as I remember and slammed the ball through the hoop.

After pressing my brain to expand my knowledge of the sports world, Leisa signed up for volleyball, which included strange terms: digs, kills, blocks, aces and assists. I refused to discuss the sport, and cheered when other mothers cheered, sometimes at the wrong times.

Leisa enjoyed socializing rather than setting school records. She came barreling home from the game, dropped her books on the kitchen table and made a mad dash to the bathroom. Her pockets were filled with wads of toilet paper where her pals had scribbled notes. She tried to read the words but couldn't reconstruct them. "My teacher said we should always set goals. If I don't set goals, I can't regret not reaching them. I've made a rule that I'll avoid sports, and exercise every now and then."

"Okay, get busy helping with chores. That's good exercise. I've got to pack for a trip."

Murder at Midnight

Twenty years brought many changes in my hometown. One reason prompted my return, a promise to help firm up plans for Saturday's reunion. The day I arrived classmate Dennis Thompson greeted me with some startling news. "I'm sure you heard about your Uncle Gil's murder."

For a long moment I stared at my apple-cheeked high school buddy, still handsome even with his gray hair. Dennis was philosophical, constantly analyzed everything. I was flabbergasted. "His what?"

"Murder. Three weeks ago. I lived next door to you, and I remember how your uncle made your life the pits. I still care what happens, even though no one else wants to get involved." He frowned. "I'm tired of unsolved crimes and lawless confusion in this one-horse hamlet. You always talked about being a private investigator. Time to assert yourself."

"Assert myself? Maybe. Even though I couldn't care less that my uncle died, the news catches me by surprise and whets my crime-solving appetite."

That afternoon a pebbly-faced farmer wearing bibbed overalls that struggled to cover his paunchy stomach told me, "Rumor and the newspapers claim that the case has been laid to rest." He puffed a Chesterfield, blew smoke in my face. "You'll never know the answer."

"There will always be answers," I replied. "Uncovering them is the problem."

During the weekend bash, I had planned to meet with giddy sweethearts who tied the knot. Those who still had no sweethearts would be there. I wanted to learn about each class member. We would laugh, swap stories, brag about our accomplishments, and thank those who helped us make it to graduation.

I turned down free lodging offers. I needed solitude and time to gather my thoughts. Lying awake in a motel room the size of a clothes closet with as much personality, I studied the matter until 4:30 a.m.

My second day in town brought another surprise. I stopped at a café near the town saloon. A tattered menu listed daily specials: fried okra, bean soup, fried ham, egg salad sandwiches. Maybe hot coffee sounded all right. The waitress displayed a faint pink scar above her right eye. She returned my hesitant smile, placed silverware and a postage-sized paper napkin on the table. Her shrill voice penetrated the room. "New in the community?"

"I grew up in this town. Left after graduation. Things just aren't the same, you know."

She plopped in a chair next to me. "You've got that right. I work here during lunch, and another job at night."

"What else do you do?"

She flipped her long bleached-blond hair with her left hand that displayed several rings. "I'm a newspaper reporter."

I read the menu again and adjusted my glasses. "Small town reporters don't make much money."

"Well, I need the money, but I also like to keep busy." Something about her looked familiar. The small pupils brought memories of grandma's squinting when she looked into a bright light.

"Have you lived in this area long?"

"Most of my life. What'll you have today?"

"Ham and egg sandwich. Wheat bread, toasted, black coffee." She headed toward the kitchen. Her hips bounced, the green and white stripes on her skirt trembled. A key dangled from her belt loop.

Three newspapers bulged in my briefcase. I retrieved the *Charleston Gazette*. The headline on page ten read: MURDER IS STILL UNSOLVED, and gave a twelve-line report of my uncle's death. I expected less information. The *Gazette* was located sixty miles away and seldom carried Fayette County news. The reporter's name was Cynthia Collard.

I unfolded another newspaper. "You have an interesting name," I said as she filled my cup and dribbled coffee on the comic section. She asked how I knew her name. "It's on your apron."

"Oh, yeah. My name is Cynthia, but everybody calls me Cin." She hung her head. "I shouldn't be talking to strangers, but you're a woman. You'll understand. Truth is, my ex-husband had an appalling temper. He beat me regularly and burned my body with cigarettes. Gave no affection. Gone most of the time. Now he's gone for good."

"Gone for good?"

"Yes, ma'am. The divorce was final last month. I'm rid of him." She ripped the bill from her note pad and placed it on top of someone's leftover pancake syrup. Rushing away, she looked over her shoulder. "Gotta get to my next job. Hey, nice talking to you. Stop by tomorrow." Stopping tomorrow had already crossed my mind. *Where have I seen her? Why did she weave her personal life into a stranger's lunch? Tomorrow, after my morning meeting, hunger pangs will prevail.*

They did. I had an urge, not only for food, but also for information. Cin greeted me at the door. She wore bright red lipstick, and had a long messy plait running down her back. "Still hangin' around, huh?"

I hung my umbrella and purse on the chair. "Needed something to eat. Think I'll have what I chose yesterday, if you can remember."

She remembered, and within minutes brought the food to my table. She poured two cups of coffee. "May I join you?"

"Feel free. I'd like to ask you a question or two. If you have time."

She brushed cracker crumbs from the chair. "Sure. Business is slow when it rains."

"You're a reporter. Are you familiar with the murder of Gil Brunk?"

Her pink face accented round scars on her chin. "Not really. I met him once. A friend of mine said his health wasn't good. Said he was living on borrowed time. I heard a something about it, but—" Her voice trailed off. "Why do you ask?"

"The victim was my dad's younger brother. When I came to town yesterday, news of his death hit me in the face. I can't get the thoughts out of my head."

Cin leaned forward on the edge of the chair and rested her elbows on the table. "I'm sorry. Hey, I just remembered something I've got to do. See ya."

Early the next morning I left the motel and ran into the vice-president of my graduating class. "Good to see you, William. What have you been doing with your life?"

"Doing great. Who'd ever think that the malicious kid I used to be would work in the police department? Just got promoted to captain."

I forced myself to sound cheerful. "Can't believe you turned out okay. Just kidding."

"Judy and I are happy in Ohio. I hear you're doing well in Michigan." He put his hands on my shoulders. "C'mon, Patty, why the downcast look?"

I told him about the murder. "Grandma and Aunt Margaret died and left the house to Uncle Gil. I wonder why the city wants to demolish the house. Gaps in police reports indicate the need for a thorough investigation."

"Who did the investigation?"

"The Fayette County Sheriff Department. Relatives want explanations and so do I."

His mouth firmed into a stubborn line. After several hard snaps of his gold lighter he lit a Winston. I thought of school days and William's almost ruthless determination. "I'm out of my jurisdiction, but I'll help you get answers. I'm on vacation, have plenty of time." He walked, military style, toward his shiny black Lincoln. "I'll be in touch." *Could I bear to revive old memories and return to my old home place, the scene of adolescent battles with Uncle Gil?* I had no choice.

Grass and weeds filled large cracks in the concrete sidewalk where I once played hopscotch. The house looked pretty much the same, except the tin roof and some of the wood casement windows had been replaced. "Those old windows used to let in too much cold air," I said aloud.

The pain of childhood swept over me as I entered the unlocked door. The same urge that encased my life long ago, the desire to run away, fought with the will to stay. Most of the furniture was gone. The rooms had shrunk. I opened a cabinet drawer. Underneath a dusty gray towel was a yellow blob, Aunt Margaret's corncob pipe, deteriorated, the stem separated from the bowl. Ailene's rubber doll, which she clutched during the nights we spent alone at Brunk hollow, had a wrinkled nose and a cracked face. Dust balls covered the familiar linoleum floors. Massive spider webs hung in clusters. The refrigerator that we rejoiced to receive the year before we left still stood in the corner of the kitchen.

I glanced toward Uncle Gil's room, the only bedroom equipped with lock and key. The doorknob turned, but the door remained locked. I checked the dusty mantle, but both the key and the black clock that concealed it were gone.

Outside, near Uncle Gil's bedroom window, cigarette butts covered the ground. Dried putty separated the bottom windowpane from the wood casing. I shoved the glass in, and nudged my 118 pounds through the small opening.

Once inside, I felt speechless, uneasy, but determined. The room looked the same, the air felt damp, eerie. The lock was tarnished and reddish-brown, like the hair on the girlie pictures that still hung above Uncle Gil's bed. The pictures had faded, and the girls' lips pale. I searched through drawers and dusty cardboard boxes filled with news clippings and old invoices.

Letters wrapped with crushed blue ribbon had been shoved under the bed. Tucked in an envelope was a note written on a white napkin:

> DEAR FRIEND,
> THE SITUATION HAS NOT IMPROVED. HE CAME HOME DRUNK. HE BEAT ME UP. I LEFT WHEN HE PASSED OUT. THANKS FOR THE SECURITY OF YOUR ROOM. GIL, YOU ARE KIND TO ME. CIN

"I'll be darned!" I said aloud. "Now I know why meeting Cin caused my insides to gnaw." I found another note written on pink stationery:

> DEAREST GIL,
> YOU ARE THE GLUE THAT HOLDS ME TOGETHER. BILL KNOWS ABOUT YOU. HE FOLLOWED ME TO YOUR HOUSE LAST NIGHT. BE CAREFUL. I FEAR FOR YOUR LIFE. ALL MY LOVE, CIN

I stuffed the evidence in my pocket, and tossed everything else in the box. A blue sheet of paper and Uncle Gil's handwriting caught my eye. The note read:

> MY DARLING CIN,
> I NEVER EXPECTED TO FIND YOU. NEVER KNEW I WANTED A LADY FRIEND, BUT YOU MAKE ME VERY HAPPY. LOVE YOU, GIL

The next day I shared the information with William. "These notes explain the connection: The girlie pictures above the bed, the key that dangled from Cin's belt loop, the blond hair that changed her identity. The features, red blush, bright lips and small eyes were branded in my mind."

"I've had some luck, too," he said. "I talked with a member of the Saturday night poker game, an old codger, threatened to silence. He told a gruesome story.

"Bill, the ex-husband, had witnessed unexpected scenes from Gil's bedroom window. Cin had given your uncle hours of entertainment and listened to his problems. But his thirst for respect was more important than Cin's reputation. The old man said that Bill crashed the poker game. Bill was so mad and upset that the smoke from his cigarette dangled up and down as he talked. Through the circles of smoke, Bill pointed a gun square into Gil's face and told him, 'you've been living on borrowed time.' I won't go into the shooting details. Bill dragged Gil's body to an abandoned coal mines, a nearby turnpike project. The next day, he watched the bulldozer bury the dead.

"Cin, afraid of Bill's repercussions, vowed to keep the secret. When the deputy inquired, she said that before Bill's last poker game he came home soused, tied her to the bed, and burned her face with cigarettes. Bill told her that no one would ever locate him in South America. She never saw him again."

After regaining my composure, I managed to speak. "Uncle Gil used to spend every weekend drunk. Was he too stoned to realize what happened?" I asked.

"Oh, no. He drank Coke for the past ten years," he concluded.

"Yes, indeed," I said. "A lot of changes have taken place in this town." Realizing that confronting Cin would end in a draw, I cancelled reservations and headed north.

Lifescapes

Sometimes we forget how much we influence others. Mel is interested in my endeavors, whether it's a special project or connections with my world of music. He helped with expenses incurred by the Gospel Lights, took care of transportation, purchased and maintained equipment. We formed a quartet and Mel sang bass. We enjoyed "singing vacations" in several states. Ailene and her Gospel Tones quartet scheduled concerts in the Michigan area. When our group piled into the Gospel Tones' greyhound bus, Gary and Leisa were thrilled with the exposure to the hectic schedule.

The bass player, Jerry Neil, taught Gary a few cords. During the children's growth, we monitored television time and the music diet. We contacted a teacher for Gary, bought a used amplifier and a new electric lead guitar. He tuned up the instrument by plucking each string in turn, adjusting the pegs to tighten or loosen them. Back and forth he went between strings, plucking, listening, and adjusting. The teacher said, "Stringed instruments don't work well if they aren't tuned with care. Too loose, and the sound is dull. Too tight, and the instrument yields a squeaky vibration."

As I observed the patience of a ten-year-old, I realized how each human being is like a musical instrument. It's easy to fall out of tune. When we want to get rid of discord, we learn how to make the music we're capable of creating. We should continually tune ourselves. When we're in tune, the world feels in tune.

Gary divided his time between sports, homework, piano, guitar, trombone lessons, and practicing with the trio. A local store had a going out of business sale. Mel asked who was going to play the Fender bass guitar that I bought. "You are," I said. "You play a saxophone. You need to advance your musical talent." After a few lessons, Gary and Mel fulfilled my dream to have all family members on stage. Gary and Leisa sang, and later formed The Sounds group. Leisa wanted to sing, but thought practice was boring. For several years, Gary played for the Gospel Lights. After two recordings, he concentrated on furthering his education.

Three weeks prior to our group's most exciting moment, our pianist resigned, claiming that she would be too nervous to perform in such a prolific theater as the Potter Center. After several interviews, we chose Phyllis Stoetzel, a concert pianist who played violin, but had never performed for a large audience.

Phyllis agreed that our most memorable performance occurred on a snowy December evening. At the Potter Center Music Hall, with elegant purple décor, Denny's Holiday House provided a beautifully decorated Christmas tree. Our guests, the Cathedral Quartet, America's number one gospel group, shared the stage. A local Christian radio station Manager, Steve Wright, acted as master of ceremonies. Phyllis smiled at the audience as she sat down on the leather piano seat. The listeners connected with the music, her relaxed touch and ease of style generated new inspiration to our group.

At intermission I noticed Steve slumped in a chair, leaning his head against the purple stage backdrop. His face and hands were winter-white. He said, "I'm so sorry, I don't know if I can finish the evening. My diabetic condition is causing problems." The Cathedrals and our group formed a circle around him, joined our hands and hearts in prayer. Within a few minutes we heard the curtain call. Steve's complexion brightened and he said he felt fine.

Our group marched into the spotlight and took our positions. Phyllis placed her hands on the ivory keys of the magnificent concert Grand piano and realized that during intermission she had taken her package of music backstage. Her face flushed, she whispered to Mel. He made a quick exit to retrieve the notebook. I stood before several hundred people, wondering what happened. My vocal and stage training had touched upon how to adlib, how to prevent the audience from knowing whether words or actions had or had not been written into the script.

Daddy's sense of humor seemed to encircle the stage. I joked about the weather, how bass players like to make a grand entrance, even at the Potter Center. My bass player remained missing so I filled the vacant time slot by giving a commercial announcement. "Let's have a hand for Denny, who arranged the stage setting and decorated the tree." I waited for the round of applause.

"The bright lights on the tree remind me of the glow that God's love gives. The stars remind me of shepherds that led the way to the good news. The beads are like strands of hope, long-lasting to those who believe. The shining tinsel tells me to let my light shine before man. The trunk reminds me of the cross where Jesus died for our sins. The gleam in children's eyes reminds me of anticipation."

Anxiety took a back seat to the melodious musical and vocal sounds we produced that night. Phyllis became a special friend, an encourager. She remained with the group for twelve years. Our seasoned friendship has stood the test of time.

Michigan winter enthusiasts look forward to the season that brings skating, sleds and ice shanties. Cross-country skiers crest wooded hills. Only their breathing, steam rising in cold, clear air, breaks the silence. In Janie and Neil's cabin at Grayling, fallen leaves rustle against the window, frost crackles in tree branches. Hills of pure snow blanket the acreage, smooth like loaves of unbaked bread.

Our weekend begins at 8:30 on Friday. As our party of nine

people on seven snowmobiles drift through Hardwick Pines, my snow-dream begins. Hundreds of trees bent with the weight of snow, formed canyons and canopies. Wildlife is plentiful. We stop at the Lone Pine restaurant that displays animal heads, horns, and antlers mounted on the walls. The place is hopping with more than thirty snowmobilers drinking coffee and ordering breakfast.

After four days of invigorating inspiration and a three-hour journey home, I settle into a routine of sleet-filled days, bitter, windy nights, and mornings when the county plow dumps knee-deep ice into snow-drifted driveways.

Leisa was in eighth grade when the telephone company secretarial positions were moved to the Lansing district. My thoughts were tossed between transferring, working six years to receive full pension, or taking termination pay. Mel could transfer, my employer would purchase our home, increase my pay, but the children's schooling took first priority. After many sleepless nights I made a decision.

Benefits of becoming a stay-at-home mom included after school conversations, sitting at the kitchen table having homemade cookies and milk. All too soon, dinner dates and telephone conversations replaced school plays and sports events. A boy's picture on Leisa's dresser replaced the attention previously devoted to her dad, the one who now stands at the door and waves goodbye. The bittersweet freedom was bearable with the knowledge that she was happy in the world she inhibited. Soon she was dressing for the prom. Memories are frozen in time, never to thaw or melt away. The hold-on-forever love is still there.

A telephone conversation with my brother Paul reminded me of family hold-on-forever love. "Haven't seen your smiling face for a coon's age," he said. "Get your butt down here or I'll have to come north. I want to see my sweet sis." The voice was serious in a gentle sort of way. I read between the lines.

The next week Mel and I visited our family in the south. Paul talked about his many occupations, how he loved driving trucks that had several gears. Problems found Paul. He had high blood pressure, various aches and pains, but he said," Don't worry sis. I don't plan to be shoveled under for a long, long time."

A few months later he drove a cement truck to the building site where a contractor wanted a poured basement. He stood in the prepared space, lowered the chute, and cement began pouring. The chute malfunctioned and slammed into Paul's chest, bouncing him backward several feet. My brother declined medical attention.

While driving home a short time later, his chest and arms hurt. He drove to the hospital emergency room. The cardiac physician said the heart was severely damaged. Paul could never work again. After a long battle, the Social Services Department granted disability. A year later he defied doctor's orders and returned to work, but within a short time he developed more problems. After another long battle, the physician signed permanent disability papers, but benefits were refused. The pain of unemployment and lack of finances caused severe depression. Within a few months my brother suffered a myocardial infarction.

In the Coronary Care Unit, the family took turns spending the last few minutes with Paul. Our prayers wafted as incense, starting in our hearts and reaching up to heaven in the power of our intercessor. The heavenly Father smelled the aroma, but knew what was best. My brother passed away. My sadness remained.

I had to know more about Paul's malady. The science and medical field has always grabbed my attention. In 1944 Dr. Vivien Thomas and Dr. Denton Cooley completed the first surgery to correct the blue baby problem. At Johns Hopkins Hospital they found that blood vessels were full of the thick, dark "blue" blood characteristic of cyanotic children.

The corrective procedure was to cut into the pulmonary artery and create an opening into which they sewed the divided subclavian artery. The two arteries were joined, thus shunting the pure blue blood through the pulmonary artery into the lungs to be oxygenated. Cyanotic children who had never been able to sit upright began standing at their crib rails, pink and healthy, the beginning of modern cardiac surgery.

The discovery came too late to help my brother, but his strong will to live helped beat the survival odds. He lived three times past the estimated age of twenty-one, maintained a high-energy lifestyle and escaped many of the medical misfortunes that had been predicted. He lived long enough to be a husband, father and grandfather.

I've had no problem being a mother. Since their birth I have hovered over our children like a mother grizzly, knowing what was happening in their lives. This connection with my kids comes from communication at mealtime as well as school activities. Youth craves direction and discipline. I probed into their heart and asked questions, combined a dose of prayer with humor and love.

I wonder how many times I've heard my daughter say, "You don't love me!" Sometimes, out of total frustration, I'd answer, "Today, I don't."

"Gary never does anything wrong. You always make me do stuff and he never has to."

"That's not true," I said.

"Fine. How long are you going to ground me? Until I'm seventy-five?

"You've spent half your life being grounded. Honey, I'm afraid you're going to grow roots while you're sleeping."

"I hate sleeping. It's a waste of time. There's lots better things to do," she growled.

I knew that someday she would understand the logic that motivates motherhood. Then she will understand how I loved her so much that I questioned where she was going, with whom, and what time she'd return home. I let her discover that her friend was a creep. I loved her enough to empty her dresser drawers in the floor, and stand over her for two hours until she cleaned her bedroom. I loved her enough to let her see anger, tears and disappointment. I loved her enough to admit it when I was wrong and ask forgiveness. I loved her enough to accept who she was, not who I wanted her to be. Perhaps the hardest part was saying no when she hated me for it. I loved her enough to ignore the phrase, "Every other mother says yes."

I'm now an expert in dealing with teenagers. My definition of a teenager is a mammal thought to be Homosapiens due to physical similarities. Teenagers live a parasitical relationship, social animals seeking contact with peer groups. They use the term, "It's my room." I tell them it's my house, and children join my life, I don't join theirs.

Females sport striking colors under and above eyes, on lips, fingers and toes. Wonder bras attract males, who indicate approval by staring at the display. Females talk on the telephone for hours. When challenged they warn intruders, "I'm doing my homework."

Males signal their kind of species with, "Yo. Hey, man. S'up?" Less vocal males sit for hours listening to violent electronic signals from radios. Males forage for food and consume three times their weight every day. They use skateboards, snowboards, surfboards and automobiles.

Teenagers spend morning hours hibernating in their nest lined with stinky sneakers and dirty clothes. They arouse from sleep, spend hours preening themselves in front of mirrors, shower until the hot water tank is empty. They use three bottles of shampoo and one bottle of cream rinse every week.

Turning sixteen means being swept up in the hectic pace of society. It means suddenly being entrusted with 3,000 pounds of potential disaster. Every parent is concerned about children being involved in a debilitating or fatal accident. When Driver's Training is over, memories of childhood with fewer concerns and less responsibility is also over. I'm thankful that our children made it through.

It's easy to be thankful for the big things in life, but we sometimes forget the insignificant things, like trying to understand other people. "Happy Turkey Day," my hairdresser said.

The words "turkey day" did not make me happy, they made me annoyed. To forget, or ignore the purpose and meaning behind our national observance, and use the day for personal celebration is hard for me to understand. This generation hasn't seen the terrible slaughter and national chaos that comes with worldwide war. The more we depend on God and try to do right, the more incentive we have to be thankful every day.

Thanksgiving and going to Grandma's house in West Virginia changed the year our son made the varsity basketball team (his sophomore year). "If I miss practice, coach won't let me play." We gave a few instructions and left Gary at home.

On Saturday he called at midnight. "Dad, I hit a deer. The front end doesn't look too good."

"Are you injured?"

"No."

Well, that's all right. The old car you're driving is ready to die anyway."

Silence. "But it wasn't the old car, Dad."

"Not the old car?"

"No. I had a date with Dawn. I wanted to impress her. I drove the Cutlass."

"You didn't!"

"Sorry to admit it, but I did."

"He wrecked the Cutlass. Dawn was with him. No one is hurt," Mel whispered to me.

While listening to one side of the conversation I pictured the scene: Gary's girlfriend is snuggling, the radio has reached several decibels. The moon is shining on the crisp November snow. The deer runs into the car, they hear a crash, Gary turns white, the girl cries. Gary figures that since this is his first offense the judge will issue a fair verdict.

The fatherly advise was, "If no one is injured, don't worry. So what if the car is damaged Tomorrow is another day."

The motherly opinion was, "That's what Gary's afraid of, dear. He has to face tomorrow."

In the teenager's eyes, tomorrow is an eternity. When the

kids reached sixteen I wrote in my journal:

> Tonight I'm thinking about you. Your dad and I used to be young and daring. We've been there and done that. We were sure we could tackle the world. We were just as dumb, silly and excited about life as you are. That's why we worry. We fell in love, got married, had you, fed you, held you when you were sick, watched you take those first steps, listened to your first words, carried pictures in our wallets and bragged to co-workers about your achievements. We kept your school projects, displayed your artwork, and cheered your team. We laughed with you, cried with you, and worried when you missed a curfew. We prayed that you would arrive home safely. Before long, you changed into young men and women. We wondered whom you would choose for your mate. We thanked God that the things we worried about didn't happen.

Seems like yesterday when I watched Gary escort a lovely lady to the prom. Tall and handsome, with poise far beyond his seventeen years, Gary was a son to delight the parent's heart. "Dad taught me how to treat a lady," he said. "I looked at my father, and learned how to become a man."

Overnight, the magical number, eighteen, transforms these creatures into adults. With this number, great expectations overwhelm both parent and child. Sometimes, in frustration and pain, it seemed my prayers went no further than the rooftop.

At eighteen, Gary found out that Mom knew everything. For the first time, he didn't seem to be listening to my advice. Could it be that he turned down a basketball scholarship at Spring Arbor University because we live one mile from campus? He had attended basketball camps and worked there two summers. He knew the coaches. Could it be that he wanted a taste of dorm life? He knew that my heart was with SAU.

Gary's friend talked him into Tri-State University in Indiana. Mel was happy with the electrical engineering choice. We toured the campus, the dining hall, met members of the staff and carried a hundred boxes into his dormitory. I dusted the dresser drawers, and stacked the socks with underwear, shorts with baggie shirts. I put the laundry bag in a prominent place and coached him on the procedure. "Separate white clothes from dark. Be sure to measure the soap. Add bleach to towels."

When we left, I shed parental-pride tears. My son agreed to take his vitamins. His even hugged his sister and whispered, "You're special."

The empty bedroom was most disturbing. Maybe I wanted the door shut, or did I want it open? The atmosphere was too quiet. Finally I decided that I must move on with life. My son was one hour away. After all, we still had one kid at home. I'll make fewer trips to the grocery store. Leisa eats like a bird.

By the time Gary got around to doing laundry he forgot my instructions. He stuffed a red shirt in with light clothes and ran the hot cycle. Imagine the surprise when he lifted the lid, his words echoing a cry for help. "Mom!" Frequently he came home with a mountain of laundry. "Mom, do you suppose you could do a couple loads while I go out?"

Gary is 6'5." He can never enter a new social situation, whether it's going to a restaurant or a party, without being asked the same dumb questions that annoy the daylights out of him: "How's the weather up there? How tall are you? Do you play basketball?"

When he has enough, he responds, "No. Are you a jockey?" The world offers inadequate facilities for "tallies." Beds and chairs are too short. Sheets, blankets and pillows are too small. A "tallie" must duck for chandeliers and doorways. Gary usually preferred the tall girls. Like Aunt Margaret used to say, "I'm right proud" that he makes the effort to bend over and kiss short mothers, little sisters and dumpy grandmas.

I clipped a cartoon to post in his dorm. It pictured an outhouse in a wooded area at a basketball camp. An open door revealed a long-limbed guy's bent knees. A basketball leaned against the building. I thought of parent's night during a basketball awards presentation. Picture this: on the left side of a lanky giant is a parent 6'1" and on the right is Mom that stands 5'2."

He skipped breakfast because of an early calculus class, and at lunchtime dashed to the cafeteria to refuel. People asked how we could afford to feed Gary. "It's easy," I say. "Work three jobs and cook enough to fill a stomach and two long legs. I purchase three gallons of milk weekly. He would never make it in the armed forces. They feed them only three times a day."

Even with carrying a full load and participating in several sports, Gary achieved high marks with a minimum amount of study. After one year he didn't like engineering. He returned home and enrolled in a community college.

The next year he began working for Tom Monaghan, the owner of Domino's Pizza empire and the Detroit Tiger baseball team. When Gary moved to Ann Arbor, he realized that the world was filled with difficult choices.

The Empty-Nest Syndrome

When the children left, I suffered for ten minutes. I'm now an empty-nest survivor. I look around at the evidence that the children "flew the coop." The cereal supply consists of Bran Buds instead of Fruit Loops. The jug of milk in the refrigerator shrank from a gallon to a pint. Pies and cakes last until they mold. You forget how to bake chocolate chip cookies.

When the telephone rings, *if* it rings, you hear mature adult voices on the line. Standing at the bathroom door with your legs crossed is a thing of the past. There is always a supply of hot water. You breathe clean air instead of nail polish and hair spray. You can walk into a bedroom without stumbling over dirty clothes.

The doors remain locked from night until morning, and the front yard never gets toilet paper decorations. The wheels on the family car are stone cold. You take an afternoon nap without the "whoop, whisk, klunk" of a basketball sinking into the net attached to the house.

My baby survived teenage years, and graduated high school. My baby turned twenty. She's not a child anymore. I don't even know the color of her toothbrush. She enrolled in a business college, worked in an office and moved into a town house.

Leisa used imagination and organization to create a neat-appearing home. We toured the apartment, Mel "accidentally" left several lights on. Leisa gave him a hefty grin and rushed to turn them off. "What are you doing, leaving all the lights on?"

Mel chuckled. "That's what I used to ask you."

A lighted aquarium stocked with tropical fish swimming through bridges and castles, glowing candles and soft music made for great relaxation. "You're my first guests," she said as Mel and I sat down to a chicken dinner, lettuce salad, macaroni and cheese. "I'm beginning to miss the food that for twenty years has appeared almost magically on the table," she said while pouring iced tea. "I baked chocolate chip cookies for dessert. Tried to make them taste like yours, Mom, but that's impossible."

"They're delicious. I love crisp cookies." Someone said that your child never stops being your child regardless of age. But sometimes you wish for yesterday.

Leisa took her office job seriously and related well with the boss. "You've been here almost a year, and you're doing well, in fact, you'll see an increase on next week's check," he told her. "We normally give raises every two years." Happy thoughts accompanied the short drive to her apartment, but a notice in the mail brought disappointment. EFFECTIVE IN THIRTY DAYS, THE RENTAL FEE WILL INCREASE 10 PERCENT. Instead of enjoying extra money, the raise in pay was already spent.

The next week, long hours of typing caused neck problems and headaches, but my daughter was determined to maintain a perfect attendance record. The family doctor recommended a chiropractor.

On Sunday Leisa's friend Mara told her, "My dad is a pastor, and he's much too strict. The family is moving to Ohio, but I need to stay in Michigan. I don't want to move away from my boyfriend, and I can't afford an apartment."

"I have an extra bedroom. We could split the rent and utility cost." They signed a lease. Leisa helped Mara move, gave lunch loans, shared her supply of Pepsi and food. "Finally, things are working out," Leisa told me at lunch.

But the rejoicing was short lived. Grocery shopping required more time as Leisa searched for bargains, clipped and redeemed coupons. Every month Leisa paid her portion of the rent, but her friend needed constant reminders. "Mara, the power bill is due. The telephone bill is due. Also you owe me for eight long distance calls."

"Hey, don't get yourself in an uproar. I'm slightly short this week, needed a new hair dryer and shoes."

"Sorry, but rent and utilities come first."

"Know what? You're a real nag. Chill out. Get a life."

"That's my goal, to have a life. You pulled the same trick last month. Grow up!"

Mara stormed down the hall and into her boyfriend's red Camero. Leisa took two aspirin and fell asleep on the couch.

On Friday light rain and a predawn haze blanketed my way to the grocery store. When I returned home, I checked the answering machine: "Mom, things went from unpleasant to terrible. I haven't called because I was trying to do things on my own. Last week I slipped on a wet floor at work, hit the back of my head, the boss drove me to the hospital for x-rays and—and more bad news. I've been threatened. I'm afraid. Call me."

I put perishables away, called Mel at work and headed for Leisa's apartment. She met me at the door. "The office sent an eviction notice. I put $250 cash on the table with a note that said: MARA, I'M LATE LEAVING FOR WORK. RENT IS DUE. HERE'S MY HALF. PLEASE PAY IT TODAY. Mara kept the money! She accused me of stealing her things. She says the office gal took the rent money, and lied about it."

My daughter's face, the peaches and cream complexion, was now crimson. Dark circles shadowed her blue eyes. I held her in my arms; we cried a river of tears. I felt blessed to be her mom. Her life had filled mine with much joy. "We'll get through this."

"I didn't want to worry you and dad, but Mara's boyfriend is here too much. She parties until two in the morning. I can't get enough sleep. I'm so tired."

"What were the threats?" Mel asked.

"Mara says she has lots of friends who will make me sorry for my unfair treatment. She says, 'I'm sick of your bossiness.' She says, 'My friends will take care of you tomorrow when I get out of work.' "

Mel spoke in a stern voice. "Start packing, honey. You're out of here. You're coming home." He went to a nearby grocery store, filled the van with empty cardboard boxes, stopped at a deli and bought chicken dinners. Leisa's friends came and helped pack kitchen items. When I opened a dresser drawer, I saw a pregnancy test kit. *Don't tell me Mara is pregnant?*

At three in the morning we finished packing, loaded the van, the car, and locked the apartment door. My daughter looked stressed. "Leave my fish in the pails. I'll take care of them after work tomorrow. You guys have done enough." She was in bed at four. At five Mel and I finished setting up the aquarium. The next morning she said, "Dad, my mind kept churning. I was awake for hours."

"Wish you didn't have to work today."

"I have to. I need my job."

"Call your boss and say you'll be in after lunch." She took his advice, and went to work at one o'clock.

An hour later she pulled into our driveway. "I told the boss why I was late. He didn't believe me. He said 'no one moves at three in the morning. You have to give a notice when you move.' I told him to pick up the phone and ask my parents where I was last night. He refused." She groped for words and fought back tears. "He said he didn't need me anymore."

The unemployment rate was high. Leisa checked newspaper ads and left applications all over town. No longer was she considered a child who needed her family, but she was a friend, a houseguest who helped without being asked.

Two weeks later Wilma and Yvonne called from Florida. Leisa told them what happened. "Honey, we haven't seen you for so long. Come down and we'll take you to Disney World. There's so much to do here. When you go back home you'll look at things differently."

We encouraged the visit. Leisa left on Friday. That evening she called. "The flight was wonderful. Florida is so beautiful."

"Two letters came in the mail today," I told her. "One is from your former employer."

"You can open them. Maybe there's something good inside. Sure could use some good news."

I opened both envelopes and began reading aloud: "DUE TO YOUR PRESENT CONDITION WE MUST SCHEDULE ANOTHER TYPE OF TREATMENT. WE DO NOT USE X-RAYS IN PREGNANCY CASES." I was dumbfounded.

A letter from her health insurance carrier—with a copy sent to her employer—gave information regarding blood work due to pregnancy. *That's the reason he fired her. He didn't want to deal with a pregnant employee. Well, I don't want to deal with a pregnant daughter.* I was speechless. Leisa handed the telephone to Wilma. "Patty, Leisa told me. I know you're crushed. But just remember that a year from now you'll look at that precious baby and forget that you were disappointed with this news."

Leisa came home a week later looking refreshed, tanned and happy. A white baby blanket and several tiny sleepers, gifts from Wilma and Yvonne, were tucked in her suitcase. "I'll never get the courage to tell Dad," she said in tears. I kept the secret from Mel until it burned in my soul. I couldn't bear to tell him that Daddy's little girl was about to crack his heart. I imagined the perfect life pattern for her: a white lace wedding dress, Mel escorting her down the aisle, violins playing, candles flickering, fresh flowers giving fragrance to a church full of relatives and friends.

On a day when we could only muster a bitter complaint, Mel suggested, "Let's get out of town, have a nice steak dinner and try to forget our heartaches." The hostess seated us at a corner table in a dimly lit section of The Steak Place. A couple with a newborn baby was seated at the next table. The baby cried and the mother gave me a fragile smile.

214

I returned a weak grin, took another tissue from my purse and wiped fresh tears. "I'm afraid of the future," I whispered to Mel.

"The future will take care of itself." Before the waitress delivered our food, we had dried many tears, and choked down a few. On the next outing we vowed that the conversation would not involve children, pregnancy or plans. Déjà vu.

On a late October afternoon, I told Gary the news. Standing under the spreading maple tree where the sandbox used to be, he wrapped those long arms around me. The parent-child relationship reversed. "Mom, this could happen to anyone. My sister isn't a wimp, and she can handle life. You know, this isn't the dark ages. No one is going to throw stones at her. Everything will be fine."

"No, it won't be fine. Not this time. I'm from the old school. You got married. *Then* had children. The world today is much different. A single parent struggles to care for her child."

"Please don't worry. As you've said many times, everything works out for the best." Hearing a song or talking with friends filled me with emotion. My feelings resembled the stages of death: anger, emotional turmoil and finally acceptance. Before long, the warmth of my tears grew stronger, and with it came a sense of tenderness. I found that the Scripture, Romans 8:28 is true: *And we know that all things work together for good to them that love God, to them who are the called according to His purpose.*

I found tranquility in unexpected places. Several times a week Mel and I sat in a darkened family room and stared into Leisa's aquarium. Tropical fish danced in the water. "Dizzy" swam in circles and ran into the glass wall. "Snakehead" was 14" long, and always swam up to greet you. He watched television. "Fat Oscar" was 8" long. He welcomed a warm hand rubbing his side.

Friends gave showers. I made crib sheets with matching comforter and draperies. Wilma painted a picture to hang above the crib, an angel guarding a sleeping baby. I hugged my daughter often and sometimes felt the baby kick.

The doctor sent Leisa for an ultrasound. The room was dark. Sound waves peeked through a mound of gel. The technician said, "Look at the baby. It's a boy." Leisa smiled, Mel, more interested in technicalities, stretched to view the computer screen. The technician slid the magic wand. "See ri-i-i-ight there."

"Mom, I see a hand."

I couldn't see what she saw. "It looks more like a blotch than anything. Don't choose the wallpaper yet," I warned. "And don't buy a football or a baseball mitt. It might turn out to be an Ashley who plays with Barbie dolls." What I saw was a new life, a head nodding in a wet universe, a creation forming.

"That's legs I think," Leisa said. "They dance to an odd rhythm."

The technician laughed. "His fist is in his mouth."

As she waved the wand across my daughter's tummy while looking for more body parts, I teased, "Maybe this modern technology can predict the future. Will the baby love Mozart or rock music? Will he be handsome or have a cowlick in the frontal area?"

"I can't answer that, but I can tell you that this shifting blur is a boy. And he looks handsome, like his Grandpa." Mel and I came to accept and look forward to a grandchild. Leisa's health was excellent. She never complained, never asked for extra attention or material things. Her face had a special glow and she looked charming in pastel colored maternity clothes.

I volunteered to be her childbirth class support person. Every Thursday evening, when the lights were lowered and the happily married couples began breathing exercises, we went to the Parlour, had an ice cream cone and drove home in silence. We dreaded going home because our beloved poodle no longer greeted us at the door. Memories of his last days returned.

With childlike faith I had carried the poodle through pelting rain and into the small country clinic. A mourning dove, perched in a small red maple tree, emitted lonely wails. I signed my name on the clipboard, and took a seat. Barney shivered and looked up as if to say that he needed a favor. He was tired and couldn't bounce around the room with eyes flashing and ears flopping like he used to. He could no longer protect me by barking at everyone who set foot onto the property.

I thought about the first time we met. Mel, Leisa, and I were sitting at the dinner table. As usual, the doorbell interrupted our meal. A miniature ball of white fur dashed into the room followed by Evelyn Lyon, our former baby-sitter. She poured a cup of coffee and displayed a bashful grin. "I want to show off Gigi's offspring. I'm on my way to Kroger's. I'll be back in a few minutes."

When Barney greeted us with a friendly wiggle and a bantam yelp, we realized that we had missed having a pet. "Pretty cagey," I said when Evelyn returned. "We can't play with a toy and put it back on the shelf; easier said than done. Is this toy for sale?"

"Just consider it as an early Christmas present."

After a long day at the office, Barney's head on my shoulder seemed to elicit a calming effect. This water retriever loved swimming and carrying something in his mouth. "Want to take a bath?" resulted in a white streak speeding down the hall, jumping into the bathtub. When we placed the telephone on the floor, dialed a ring-back code and gave a command, he answered with a left paw and a loud bark. He mastered the feat after three attempts. He turned out to be a super dog and had a sixth sense about behavior.

The intelligent canine line began with Mimi, owned by Mel's sister. Our children were toddlers when Mimi's black puppy became ours. When Flipsy was two years old, we kept our agreement to continue the line of thoroughbred show-dogs, and Gigi, his offspring, had livened the Lyon household.

At the age of seven, Barney had sleep disorders, tremors and trouble digesting food. The weight loss was obvious, even with the thick poodle curls. The vet prescribed basic tests and special food formulas. At the recommendation of a friend, I took Barney to Dr. Kelley, a sturdy man of forty with firm muscles that bulged from under the crisp white coat.

Barney, sitting quietly in the cage, seemed to comprehend the results of the doctor's examination. "I suspect that he is full of inoperable cancer. I'll confirm my suspicions with a biopsy, but I'm sure of the result. The best and last good deed you could show him now is to let me end his life." He folded his arms and stared at the floor. "This never gets any easier."

There I was, all alone and about to learn one of life's toughest lessons. Understanding death can be life changing. Death happens to every living thing. I felt thankful that Gigi had produced Barney, but regretful that every time we considered breeding him, our busy lifestyle had crushed the thoughts. Now I was to be the one to guide him through the conclusion of his generation.

Remorse overwhelmed me, feelings of guilt about what I could have done differently. I paced the floor. My breath seemed to drag its way from my lungs. I stared at the rain forming puddles in the parking lot, and wished I could escape the aching emptiness. It would have been easy to shirk this task and summon Mel at work.

Then another thought came to mind. "But doctor, my daughter's baby is due. She'll be crushed."

"Pick up that phone and call her, she'll want Barney's pain to end."

I tried to delay the decision. "But it's long distance."

"That's all right."

I explained the situation to Leisa. Her voice broke. "He has suffered enough. Don't worry about the baby and me."

I told the doctor that we decided to put Barney to sleep. No denial. No nervous outburst. Only acceptance. "I'll give you a few minutes," he said as he left the room.

I held Barney's sweet face in my hands. I looked into his innocent eyes and imagined him standing with one paw braced against the bathroom wall, the other unrolling toilet tissue.

When scolded, he seemed to say, "I'm sorry, but when you're not looking I'll do it again." A muffled yap as he wandered down the hall was a reminder that he would have the last word.

Now it was my turn to have the last word. Through my sobs I whispered, "I love you." Barney tipped his head sideways, and seemed to convey a different message. He understood.

I rushed from the room and said I was ready. Dr. Kelley explained, "He'll drift into a restful, peaceful sleep. You're giving him a fine gift, to assume his pain. The dark-rimmed glasses dominating his face failed to cover up his moist eyes. "I'll bury Barney in the pet cemetery."

I lingered at the desk with checkbook in hand. "Don't worry about paying now. Just take care of your daughter and the baby. I'll mail the biopsy photographs."[Mel spared us the pain of viewing the horrible proof that cancer had claimed Barney. Several months later, I found the photographs in a drawer.]

The next week I received an invoice that read: PAID IN FULL. "But who paid it?" I asked. The secretary said she didn't know.

"It won't be too long before we get to know our new grandson," I told Mel the next morning as we headed to Ohio for a family picnic. "This sunrise gives birth to magnificent mornings."

"Uh, huh."

"I wonder if the baby will be hardheaded like Grandpa?" I teased.

"Why do you say that?"

"Do you know where you're going?" We had directions, but Mel drove for miles and we saw nothing to indicate that we were on the right route.

"Yes, I'm going to Ohio. Lake Erie to be exact." By now he's driving faster. *I'll bet nature is calling. He's twenty miles from a rest area. I suppose he wants to get loster faster.*

Then the famous second question, "Do you know where you are?"

"Of course I know."

"There's a mom-and-pop grocery. Why don't you stop and ask?"

"The person I ask won't know any more than I do."

"Get a second opinion. I have a thermos, want a cup of coffee?"

"Don't have time. Had enough coffee. Steam on my glasses could cause me to miss a road sign."

"What road are you searching for? I'll help you look."

"You mess me up. You mention the name of several roads and then I forget what I'm looking for?"

"Are we programmed to drive each other crazy?"

"I don't know. I need to find a rest room."

" I *knew* it! At least when the baby comes we don't need a map to get to the hospital. Only one week to wait."

Grandma and Grandpa

"Contractions are five minutes apart, lasting one minute," I told the nurse on the phone.

"The doctor will meet you at the hospital." I grabbed Leisa's suitcase. Mel helped her into the car. She had previously signed admittance forms.

Her room was pleasant, with an eastern view of the city. The doctor told Leisa, "I hope you have this baby tonight. I leave for vacation tomorrow." He waited until 2:00 a.m. The contractions stopped. He decided to induce labor. We assumed that birth would occur within one day, but we were told to go home and wait.

Twenty-four hours later we returned to the hospital. Leisa didn't complain, but the pain was severe. Mel rubbed her back and sat by her bed. The contractions occurred every two minutes, with no resting intervals. Every ten minutes a nurse performed an examination and the pain increased to almost unbearable status.

An overweight male with a shaggy beard hastened into the room and lifted the sheets. He was wearing a dingy white tee shirt. I thought he was a disgruntled patient. "Who are you?" I asked.

"I'm filling in for Dr. Crawford. I'm Dr. Grubs." The name suited his potbellied figure.

"Have you seen my daughter's chart?"

"It's at the nurses station."

"The *nurses* station? Do you know what you're dealing with here?"

"Yes. She's having a baby."

"I'm aware of that. My point is she has been in labor thirty-one hours. You've got to do something."

"I *am* doing something." The nurse took Leisa's blood pressure. Numbers on the monitor increased. Her face blended with the white pillow. Her heart raced. Another nurse, on the opposite side of the bed, checked the fetal monitor's steady beep-blop. Soon the continuous round of beeps became a buzzing sound. The fetal monitor registered 255. The nurse pushed the machine from my view.

Three nurses and a doctor rushed in. "BP dropping!" A nurse nodded, "Please leave the room." Mel and I moved aside as a nurse lowered the head of the bed, another pulled an oxygen mask from the wall. The doctor gave an injection.

Running down the hall I cried out," Oh God, please don't let my daughter die. Please take care of the baby." We waited outside the door. The nurses left and quickly returned to the room. Once stabilized, they prepared for a caesarean section. Dr. Grubs summoned Dr. Jones, a specialist in obstetrics, and a pediatrician.

"Mom, should I stay awake for the surgery?"

"I would opt for anesthesia. Leisa, you've had many hours of pain. You need to rest."

The next few minutes brought two special events. The date was June 18, 1987. The pediatrician, Dr. VanSchoick, who took care of our children, came into the waiting room. "The Apgar rating is nine. Leisa is okay," he said with a broad smile. "Would you like to see your grandson?" The nurse brought surgical gowns and masks, and the doctor placed Nathan Mark in my arms. We posed for Mel's camera shot.

In the recovery unit Leisa was extremely weak and tired. Mel took pictures of Nathan cradled in her arms. An hour later she looked around the room. Her voice expressed panic. "Where's the baby? Something has happened. Why isn't the baby here?"

"Don't worry honey. Don't you remember holding him? Your dad took pictures."

"Tell me the truth!"

"The truth is, the nurse is bringing your baby right now." One look and our daughter's fears diminished. Before long, mother and baby were sound asleep.

One of my favorite songs was written and made popular by Jim Reeves. The words now took on a special meaning:

> Welcome to my world. Won't you come on in?
> Miracles, you see, still happen now and then.
> Come into my life. Leave the old behind.
> Welcome to my world, built with you in mind.

A month later I introduced Leisa and her baby to Dr. Kelley. "Blissful gift from God. He's a fine boy. He'll bring much joy to your world." Dr. Kelley was right. A new life had replaced the pain of our poodle's death.

"I need a miracle," a friend told me the next day.

"I don't need one. I've had the miracle of giving birth to a son and a daughter. I've had the miracle of holding a newborn grandson." She nodded agreement. "Every day I experience seeing green trees, the blue sky, I read newspapers, books. I have the miracle of fresh water, heat and air-conditioning when I need them. I enjoy the miracle of clicking a switch and listening to my favorite recording artists. I've survived cancer surgery. The greatest miracle is being able to attend church and believe in a living Creator, the author of happiness."

Happiness is the willingness to help others. We had helped our daughter through difficult circumstances, and at the same time fell in love with her son. Nathan and Leisa stayed with us for a few months then moved to a townhouse. Happiness had returned.

After thirty years with Consumers Power Company, Mel and three others were honored with a retirement dinner. Our friends Nancy, Lyle, Chris and Dick planned a Caribbean cruise to celebrate the occasion. On Valentine's Day I started packing for the trip. An old Writer's Digest magazine tucked in my suitcase had an article about writing confessional poetry. Music from a love song album floated through the room. As I began jotting down some of my past heartaches that had brought happiness, Gary appeared at the door.

"Got anything to eat?"

"There's always a quick meal in the freezer."

"Look at the gold necklace I bought Sue for Valentine's Day."

"Ooh. She'll love it. I have some nice paper. Want me to wrap it for you?"

He bent over and kissed my cheek. "I need a cup of coffee." He leaned against the door and put one hand in the hip pocket of his faded blue jeans. He knew he could count on me for food, a good cup of coffee and a strong piece of advise. He probably didn't want any of the three. Intuition led me to believe that the main purpose for his visit was not food or drink.

"I could use a break." I heated a bowl of chili, and poured coffee. Life is full of surprises. The shocking news brought by this dreamer-of-dreams who sat before me silenced the music in my heart. History had repeated itself. I tried to sort out the words I was hearing. I held my breath and gave a long, hard look. The news rocked my world.

"Mom, you're going to be grandma again. In April."

"Grandma? In *April?*" I screamed. Tears flowed for an eternity—actually, a few minutes—and hardened into a lump that settled in my chest. After my heartbeat slowed a little, I forced a smile and gave him a light hug. "You know how much your dad and I love children. I've adjusted to the role of grandma."

I will cling to the anticipation of our first cruise. I will evade agony, and break the news to Mel when we return home. The idea worked through daylight hours, but lying awake at night brought questions about the future, the same concerns I had just a year ago.

During the flight to Miami, my thoughts were elsewhere. I had a sinking feeling in my stomach, the kind that makes you want to blubber, but I refused to blubber, even with best friends. I was in a group of six, but felt alone. Telling Mel would ruin his trip. We never kept secrets from each other. Guilt feelings overwhelmed me. I found it difficult to follow the suggested reasons to cruise: indulge your senses, renew your spirit, and relax completely. When we walked up the Sovereign of the Seas gangplank, the crew welcomed us aboard. I was able to smile through my caustic feelings, and realized I could still have dreams, just different ones. I determined to explore a fascinating part of the world.

The cruise ship had a dream-like environment. Hundreds of people took care of your every whim. We dined on glorious food that was served several times a day, from burgers and pizza to filet mignon, mousse au chocolate, escargot, and the colorful midnight buffet. Dining room waiters seated the ladies, placed a linen dinner napkin on their lap, and treated everyone like kings and queens. The first night I requested Coke with my meal and coffee with dessert. Pierre didn't have to be reminded.

Mel walked several miles daily, and helped our group earn ship shape dollars, points used to purchase sun visors and shirts. Onboard fitness programs promoted aerobics, stretching exercise, dance classes. I learned the tango and rumba. The guys enjoyed a bikini contest at the pool. (I skipped that one.)

At Labadee, the Royal Caribbean Cruise Lines' private peninsula, we enjoyed snorkeling and sunbathing. St. Thomas features white sandy beaches, palm trees, breathtaking views, and duty-free shopping. The natives sell hats, hair braids, sweatshirts that say JAMIN' IN ST. THOMAS.

We listened to an excellent orchestra, and danced on a lighted floor in the main ballroom, or in the moonlight on the upper deck. I enjoyed the atrium-view balconies, and soft lighting. The dazzling Broadway-style entertainment was an excuse to sit and daydream. I felt alone in the 900-seat theater.

Frank, our invisible cabin boy, took care of our needs and wishes before we asked. While we were in the theater, he turned down the white sheets, and placed chocolates on our pillow. He found my pink gown hanging on a hook in the bathroom and formed the gown into a bathing suit. Mel's cap appeared to view the scene from a window ledge above the bed.

Ship photographers prowl all over. "Your memories must be preserved," they say. On the final day of the cruise, a computer printout affirms charges incurred. The last night of the cruise, fifteen-foot waves forced some passengers to visit the ship doctor. Clinging to the rail on the promenade deck, I made my way to the circular stairs and took the glass elevator to the eleventh floor. I sat in the butterfly room enjoying nature's beauty. A couple with a young child passed by and quickly returned. The child stood in awe at the transformation stages of butterflies. The mother told the asker-of-questions, "Being born is a special pleasure to enjoy."

Following the cruise, we spent a week with Yvonne, Jerry, Wilma and Herb who had recently moved to Florida. On Wednesday I broke the news about Gary. Yvonne said, "Honey, don't worry about telling Mel. When the time is right, you'll tell him. This child will bring blessings."

In April, five minutes after his birth, the nurse handed me another miracle. When I cuddled Gary Scott in my arms I enjoyed the pleasure of holding another precious grandchild. Grandpa was there with camera in hand.

Two years later we were drawn to the graceful Caribbean Islands to photograph a wedding on Megan's Bay. Janice was a tall bride with a bronze tan and a movie star smile. Darin, the handsome charismatic groom with deep blue eyes, fixed them on Janice and gave affectionate smiles. It was an awesome scene that will forever remain in my mind, a most breathtaking memory.

I designed a longer than usual wedding bouquet, miniature white roses trailed behind tall orange daylilies, bird of paradise and cinnamon fern. A white runner, anchored in the sand by tropical flowers, created a pathway through palm trees that formed an arch above the happy couple. Sequins and pearls on her long white dress glistened in the morning sun. A fingertip veil flowing in the gentle breeze, kept time with the waves lapping against the shore.

The Jamaican minister in a dark suit over a white shirt wore gold cufflinks and a turquoise-blue tie that emphasized his flawless dark skin. After he introduced the new Mr. and Mrs., the picture-perfect day prompted me to burst into a song that seemed to fit the occasion; "Only God Could Love You More Than I Do." The Caribbean sun accented the happy couple's tears. They drew a large heart and left their signature in the sand. Twenty friends and family cheered. Mel's camera froze the day in time, and captured the week's glorious honeymoon events. (Well, not *all* of them.)

A few months later, the silence of a lazy Saturday morning was shaken by the telephone. "Hey guys, summer is half over. We planned to fly to Put-N-Bay and Cedar Point, and haven't done either. How about going to Mackinac Island tomorrow?"

"Wonderful idea," Mel said.

"Okay. We'll leave at nine."

Our flight on the Eiler's red and white Apache to the picturesque island revealed many of Michigan's thrilling secrets. After ninety minutes of viewing the vast woodland and blue-green water, we arrived at the airport. Shirley and I headed for the restroom. John called a taxi.

When the horse and carriage arrived, I said in jest, "*This* is our taxi?" The mile ride through shaded one-lane roads gave a sense of pastoral serenity. Silence reigned, except for an occasional horse snort and the beat of hooves pounding the paved road. Sunlight sifted through oaks and cedars. Hardy maples sheltered the soft trilliums. Ferns expanded the floral grace of green. Purple mounds of violets blooming near the brown earth added to the tranquility.

Mackinac Island is a place where the horse is king. In 1900, when a summer resident tooled around the park in his car and caused several injuries to horses, the Common Council of the village passed an ordinance to ban most forms of motorized transportation. The Hackmen's Association, which represented horse-drawn transport companies, feared that the "horseless carriage," the "mechanical monster" would invade the residents' lives. They feared that the automobile might cause frightened animals to stampede down busy streets. The policy is strictly observed to this day, except for a handful of emergency vehicles. The ban, while sometimes inconvenient and ironic in a state whose fortunes are linked to the automobile industry, is central to what many tourists consider the island's charm. Snowmobiles have been allowed since 1970, however winter seems quite isolated.

The island is referred to as "Somewhere in Time." The title alone gives tourists comfort in knowing that in this hustle-bustle society there is a spot in America where you can go and enjoy a slower pace. You truly feel that you're going back in time. Gift shops market paintings with a scenic theme, compact discs, cassette tapes, and a video "Somewhere In Time" that was filmed at the Grand Hotel. We purchased purple sweatshirts imprinted with the well-known logo, a white gazebo and horse-drawn carriages.

Snowy seagulls produce a desperate sound as they soar above Lake Michigan's foaming waters. On a large patio restaurant overlooking the serene lake, they waited in line for a lunch handout. After several hours of window-shopping, sightseeing, and munching the famous Mackinac Island fudge, we looked forward to resting tired feet while riding through the woods to the airport.

The twin engines roared. Our pilot completed the pre-flight check. "Okay gang, there's no control tower on the island. Look for planes, or birds, or anything that might interfere with take-off."

The request made me a little apprehensive. "I've flown many times. Never thought about birds creating a dangerous situation." The plane lifted off the runway. We soared into the blue sky with the knowledge that our somewhere-in-time encounter will last a lifetime, or at least until next year.

Three weeks later Shirley, John, Mel and I took American Airlines to Las Vegas. Our itinerary included stage plays, viewing desert flowers and visiting Hoover Dam.

Thoughts of death and the hereafter came to mind when we decided to pay $130 each to fly over Grand Canyon in a seven-passenger Cesna. I can now give you an excellent description of air pockets. Shirley and I gripped the seat; our knuckles were white, although we felt comfort in knowing that if the pilot failed to do his job, John was sitting in the co-pilot's seat. He was well qualified, having flown for a dozen years. To distribute weight properly, Mel sat in the cargo area. His head and camera met with the ceiling several times during the flight, but he still managed to get great shots.

We landed on the paved Arizona airstrip. Strong wind whipped our spring jackets. The pilot, our tour guide, stood facing visitors with his back to the canyon rim. He weaved back and forth as he talked. There was no guardrail, no warning signs, and no evidence of humanity except for tourists and employees.

"Pictures and dreams can't prepare you for the real thing," I said as we entered another viewing area. The smell of desert dust, and the sound of a gentle breeze swept through one of the most spectacular views in North America. The shadings of red, pink and tan on the rugged color-washed walls seem to form pictures. Round boulders and smooth pebbles tuck into the feet of willows and slender pines. The 277-mile canyon, more than a mile across, seems to swallow most noises. It was so quiet you could almost hear the shadows tugging periwinkle twilight over the scrub pines. The Grand Canyon is about 5,000 feet elevation on the rim and the weather is notoriously changeable. One mile below, the Colorado River winds its way to Lake Mead.

The return flight to Las Vegas was delayed due to a spring

snowstorm. Wind whistled and sleet beat against the National Park Welcome Center. Shirley and I saw a greyhound bus waiting for passengers. We said in unison, "Let the guys fly back. We'll take the bus."

"But we have a problem. The bus trip will take eight hours and we have $35 show tickets. We'll miss the show," I told her. The flight was smooth, or maybe we were still too dizzy to notice. We had charted something new in the memory category.

Speaking of memories, you just get over the empty-nest syndrome and along come grandkids. You can't help but wonder if this journey will be a walk in the park or a root canal. Grandkids are usually happy creatures. But there must be a dark side to these small humans. Maybe they resent being plucked from the ether into this plane of existence with being force-fed vegetables when they prefer ice cream.

You see Gerber babies with round, smiling faces. Teeth appear on the bottom gum. They coo, gurgle, and pose when Grandpa brings out his camera. Babysitting is different now. Your energy level hits bottom. Your patience flew out the window. Watching two at once is like commanding an army. The smallest one screams while you heat the green beans and pureed turkey. Turn your head momentarily and you see the three-year-old use kitchen supplies to perform oral surgery on the dog. You tell him, "Look out the window. The birds are sitting in a row on telephone wires. They're waiting for their mama to bring food. Or maybe when people talk it tickles their feet." They weren't impressed.

Meanwhile, the baby is crying because his round bottom slid to the front of the high chair and tightened his diaper, perhaps causing a hernia or sterilization. You grab a rubber sink mat to cure the sliding problem. Cleaning up the lunch mess includes mopping the kitchen floor. The baby grins and crawls toward the white couch. You yank a wet dishrag from the sink. "No. Stop. I forgot to clean you up."

Turn your head and the kid falls off the couch. Swan dive.

230

He grins and crawls after the newly purchased $30 houseplant that is guaranteed to clean the air and provide a relaxing atmosphere. He finds a toy and plays with it for ten whole minutes. Silence reigns. You pick up a magazine, become involved in a romance story (the culprit that started all of these glorious events) and suddenly you sense the absence of the three-year-old. When you find him, should you velcro him to the wall? No. Parents would complain. Frantically, you rush to the bedroom and find him asleep on the floor.

When I was a kid I dreamed a lot. As I get older I realize that the silly dreams no longer occur. I won't be the next Danielle Steele or Patricia Cornwell. I won't be a millionaire or a famous singer. I now dream about my grandchildren becoming valedictorian. I wish for good health, and lowering cholesterol. I dream about sleeping eight-hour shifts. I've stopped dreaming impossible dreams.

Bing Crosby's words in the song "I'm Dreaming of a White Christmas," have taken on a new meaning. Pictures in albums bring back memories of traipsing from one pine to the other then choosing the first one we looked at. We stuffed the trunk full and tied the lid down. We decorated only the top two-thirds of the tree, putting the glass ornaments out of the reach of creeping babies. I told Mel, "We've given our children memories to teach their children. We've done our tradition of wrestling a tree, hauling it outside after the holidays and picking needles out of the carpet until fall. It's time for an artificial tree."

For the first time in thirty years, Mel would be free from making a crooked trunk look straight, and cutting two feet off the top because trees looked much smaller in the lot. Even though guilt overwhelmed me as I hung bulbs and lights on the phony tree branches, the five-foot fake tree has its place in the corner, a straight trunk from any view. To set it up requires thirty minutes. It's down and in the box in ten. We don't miss frostbite in sub-zero temperatures, although the artificial tree didn't smell right. I sprayed pine scent that gave me an allergic reaction. On the other hand, never again will I find pine needles in the trunk when I pack for summer vacation.

Just prior to summer vacation, we invited Leisa's childbirth class to a cookout at our house. Mel took pictures of eleven smiling, drooling, sleeping one-year-olds lined up on the couch. He gave prints to the proud parents.

LEISA IS NOT ONLY a chocoholic. She's a pizzaholic. On a regular schedule, she and Mel had lunch dates, usually at the Pizza Hut. One day he said, "Well, you've been at Ameritech two months now. How do you like it?"

"Greater every day. I really don't mind driving thirty miles to work. In the Centralized Intercept Bureau, there's nothing to do between calls, so I chat with a really, really nice guy that sits next to me. His name is Mike. Ooh, he's soooo good looking.

"Uh, huh. Tell me more."

"Yesterday we were talking about our office being the only CIB in Michigan. He said we weren't. I said we were. He bet me a pizza. I won, of course. How could he not know that? He's been with the company a lot longer than I. He wanted to lose so he could take me out."

The next week when Mike came home from a date with Leisa his mom asked about the first date with that beautiful girl he'd been talking about. "Mom," he said, "I'm going to marry that girl."

She gave him one of her patented head-tilted, side-glance grin. "So this is your first date and you tell me you're going to *marry* her?"

"Yep." During the year they developed a special friendship. On Valentine's Day he asked Leisa for a date. He forgot to tell her that he had a reservation at the Country Club. She wore her favorite "dress," her best blue jeans. After dinner she went to the powder room and returned to find a single red rose on the table. A brilliant cut Marquise diamond with a gold band was tucked in the petals.

The next day Mike asked me, "Is it okay if I call you Mom and Dad?" You bet it was okay.

Each moment of planning carried an air of anticipation. Music would capture the mood. A balloon launch would capture the essence of high expectations. Pictures would freeze the moment. Leisa knew that the day would be perfect except for one thing. "But Dad, you take everyone *else's* wedding pictures. Why can't you take mine? You're the best."

"1 know, but the father of the bride has too many duties. I have two photographer friends who will do the job." Leisa and I selected white satin fabric, several yards of lace, sequins and pearls for the wedding dress, silk flowers for the bridal bouquet, attendants, parents and grandparents. Since she worked a distance away, Mel and I offered to help plan the special September day. Leisa ordered invitations and response cards that featured a red rose on white paper. She scheduled the wedding in our home church located two blocks from our house. The church organist would take care of the music.

After dinner with our future son-in-law and his parents, we toured Point East, a top-rated restaurant that had been in business for thirty-five years. Something didn't seem right. *This room looks deserted, chandeliers are dusty, drapery needs cleaned and pressed.* I questioned the owner who explained, "There's not much going on in the springtime. We'll have this place in mint condition for your September date."

"Sounds good," Mike said. Leisa and everyone else agreed. Mike's parents paid a deposit for the rehearsal dinner, and we made a deposit for the reception.

Six weeks prior to the big day, the newspaper headlines jumped out at me: POINT EAST RESTAURANT DECLARES BANKRUPTCY. No refunds were issued. Several reception halls that I called couldn't accommodate 300 people.

I picked up the phone several times that day, but delayed calling Leisa until late afternoon. Suddenly, headlines flashed in my mind, "Call the Country Club." I called, the date was available, but I needed a sponsor. I hung up the phone and an immediate mental news flash demanded that I call a bowling partner who was a member.

"Do you want the good news, or the bad news first?" I asked Leisa. "Never mind. Guess the best thing to do spurt it all out. Point East declared bankruptcy. We have to select a location for the reception. The good news: we've scheduled the Arbor Hills Country Club. Our bowling partner agreed to sponsor."

"Can't believe what I'm hearing. Thanks, Mom. You did good."

"Hold on for a combination of good *and* bad news: the invitations are addressed and stamped. Another bit of good news is we had planned to mail the invitations yesterday, but became so involved with making decorations for the reception that we didn't mail them. The bad news: they're sealed and we have to open the envelopes and change the reception location."

"I can handle that. I'll come over after work."

Three weeks before the wedding, the dresses arrived. Instead of black and white, they were red and white, and all but one was the wrong size. Two had to be altered. The girls traded with each other to get the right size.

The next week, the day the programs were printed, the maid of honor developed a serious medical condition. Teri, Gary's fiancé, filled in for a bridesmaid who replaced the maid of honor.

On Sunday morning, one week before the scheduled event, the Assistant Pastor dropped a bombshell when he announced to the congregation, "The pastor and organist had a dispute and both have resigned." On Tuesday night, I dreamed that I was in the front yard, looked to the west and saw Leisa and Mike sitting on the church steps crying. The preacher had failed to show up for the wedding. *Why would I dream something so silly? I've got too much on my mind. On the other hand, could this be a premonition?*

The next day I called the pastor. "Sorry I can't go into detail, but I don't feel comfortable performing the ceremony in that church. The organist has caused a serious problem."

"Thanks very much for letting us know."

"I just assumed you would get someone else."

"What about the organist?"

"Don't want to talk about that. You'd better call him."

I called the organist. "Sorry to disappoint you. Can't do the wedding. Can't talk about the problem, only to say that the pastor is at fault."

As I said a few chapters ago, my guardian angel works overtime. Angels not only help during disasters, they also care about weddings, especially when it's my *daughter's* wedding. My third news flash recommended that I call a minister friend and explain the situation. "Yes, I heard some rumors. I'm available and willing, but I'll have to get approval from the church and call you back." He called within the hour.

At this point I absolutely dreaded calling Leisa. "I have news. Knowing how busy you are, and facing the fact that Mike gets spastic when plans don't go as scheduled, I took it upon myself to offer some suggestions. Hope it's okay."

"Sure mom. Hey, we appreciate your help. Couldn't have survived all these years without you and Dad."

"Which do you want first, the good news or the bad news?" Silence. "I'll give you the bad news. While you were out of town our pastor resigned." A sigh mixed with a deep groan soared into my ear. "The good news is this. Another minister will be available to perform the ceremony. You're scheduled to meet with him at seven on Thursday evening. The rehearsal is Friday at six." She recovered from shock and said she and Mike would be there.

The next morning she told me, "Pastor Stout is friendly. He's humorous. I'm so glad he's doing the ceremony. And guess what? Mike doesn't go to church, but he decided to attend services next Sunday. I sure thank you."

"Hold on, I'm not finished. The bad news: the organist resigned. The good news: I have interviewed another one, a very gifted musician."

"Nothing surprises me these days. Anything you do or say will be fine with me."

Hold on. More news. My husband just looked out the door and yelled, 'Honey, call 911. The church is on fire.' Hold on. I have to go look."

Instead of a deep groan, I heard a spine-tingling yell. "No!"

"Don't be upset, baby doll. He's only kidding."

Leisa looked radiant in a white satin dress that I spent seven months sewing, thirty-two hours applying sequins and pearls. Satin bows trailed down a 9-foot train edged with Venetian lace. The fingertip veil, created by Nancy Sheets, was made of French tulle, and featured a crown of sparkling cut glass and white rosebuds.

Red rosebuds and Grandmother Bertha's tatting lace on the unity candle blended with red and white alter flowers. Just before the ceremony began, Gary, the groomsman that used to call his sister Bonehead said, "I look like a penguin in a black tuxedo with a red bow tie." He was proud of his sister.

Seven groomsmen wearing black tuxedos, and Pastor Stout filed in. As Phyllis Stoetzel accompanied the organist to the song, "Ice Castles," seven bridesmaids, wearing red satin dresses drifted down the center aisle. The ring bearer, three-year-old Nathan, wore a black tuxedo. Christina, the five-year-old flower girl, was dolled up in a miniature white satin wedding dress and carried a lace parasol. They marched down the aisle without somersaults or fingers up noses.

After Ailene sang a song she wrote for the occasion, the congregation stood. The "Bridal March" began and Leisa's Cinderella story unfolded. Today was the crowning moment of Leisa's life. She said, "I feel like I'm queen for the day."

Mel whispered, "You *are* the queen. A beautiful one." She squeezed his arm. When Mike saw Mel walking our happy daughter down the aisle, his face turned a delicate pink. Mike's

Cinderella wore a silver slipper. As she stood by his side, he flashed an unrestricted smile. Mel stepped back and put Leisa's hand into a new future. It's saying goodbye to childhood, hello to a new family member and a new relationship. Gentle hands touched, and loving words acknowledged togetherness. You wouldn't expect tears to stream down the handsome face of this muscular man. His mom had a hanky ready. The candlelight ceremony was all that we had dreamed about.

We had decorated the reception hall with white twinkle lights and nylon netting. Jeanette and Chuck helped with a balloon arch for the couple to walk through. Chef Bengie outdid himself with an elegant display of food. Red roses and white carnations accented an ice sculpture. Between the floral centerpieces on the head table, large white bride and groom bears greeted the guests. The wedding cake had an element of creative flair, a fountain spraying colored water over fresh flowers. Two winding staircases—with fourteen figurines standing on the steps—led to a three-tier cake that featured a lighted "Precious Moments" bride and groom. This was indeed a precious moment. Photographers captured the chain of romantic events.

Several months ago Mel cut the pattern and I sewed a white satin replica of a hot air balloon with a bride and groom in the basket. When the disc jockey announced the newlyweds' first dance, the balloon, rigged on a pulley, "floated" above the happy couple. He announced the bridal party dance, and only four of the sixteen attendants showed up. Mel went outside and was told that on the way to the reception, one of the groomsmen let a friend drive his rental car. His friend rear-ended a bridesmaid's new Impala, which resulted in a whiplash. A chain reaction involved five cars belonging to the attendants. The groomsman had to pay a $2,000 penalty, plus repairs. After a heated discussion and police involvement, they returned to the reception.

When I danced with Mike he said, "Mom, I've waited all my life for a gal like Leisa. I give you my word. I'll take care of her and make her happy."

A bridesmaid volunteered to put Leisa's suitcase in Mike's car. The next morning, five minutes before time to check out, Leisa called, "Hi Mom. Everything was wonderful. Several guests said we had a storybook wedding, a fairy-tale wedding. I have news. Which do you want first, the good news or the bad news?"

"That question sounds familiar."

"The good news: I'm *so glad* you're home. We had a wonderful night. The bad news: My suitcase is missing, and all I have to wear on the honeymoon is a wedding dress. Will you bring me some clothes?"

Gary's friend Kirt arranged a blind date with Gary and Teri Lynn, who was married previously and had a son Michael. They dated for a year, he gave her a diamond, and I gave a bit of motherly advice. "Now, Son, you'd better follow the straight and narrow. Her dad is a preacher."

Teri asked if she could call me Mom. "You bet it's okay. I always wanted two boys and two girls. Now I have them." Teri is a tall, attractive blond with delightful qualities. She designed and sewed an off-white silk shantung, ankle-length dress and a short English tulle veil with silk flowers and pearls. In a small ceremony, they almost laughed out loud as they repeated the vows. At the reception, I was surprised that they didn't smash cake in each other's face.

A few months later Teri said," Mom, it's all your fault."

"My fault? What did I do?"

"You gave us a night in an elaborate hotel. Now we're going to have a baby."

"I had nothing to do with that part, honey. Could I request a girl?"

The next spring Gary called from the hospital. "It's a girl! You have a cute, adorable granddaughter."

"You're kidding."

"Would I kid you?"

"You've been known to."

"Not about such an important thing in your life. We named

her Lauren Nicole."

I felt blessed to be able to turn back the clock and remember the enjoyable days with Leisa. Lauren had the same petite features, a tiny voice, small face with a creamy complexion and deep blue eyes. Can it *get* any better?

The telephone company came up with a plan to make service better. Our church secretary was proud of her ability to answer several lines while taking care of callers' requests. Switching from seven digit numbers to area codes, to touch tone service threatened her intellectual pride. She wondered if the newly installed telephone system was too fancy for God. As you know, I have a great imagination.

God answers the phone. "Hello. This is God. Please listen to these options. Use a rotary dial for the King James Version. If you have Touch Tone, stay on the line and an angel will answer."

"Hello. This is your angel. Carefully listen to the menu choices. To confess a sin, press one. To pray for yourself, press two. To pray for someone else, press three. To request support for a creditable cause, press four."

The voice continues. "To express a simple 'Thank you,' press five. To make requests, press six. If you cursed at your husband or wife and you're sorry, press seven. If the sin is more than eight days old, press eight. For all other requests, press nine. Press star seven if you need the choices repeated."

The angelic voice says, "If you have violated the Ten Commandments, call the toll-free number 1-800-NEWAGE.

I learned in Aunt Hannah's Sunday school class that you don't have to find a telephone to hook up with God. You simply start talking and God listens. Aunt Hannah used to say, "Confession is easy." I've learned that God's line is never too busy. His communication system will never encounter a service interruption.

Sometimes it seems a misfortune that Bell invented the telephone. The phone rang yesterday. The solicitor gave a memorized sales pitch. "Good evening, Ma'am," the foreigner said. "By switching to our company you can save big money on your long-distance rates. Ma'am, you must have at least two important items. May I explain call waiting?"

"No. Wouldn't have it. Call waiting is like being in a restaurant and looking around to see if there's someone at another table you'd prefer talking to. You feel unimportant, like tossed out garbage."

"But Ma'am, you *must* have caller ID."

"I have it. You people block the number. Sorry, I'm trying to be a nice person, but I don't feel nice right now." I plan to change my answering machine message: "Hello. I'm too busy to answer the phone right now. Please leave a brief message. If you are a telemarketer, leave your home number and the time you eat dinner. I'll return your call at that time."

A familiar cruise lines called with a two-for-the-price-of-one offer that was too good to turn down. Someone said, "I can't imagine being cooped up with my daughter for seven days." I stole Leisa's journal entries:

Sunday, September 1:
Mom and I left Metro airport at 8:15 a.m. (late due to air conditioner problems). We will celebrate Aunt Wilma and Uncle Herb's 50th anniversary with a Western Caribbean cruise. Cousins Joy and Rich arrived at 12:05, Herb and Wilma picked us up and we arrived at the ship around 1:00 p.m. We checked in, toured the ship. The travel agent sent a basket of champagne, crackers and cheese.

The Bon Voyage party, with streamers and party favors, began at 5:30. Cars on the highway honked, arms waved as we left port. Our cabin is roomy, the toilets are aggravating, like a giant suction when you flush. We unpacked, showered and dressed for 6:30 dinner.

After stuffing ourselves on steak, lobster, and flaming desserts, we went to the Cabaret Lounge where the captain and crew introduced themselves and gave activities talks. The midnight buffet displayed several ice sculptures, nautical items made from butter. Trees, vegetables and flowers were made from chocolate. We had yummy desserts, fruit, cheese, rolls, and several meat dishes. We fell into bed at one.

Monday, September 2:

Wilma knocked on our door at 7:30. Had breakfast in the dining room. Waiter made a paper rose, kissed me on the cheek and put the rose in my hair. We anchored in the Bahamas. The "Little Seaward II" shuttled us to Pleasure Island. The small boat was rocky.

From the island, the ship looked large, elaborate. After a picnic of BBQ chicken, burgers, hot dogs and delicious fruit, we rented a raft and swam in the beautiful blue water that left the gross taste of salt on my lips. We snorkeled, swam through schools of saltwater fish. Saw a jellyfish. We rented a beach umbrella. The temperature was 94 degrees in the shade, 115 degrees in the sun, but comfortable, no humidity. Rich and I got real burned. The rest of our party tanned a golden brown.

The captain's party began at 5:30. Met and had pictures taken with the captain, toasted with campaign, tasted caviar. Uck! After dinner we saw a Broadway musical "Anything Goes." At midnight, after the grand buffet, we changed into jeans and headed for the casino. Sure miss my sweetie!

Tuesday, September 3:

Herb knocked on our door at 9:00. Today we sail all day. A group of guys at the pool played tapes and sang. Reminded me of Mike and his friends. Made me miss him more.

After dinner the "Roaring Twenties" play was terrific. Called my sweetie but he wasn't home, so we headed for the midnight buffet and limbo contest on the 11th floor deck. Retired at 1:30 a.m.

Wednesday, September 4:

Today we docked in Jamaica. The culture was so different. People beg on the streets, high crime rate. Natives are asking you several times to buy drugs from them. Their policeman friend is about four feet away, waiting to land you in jail.

In every store, about a dozen sales people approach you

with shirts, etc., and tell you, "Nice. Well made. Look good on you." On the street, they sell Rolex watches for $30. The gas price is $20 a gallon. Cars are run down, rusty. Most buildings are ready to fall. I see two classes of people, either the very rich or the very poor. The rich have expensive clothes, expensive shoes, lots of gold jewelry and several rings. The poor go barefoot, have dirty clothes, beg you to buy and get irritated when you don't.

A small candy bar costs $1.95 U.S. dollars. Coke or Pepsi is one dollar. I notice that beer is $2.00 for 10 ounces and $48 a case. Rum, Vodka, etc., is inexpensive. We went to the Dunn's River Falls. Some people climbed the falls; very strong current. You climb up the mountain on wet, slippery rocks, looked interesting but not for me! One U.S. dollar is around $12 to $20 Jamaican dollars, in the morning. If you go back to the currency exchange just before the ship docks the value is much less. You feel cheated!

I noticed a Burger King and Kentucky Fried Chicken in Jamaica. The ship's gift shop manager told us to "dicker" and ask if they will take at least half off. Most of the time they will. I called my sweetie; it was nice talking to him. My three-year-old is riding a two-wheel bike without training wheels. I miss home!

The ship personnel warned us to take taxi with red license plates. The other plates belong to the natives who want you to ride with them. They take you places, but don't bring you back. No speed limit here, no stoplights, and no stop signs.

Thursday, September 5:

We anchored ship and took tenders to Grand Cayman Island. On the glass-bottom boat tour, everyone sits on the outside edge of the boat. You look through a window in the bottom. Saw lots of coral, and several shipwrecks. A diver fed the fish; so many surrounded him that we couldn't see the diver.

We went shopping, had to pay $1.25 to equal one of their dollars. Items cost more on this island; didn't buy much. The island is small, neat appearing, and easy to walk everywhere.

They drive on the left side of the road here. Mom owes her life to me. She crossed a parking space as a car whizzed in, I grabbed her just in time. They have a Burger King here. The temperature was 100 degrees. The cruise director said today was a cool day!

Found coral on the beach. Returned to the ship for a late lunch. After dinner the waiters sang, marched around the room. Mom sang at the talent show and dedicated an anniversary song, "Nobody Loves Me Like You Do," to Aunt Wilma and Uncle Herb. Saw a terrific Broadway show "Sea Legs Express." All dancing! We'll go to "Comedy Hour" then to the midnight buffet to satisfy my chocoholic desire. Miss my sweetie. I have already called twice at $15.50 per minute.

Friday, September 6:

We docked around noon in Cozumel, my favorite island. Street vendors are a bit annoying. Most shops were good, some were run down, but we were advised as to which shops to buy from. At the Bye Bye store, we looked out and rain poured so hard we couldn't see across the street. Five minutes later the clouds moved out, the sun shinned and temperature soared to ninety.

The natives drive on the right side of the road here. We asked the taxi driver what the speed limit was. He said, "Be careful." No speed limit, but they had stop signs. Our dollar was worth 3,000 pesos. We returned to the ship in time for the midnight buffet. As we slept, the ship headed back to Miami.

Saturday, September 7:

After saying goodbye to the cruise staff and family members, we had an excellent flight to Michigan. The week with Mom was a pleasure I will always cherish. Dad, Mike and Nathan met us at the airport. Our welcome home gift was flowers, non-alcoholic "champagne" on ice, served in long-stemmed glasses, cheese and crackers. Tomorrow, Mike and I will celebrate our first anniversary. I'll write more next week.

The next August Leisa's doctor performed a caesarean section. Unlike the previous pregnancy with thirty hours of unbearable pain, the nurse wheeled her into the operating room. Ten minutes later five grandmas and two grandpas welcomed Joshua Michael into the family.

When Joshua was two, he discovered many new words. After lunch I put him in bed for a nap. An hour later I heard a strange squeaking noise, and looked up to see the pedals on his large red plastic car whirling down the hallway. He clutched a teddy bear around the neck, stopped the car and sat there grinning. "I fooled you, Grandma. I want, I need, bobble. Right now." He looked through the toy box, the refrigerator and yelled, "Juice cup."

"Honey, if you know so much about juice cups and bottle locations, you're old enough to forget." He had a drink of water and fell asleep.

When he awoke he took a supply of pencils, markers and paper to the dining room table. "Hassa do homework. Brother does homework." They say that three-year-olds control their environment and declare independence by punching and kicking other kids, especially big brothers. Leisa taught Joshua the art of sitting in a chair and experiencing time out. The punishment didn't fit the crime, so the first chance he got he pounced on big brother again. Both boys often asked for a baby in the family, preferably a sister.

On January fifth, a cold blustery night, the phone rang. Gary's voice had a calm, cheerful sound. "Well, I know you're not eager to drive to Indiana in this awful winter weather. I'm taking Teri to the hospital and dropping Lauren at Betty's."

"Babies aren't concerned with the weather, you know. We're all packed. Ready to stay a week if necessary," I said while putting on my jeans and sweatshirt. It was the worst snowstorm in seven winters. Snow-covered I-69, with no visible divider lines, reminded me of the vast Midwest winter wheat fields. Our Ford van swayed when semi trucks passed and caused a thirty-second whiteout. The heater quit working. I put a scarf over my head and wrapped a wool blanket around my feet. "Glad you're behind the wheel," I told Mel. "I would never attempt to handle this situation." The normal three-hour trip took five hours.

The next morning we held another miracle. Lindsay Michelle came into the world with a bright smile that never faded. I called her our "Snow baby," a special ending in a generation of family love. Our last grandchild didn't remain a baby long enough. Each time I held her I thought of Gary and Leisa's announcement, "No more babies, Mom."

Lauren loved sharing her kindergarten gossip and reasons to loathe her big brother Michael. She's a delightful luncheon companion. "Let's go to McDonald's and get a Happy Meal. Puh-leez," she begs. She has sparkling conversation and good table manners. Sometimes her favorite doll or Beanie Baby joins us. I've been tempted to slide a plate of veggies in front of her and see what happens. While Lindsay eats another burger and plays with the movie-based toys, Lauren heads for the play yard. The sun shined down on her golden hair as she chased butterflies. She held her hands in the air while spinning in circles. A cool breeze wisped around her angelic face. It was a magical moment.

"Your room resembles a New York toy store," I said. "Gadgets spill out of the closets. The drawers won't close because they're too full."

"Let's go home and you can help us put things in order."

We shoved the leftover food into the tall wood box marked, THANK YOU. "Good suggestion," I said as we headed for the car."

Being with Lauren and Lindsay gives me an extra shot at life, a second time around. Lauren reminds me of Leisa. The scene reminded me of Leisa's room. My comment was the same. "Just look at poor Barbie. She's sprawled on the floor. Her hair is a mess, her clothes wrinkled." Leisa was two when she first met Barbie. They grew up together, and remained friends through elementary school. Barbie played whenever and whatever Leisa wanted. She wanted her dolls to be free to dance in the wind, unrestricted by clothes. Barbie has a swanky, Pepto-Bismol pink townhouse. Barbie is now past fifty. Most of her playmates are married and had children, yet Barbie is still dating a dorky guy, still dressing like a teenager, still giving a flirty smile.

Lindsay matched up several pair of socks. "Why do you two own thirty pairs of socks?" I asked. "You aren't centipedes."

Lindsay said, "But the dog has four feet. He's cold. I put socks on him." Two hours later we admired the changes. They gave me a "pinkie promise." I offered a dollar if I made a surprise visit and found everything in order.

Both girls spent the next day at my house. After crafts, we watched a Disney movie, had popcorn with lots of butter and hot chocolate with lots of whipped cream. When Gary came to pick them up Lindsay said, "Grandma, today went too fast. Wish I could push rewind and start *all over* again."

Three weeks later she tugged at my arm. "Come upstairs, Grandma." A platoon of stuffed animals, rabbits, puppies, kittens and bears were lined up against the wall. A squad of fuzzy bodyguards had interlocked arms. She lifted the covers. Dolls were lined along the side of the bed. Under her pillow, dolls stared at the ceiling. "See my friends. They watch me sleep," she said. Their room was spotless. I gave them two dollars. Her personality and loving ways reminded me of Brenda, the "sister" I'll always miss.

Like Brenda, Lauren and Lindsay loved climbing trees. That summer nimble, long-limbed Lauren climbed a white pine tree and stood on a limb that measured one inch in diameter. Lindsay couldn't be outdone, so she advanced to the same limb, which broke with the weight. Lindsay grabbed another branch and held on for dear life. Lauren fell twelve feet. "This wrist hurts," she told the doctor. "This arm hurts really bad," she cried. She had a broken left wrist, and two fractures in the right arm.

My grandchildren are growing up into their own world. I hope they'll remember special times with Grandma. We bake cookies, tour the flower garden and count the colors. We play simple games for a brief span. In next to no time we move on to chess and monopoly.

Grandchildren know that Grandpa can fix anything that's fixable, and it stays fixed. When Nathan was six, he wanted Grandpa to fix an injured snake that slithered up the driveway. Grandpa laughed, the sitter screamed. Nathan applied a tooth-pick splint and a band-aid. The snake went merrily on its way. On a field trip to the teacher's house Nathan says he caught a mouse, hid it in his backpack and released it on the playground. The girls tried all recess to find the mouse. Nathan has quite an imagination. Grandpa was the only one who believed Nathan's story.

All summer the fireplace has been collecting dust. I chuck in a log, light it up and watch orange shadows dance on the wall. Most people are aware of how defective fuel-burning ap-pliances and fireplaces can release carbon monoxide into the home. There is another source of this gas that most of us never think about.

Leisa's house, in a wooded subdivision, was one of thirty million American homes with an attached garage. On cold win-ter mornings, Mike opens the garage door, starts the car to warm it up. After a few minutes he pulls out of the garage, shuts the door and drives off.

One November morning, Nathan headed for school on the bus, Leisa dressed for work while trying to convince five-year old Joshua to brush his teeth. "I'm too tired," he said. Shortly after Mike left, Leisa developed a headache, and remembered reading a magazine article about carbon monoxide poisoning. She called 911 and explained that she and her son were experi-encing symptoms. The ambulance driver picked them up and drove to the school to get Nathan. Emergency room tests re-vealed that two of the three had high poison levels "The needle hurt, but riding in the ambulance was fun," Joshua said. The next day Leisa called friends and relatives to recommend that they purchase carbon monoxide detectors.

In kindergarten, the teacher said Joshua socialized too much. "I have a friend named Kelsey. She's my girlfriend on Tuesdays. She's Cody's girlfriend on Fridays. She's got pretty blond hair, just like Lauren and Lindsay."

Lindsay asked her mom if she could have ice cream. "What is the magic word to get what you want?" Teri asked.

"Grandma! If that doesn't work, ask Grandpa." Children think Grandpa Mel is real cool, real relaxed. Sometimes kids fight with their siblings, hate their parents, but they never hate grandpas. Michael, Lauren and Lindsay had their share of rivalry. Michael and Grandpa had many open discussions. Talking with Grandpa seemed to clear the air. Grandpas have the power to ask blank, embarrassing questions that parents don't ask. The same kid who cons his parents is ashamed to lie to Grandpa. Kids open their hearts to him because there is a special place in Grandpa's heart, just for the grandkids. Even Grandma can't go there.

The ding-a-ling ice cream truck meanders down the street, Grandpa fishes money out of his pocket. So what's the big deal if he ruins their dinner, or forgets nap time? When they get old enough, Grandpa will teach them how to shave, and tie a tie. Grandma cleans house and takes lovely artwork off the refrigerator door; Grandpa puts them back. "You can't hide this artistic creativity," he says. The heart music and Grandpa's drive will give grandchildren confidence to make wise decisions, and encouragement to learn responsibility.

Nathan's first job, delivering the local weekly paper, The *Holt Community News*, brought him $12 for a fifty-minute jaunt. He won $100 for delivering papers on time. Grandpa thought that was a nice rate for a nine-year-old. He also believed that the job was the reason Nathan's spelling and math grades improved that year. I think the reason is that his teacher's husband, Sheriff Wrigglesworth, came to the school often, and talked about being a successful, responsible citizen.

Family parties, with children and laughter, give parents proof of their child-rearing success. I don't take these gatherings for granted. When family members return home, we expand the dining room table as far as it will go. Babies toddle underfoot. Toddlers hold court in high chairs. Older children head for the computer or the family room to play board games. The adults camp out in the kitchen. They conduct simultaneous conversations, and prove they can enjoy each other's company. I hope my children won't splinter apart under the weight of long-standing wounds and petty resentments. Cutting slack and biting your tongue is hard work, but the choice is worth it. Harmony doesn't just happen. Each generation has a different set of problems.

Mel and I were born in the last half of the "Builders" generation, 1902-1945. Builders remember when a computer was something from a science fiction show, memory was lost with age, a CD was a bank account, a cursor was profanity and a keyboard was a musical instrument. Log on meant adding firewood to the fire and a hard drive was a long trip on the road. A web was a spider's home. A virus was the flu.

Builders believed in strict moral ethic, you married only once. You listened to the big band and swing tunes. You didn't buy on credit. Builders were committed to fulfilling tasks. The "old country" work idea helped build this country and get us through difficult times.

The Postal Service invited the public to choose fifteen stamps to commemorate the 1950s decade. The leading vote getter was conquering the dreaded disease, polio. Second came drive-ins followed by cars with chrome and tail fins. Then came rock 'n roll. The popular television sitcom *I Love Lucy* rounded out the top five.

Gary was born the last year of the "Boomers," 1946-1964. The 60s saw: Vietnam, President Kennedy shot. Women and minorities wanted change. "Chairman" became "chairperson." Walter Cronkite was a CBS icon. The conquest of space, Apollo landed on the moon. Saturn was tall (363 feet).

The Boomers were united by anti-war demonstrations, Woodstock, the Civil Rights movement, and music their parents found appealing. During that time, more mothers worked outside the home. The Boomers—with their fast-paced lifestyle, rejection of traditional values, and focus on their own needs—saw divorce as a solution when relationships became difficult. The divorce rate increased, and extended families became more dispersed as families moved to follow careers.

Gary and Leisa's generation was separated by one year. The "Tweeners," sometimes called "Xers" born in 1965-1976, were the tail end Boomers, the twenty something's or early thirty something's. With Generation X came an increase in single mothers, as well as dual-income households. Many Xers came home from school to empty houses. Several Xers were hesitant to get into marriage. The trend of living together without being married was a real option. They grew up with television, the sexual revolution, and space exploration. The "me" generation involved AIDS, MTV, Watergate, rap and a struggling-to-buy era.

When the Tweeners entered the job market, they had more competition for a smaller number of jobs. There was a crunch in the housing market. The most significant political event many Tweeners remember is Nixon's resignation. Gary said, "I used to think that presidents are infallible, but a president is a person, not a god."

My grandchildren, the "Net" generation or "N-Geners" born after 1977, suffer from the environmental blitz of video games, e-mail, cell phones, pagers, behaviors of squirming, blurting out, and Attention Deficit Disorders. Children are seeing the rise of joint or shared custody. Many are growing up in multiple households. They live with single moms and single dads. They are acquainted with domestic terrorism and a booming economy. The N-Geners enjoy all types of music. They love to celebrate.

Crossing Mountains

Signs of spring sprouted in her backyard. April rains produced emerald green grass. Forsythia exploded yellow over the neighbor's fence. Purple hyacinths cast fragrance that encircled the neighborhood. Her thick, dark hair glistened in the sun. Her eyes were blue, opaque blue. On a sunny day, the light turns them pale, the blue of a cloudless sky. The eyes flutter between short lashes. My sister Yvonne, the owner of these eyes had many pictures stored in her head, retrievable images fashioned by the people who loved her.

She wanted to touch everything, see everything. Many places of beauty reminded her of heaven. She said, "When driving through Tennessee, you're not sure whether you're entering heaven, but you know you're in a favorite place. Let's have a reunion in Gatlinberg. I want to see every family member this summer."

I sent out a "Cousin Cluster" newsletter: "Upon conferring with the mamas and papas of the group, we agreed to meet on June 16, 1995, at the Holiday Inn in Pigeon Forge."

As our group of eighteen said goodbye to a weekend filled with chatter, parades, food, and fun, we spent over an hour posing for pictures, some hamming it up on a brick wall, some serious. During our "sister hugs" Yvonne told us about a vision problem. "Something is terribly wrong. It's like a shade being pulled down, covering over half of my right eye."

After spending most of the next day calling to explain a

condition that appeared to be a detached retina, she scheduled an appointment. The doctor suspected a tumor and arranged a private plane flight to the University of Virginia Medical Center in Charlottesville. Many tests were administered, and several doctors discussed the case.

Two days later the doctor called Jerry who called family members the same day. "The team of specialists found liver and lung scans to be negative, but an aggressive tumor located in the right eye near the optic nerve, must be removed. Surgery is scheduled the seventh of July." Several family members from various states arrived at five that evening. A friend of the family who owned an ultrasound clinic asked if she could videotape pictures to use for medical research. I'll never forget the anguish that ripped through my body as Yvonne's children and siblings viewed the screen. An 8.6 mm tumor was surrounded by dark red blood vessels. Another tumor measured 4.3 mm. Darkness filled other areas of the eye.

The next week Jerry scheduled a second-opinion appointment at Johns Hopkins Eye Center in Baltimore. "The van is more roomy and comfortable than a car. I'll drive you there," their daughter-in-law Nancy said. "Mel and Pat can follow behind in case we need them."

During the four-hour trip, rain pelted the windshield. We reached the Marilyn state line, the sun came out, and a rainbow encircled our car. Was the rainbow a covenant that Yvonne will be all right?

The parking situation was insufficient for the amount of patients seen at this well-known place of medical research. After looking for several minutes, I asked a city policeman for a suggestion. "No problem. Park on this street."

As we crossed the threshold of the building where Mom had entered and left with life-threatening news, my childhood uneasiness returned, and with anxiety came nausea, an irritable sense of doom. We sat in the large room waiting for test results. My sister didn't mention how tired she had been lately. "Maybe God will grant healing," she said.

A woman sitting next to us in the waiting room looked healthy and happy. "I came here in 1985. They ran me through two days of tests, and took my left eye. You'll be fine. Here's my phone number, call if you have questions."

"We must believe that the news will be positive," I whispered as the doctor pulled up a chair and sat across from us. He said, "Mrs. Stover, your general health is good. You have determination, and tremendous faith. I will confer with colleagues, experts in the cancer field. We don't want to give you false hope, neither do we want to speculate."

We left the building and passed by a shabbily dressed man leaning against a weathered bronze statue. I glanced up the street just as a wrecker with a car attached pulled away from the curb. "No." I yelled. "That's our car."

Like an expert sprinter, but several years too late for the sport, Mel ran after the wrecker while yelling for the driver to stop. As he made a right turn, a passerby rolled down his window. "Is that your vehicle?" Mel nodded. "Climb in. This city pulled the same darn trick on me once. I'll help you get your car. At least we'll find out where they take it."

Yvonne and I leaned against the brick building, hot from the summer sun. Jerry went inside to get information from the security guard. "Sorry. City wreckers stay busy day and night. It's a game they play. If you look carefully you'll see, in small, faded letters, a street sign saying that no parking is allowed between the hours of four and six. Once they pull your car in, it'll cost big bucks to get it out of hock."

I remembered that the time was 3:55 when the police officer stood in front of the sign and told us to park on the street. By now the humidity was high, the temperature had reached ninety degrees. Yvonne's exasperating day, with several hours of eye examinations and discussions by pre-med students, had left her exhausted and drained. "Let's go into the emergency room, find a comfortable chair, and enjoy the air conditioning," I suggested.

The room reeked. Marijuana? Impoverished-looking people

slumped in chairs. Mud from the morning rain had dried on the tile floor. Office personnel looked frustrated as they hurried from room to room. Several security guards stood at attention. Yvonne leaned on one arm. I stroked her hair. An uncomfortable feeling swept over me. "Let's go. You don't need an infection or some other illness."

An hour later Mel returned with the car, but minus $180. At the hotel he and the manager struck up a conversation about the "wrecker scandal." The manager shook his head. We called to request a rollaway bed. Two maids came with ice, shortbread cookies, coffee beans, and extra chocolates. "If we can do anything just call," they said. The aroma of fresh-ground coffee penetrated our large suite. Sipping the wonderful brew and telling "knock-knock" jokes took the edge off our troubled minds.

Before bedtime Nancy (Jerry and Yvonne's "taxi") received a telephone call from an employee she had placed in charge. By the sound of the conversation, many situations had surfaced. Mel didn't sleep because of pain in his left knee. At 4:00 a.m. Jerry knocked on our door. "Yvonne has a splitting headache. She wants to see you." My precious sister reminded me of a scared little girl. I rubbed her head and back, and applied cold cloths. A streetlight cast shadows on the wall and softness in her lovely but strained face. I prayed for relaxation. Within a short time she fell asleep.

Early the next morning we learned that a turn of events demanded Nancy's attention at her place of business. We threw our belongings into suitcases, ate a banana and drank a cup of fresh-brewed coffee. A carhop brought our valet parked car. The hotel staff knew about our many troubles and charged half price.

We maintained daily contact with Leisa. Her positive approach to life lifted our spirits. "Be careful," she advised. "Remember that this is a holiday weekend." We left the hotel at 9:15. During the trip home we encountered a flat tire, dense fog, dark clouds and a downpour. As we read the "Welcome to Michigan" sign Leisa called on the cellular phone. "Where are you? I missed you two so much. I'm glad you're coming home."

Three days later my sister was very nauseous, listed as critical at Beckley Hospital. They administered medication for food poisoning. She stayed overnight, slept fourteen hours. The doctor scheduled an appointment that afternoon at the University of Virginia Hospital. The doctor in Charlottesville ordered several tests, and said the problem was much more serious than food poisoning. He scheduled surgery to remove the right eye.

Mel and I left Michigan a few hours after hearing the news. Leisa's office became a mediator for traveling relatives. She booked three rooms at a motel near the hospital. We arrived at three in the morning and left a note under Jerry's door. His children from Indiana arrived at four.

At five, we walked the halls that are never dark, never quiet, and entered the Critical Care unit, where tubes and monitors beep and blink, a room with no sense of day or night. Chapters of life and death were being written. Waiting rooms were filled with people afraid they were losing their loved ones. Some lost sleep, dignity and control, some lost hope. We had hope for tomorrow.

Yvonne displayed her usual facial glow as she doled out hugs. "I'm better today. I'm ready to get with the program. Don't worry gang. Dr. Britton and I will do fine. He knows that I'm prepared to get rid of this eye." She waved slightly as the nurse wheeled her into the operating room.

At seven, a technician checked the X-ray films hanging on a lighted panel. A nurse laid out instruments. My sister was placed on a stainless steel table with bright lights overhead. A sensor was connected to electronic instruments. The anesthesiologist checked the waveforms that moved rhythmically across the screen. A loudspeaker produced a heartbeat that dominated the operating room. A steady pop, pop, pop. Seventy beats a minute. The normal eye pressure is fourteen. At first there was no pressure, then nineteen. It soared to seventy-six.

The tumor directly behind the eye was most dangerous. Dr.

Britton studied X-ray films. His draped my sister's body with green sheets and placed her head in a clamp. The nurse put a scalpel into Dr. Britton's rubber-gloved palm. Gently, for two hours, he probed and teased the eye apart from the tissue. A steel tray possessed evidence of an invasive monster that was sent to the laboratory. The television screen turned red. The suction hose hissed. Tweezers removed the white trunk of the optic nerve. The large malformation of arteries and veins had leaked blood into the brain and released torrents of agony. The heart monitor remained steady. Dr. Britton closed the incision. The anesthesiologist approved vital signs.

The waiting room door opened and a friendly receptionist led us to Dr. Britton's office. He shuffled through papers on his desk. "The surgery went well. The monster was stubborn, but we won. Twenty cases of this rare cancer have been reported in the United States. I believe the malignancy was confined, however I rarely find this kind of tumor in only one eye." The reality hit like a fighter's punch. *Will she lose the other eye? Her beautiful face is forever marred.* Dr. Britton patted Jerry's shoulder. "Our first-rate eye replacement team will call in two weeks."

The recovery room nurse wheeled Yvonne to her room. She was alert and optimistic. After a kiss from Jerry, she asked for "Diana" [her firstborn] then "my brother," [She claimed Mel as her brother. Our brother, Gee couldn't make the trip from California.]

Yvonne maintained a fine outlook. The next day we wheeled her through a branch-covered pathway where honeysuckle and pink roses, arranged in several levels, led to a large patio overlooking another flower garden. The white lattice fence was lined with morning glories and dark pink impatiens. She enjoyed the soft evening sun. I sat in a white wicker rocker, rubbed lotion on her hands and arms. We talked for two hours. "Well, sweet sis, the surgery is behind you. Your health condition will be uphill now." Tears fell from her one good eye. I walked to the railing, pretending to be interested in the many flower gardens that surrounded the area on the next level. Through my sniffles, I thanked God for understanding the language of tears.

On Saturday the nurse took care of release papers, and told us how to care for the incision. The eye was swollen, but looked quite normal. My sister was happy to be home again. Her outlook was great, but her face looked stressed. "I'm sleeping well. I'm counting my blessings and trying to forget the pain. I'm surrounded by love." The next few days were filled with unexpected events.

On Wednesday a neighbor called. "I'm a nurse and I know all about taking care of the sick. Let me wash her hair." She handled my sister's head like you'd wash a mud-soaked head of cabbage. My sister violently struggled to get out of her reach. I remembered the doctor's cautions, no bending, no sudden movement.

"Hey, stop. You're pulling her hair. You're scaring her," I yelled while shoving the troublemaker aside. Yvonne had been progressing, but not after the hair-washing ordeal. "That pest will never touch you again. I give you my word."

The next day I cradled her head in my hand and gently poured water over her hair. My sister grinned, almost went to sleep as I shampooed, rinsed and caressed. After her morning nap I said, "You're all prettied up. You need some place to go. Let's sit in the patio swing." I poured a glass of iced tea, with sugar.

While chatting about writing goals, poetry, and the summer flowers, a strange noise came from behind a clump of pines. A large German shepherd was standing behind the swing. My sister trembled at the sight of the animal's white teeth and the growling sound. "Sit still, honey." I grabbed a broom and began swinging. "Go away," I yelled. The dog tucked his tail and left.

Once she relaxed, she began to reminisce. "Reminds me of last summer. I was visiting Wilma; Herb and I had words. You know, Herb and I never did see eye to eye."

"Oh, yes, I remember. I came to pick you up for lunch. You were sitting on the back steps. You'd been crying. I asked what was wrong, and between sobs you told me the story."

"I'll never forget that day. I had the feeling that I'm no good, wanted to leave this world. I never cared much for dogs, and thought Wilma's little terrier hated me. Candy never acted friendly, but that day, when I sat there blubbering, she climbed on the couch, put her head in my lap and licked my hand. She pawed at my arm, stared at me and whimpered long, sad cries. All at once I felt comfort and peace. Candy convinced me that life is worth living. Herb apologized and I accepted, all because of an animal's love."

Yvonne loved having the family drop in. That evening several came to visit. My sister used any excuse to celebrate. "Jerry picked raspberries today. Let's have a party," she said as she rested on the couch. "There's ice cream in the freezer."

Her health improved daily. Each time we changed the bandage, healing was obvious. Two days later, I left without waking my sister. I just couldn't say goodbye.

The next week she returned to Charlottesville for a check up. She told the doctor her eye had been uncomfortable for several days. He prescribed two medications and said that everything was fine. She attended church on Sunday.

Nine months later, On April 18, 1996, flashes of light appeared in my left eye. At breakfast the next morning, Janie and Jeanette insisted that I go directly to my ophthalmologist. "Please don't diagnose your own case. You're not trained in that field."

The receptionist said, "Have a seat. The retina specialist will work you in." *This is exactly the way Yvonne's trouble started. Please, God, don't let that happen to me,* I prayed silently.

Dr. Werner told me, "Like wallpaper that starts in one corner and works its way down, you have a torn retina, that separates the retina from the back wall of the eye and allows vitreous fluid to seep. I'm glad you came in right away."

I called Yvonne's room and explained that I needed eye surgery the next day. "Oh, no," she said. "Don't worry about coming to see me sweetie. Please don't be too concerned about your eye. You'll be fine."

At St. Joseph Hospital in Ann Arbor, cryotherapy, extremely cold probes, were applied to the overlying tear to "freeze-burn" the tissue, seal the tear, and create an eventual scar. The retina adheres to the scar. Two days later, the doctor removed the patch and said that everything looked fine. The same day, surgery revealed that Yvonne's brain was filled with numerous inoperable tumors. There has to be a room for everything in life, a happy room, a playroom, a sad room. That day, I was in the sad room.

Ailene called Yvonne's room and made notes of their hour-long conversation. Yvonne said, "Ailene, write this down. Tell your sons Mark and Kevin that I love them dearly. They're like grandchildren to me. Tell Kevin there's joy in serving God. You've been my daughter. When you were born, you were so cute. Your golden curls and blue eyes had us all in love with you. One day Mom and I were bathing you, and admiring your little toes. I asked if anything happened to her could I have you. She said, 'Yes. She's yours.' We've had a few ups and downs, but we always knew we loved each other." They cried and Ailene told how much she loved her sister-mom. They talked about the good times, laughing together, praying together.

Yvonne said, "Ailene, I don't know why God chose me to reach people during my dying hours. I don't have long. I've got to get this work done. God has revealed that Satan will try to stop me from reaching everyone He wants to bless through me. God will win out over Satan. God will get more glory out of my death than He did out of my life. Oh, the glory. It's so wonderful. I'm so glad He's using me to touch people. All I want is to glorify Him until I draw my last breath. Pray that God will let me keep a clear mind so that I can do His will up to the very end."

"Yvonne I know you're—you shouldn't talk so much and

wear yourself out. I think we should hang up now."

She said very adamantly, almost angrily, "I've got work to do before I can go home. What's a few hours of being tired when I've got thousands of years to rest? Just a few more days and after God has helped me finish reaching everyone I'm supposed to reach then I can rest. But for now I've got more work to do. Fast and pray that Satan won't defeat me in my final hours of work for the Lord."

She named the people she wanted to see before she died, the grandchildren, great grandchildren, her sisters and brother Gee. "Tell Herbert we've had our bad times and maybe I didn't handle it well. I've been so protective of my family trying to shield them from hurts. Tell Herbert God wants him to get back to serving and loving him the way he did when he was first saved. God wants him to use his singing talent. Tell him I hold no grudges. If I don't see Wilma again, please express my love. Sometimes I thought nobody loved me. I know I was wrong. Sometimes our brain just doesn't work right, and we imagine that people don't love us."

Ailene told her, "Wilma loves you. She just can't express her feelings. Because of that cataplexy, she has to hold a tight reign on her emotions."

She said, "I want to see Patty. I talked to her on the phone one day and I wondered if she loved me. I don't know what was said, but I cried for two days. Now I know it was just the cancer working on my brain. There were times I was mean to Jerry and he's been so good to me. I could kiss his feet. God gave me a wonderful husband and family. Tell Arnold I love him. He's been so good to me lately. We had some harsh words, but I was trying to protect you. But all that has worked out good. Tell him God is going to use him these last days more than He's ever used him. He's always done a lot for people. I'd like to see Mel. He's like my brother. I love him. [When Mel arrived, she was incoherent.]

"Oh, it's so wonderful! I feel the power of God so real. Death is not bad. I hate to leave my loved ones here, but God

will take care of them and I'll see them all in a better place."
She refused Ailene's request to end the conversation. "No. I've
got more to say. I wanted to write more songs and poems. I
love Mom's favorite song."

She and Ailene repeated lines from "In the Garden." Ailene
asked if she wanted that song at her funeral. She said, "Yes,
that's what I've been trying to think about. It keeps slipping
away. God has been with me through it all."

They began to sing, *Through It All, I've learned to trust in
Jesus. I've learned to trust in God, through it all,* [she began to
sing alto.] *I've learned to depend upon His Word."* Ailene told
her she would finish the songs and they would be sung.

"Oh thank you. I keep trying to write a song called
"Blinded By His Glory" but can't get it together." Ailene offered to help. Yvonne said, "The love kept flowing, and His
glory kept glowing. I see His face more clearly now, as I prepare to cross the brow. Can't think of the rest. You finish it.
God will tell you what to say."

The next day Jerry called. "Patty, time is closing in. Hos-
pice is here. We have a hospital bed in the living room near the
sliding glass door. She looks out over the city. Sometimes she
sleeps all day. She's asking for her brother and sisters."

That evening I stood by her bed and read portions of
Psalms 116. *"I love the Lord; He has heard my supplications.
He has delivered my eyes from tears. Precious in the sight of
God is the death of his saints. I called upon the Lord in dis-
tress. He answered me and set me in a large place. Blessed be
the Lord."*

I stroked her hair. "Have I done everything right?" she
asked.

"Yes, honey, you have."

"Have I pleased God? Did I do what God wanted me to
do?"

"Sure you have. God is pleased with you. You have followed Him most of your life.

"Can I go now?" she asked.

I didn't answer. Her oldest daughter Diana stood on the opposite side of the room. "Tell her she can go now if she wants to."

I backed away. "I *can't* let her go."

Diana took her hand. "Mom, you can go now." My sweet sister smiled and fell into a relaxed sleep.

After a few minutes she awoke with the same facial expression. "It's Patty here," I said. "I've been watching you sleep."

"Oh, Patty, I love you so much. Have I pleased God?" she asked again.

"Honey, if *anyone* has pleased God, *you* have." She asked for Gee. After a long embrace she told him she wished everyone could have a brother like him. I repeated the Scripture notes that gave comfort to Gee and me as we made the ten-hour trip. I whispered, "I love you. I'll see you tomorrow."

I kept my promise. I saw her the next day, but I saw the shell of a beautiful person. During the night, angels carried the spirit of my darling sister into a glorious land, a land free of pain, sorrow or heartache. I don't think Yvonne questioned her fate. She knew why we endure the low spots, the valleys and bridges. Yvonne and Jerry crossed many mountains. They were inseparable for fifty-five years. At her funeral, the minister read a poem that she wrote on her wedding day:

Come walk with me, our hands entwined across the bridge of love. We'll climb the highest mountain peak, and watch the stars above. I'll be with you in valleys deep. We'll view the rippling stream. I'll look into your eyes sublime and know the thrill that you are mine. Oh, dearest, my life I give to you. How precious our love will be. This journey we'll explore today will last eternally. I'll hold your hand. We'll take our vows as God looks from above. Oh, come with me and we will walk along the path of love.

The night of her funeral I had a pleasant dream. I was driving to the grocery store. The weather was a gloomy mix of clouds and misty rain. Suddenly the sun began shining just in front of my car. For several miles the sun hovered over the roadway. All other areas remained cloudy. As I entered a curve, I saw an image of seven angels and clearly heard my sister speak, "I'm happy. I'm walking streets of gold, just like you sing about." She was laughing. The images disappeared and the sound of her voice became silent. My sister is in a happy room, even though I'm still in a sad one.

"PATTY, WOULD YOU help celebrate Frank's birthday?" Mel's cousin asked.

"Sure. What do you have in mind?"

"I can't believe my son is almost fifty. I want you to dance for him."

"Dance? You want me to dance?"

"I got the idea from a program I saw last night. You're perfect for the part. You have to bring props."

"What kind of props?"

"Just get a tape of "The Stripper." Dress in a bathing suit and swing your hips. Carry a bag of candy to shower the guests. Then you could tease the birthday boy with hugs and a kiss on the cheek."

"No. No. Not me. I've never done that."

"Sure you can do it. You love the stage. I want something really different." I hate to disappoint relatives so I agreed to go along with the act.

When the big night arrived I was ready to roll. After the guests arrived, Mary gave the signal. I rang the front doorbell. Mary answered, "Ooh. We have another guest. Come in." I almost had a heart attack to find the room full of people sitting in a circle. I pranced in, wearing a black top hat, black boots and a black overcoat. I carried a shopping bag with "K-Mart" written on the side.

I puckered my lips, fanned my face and danced to the music. Passing in front of the video camera, I unbuttoned the overcoat and tossed it in the corner. I removed the boots, threw my hat in the dining room and sashayed up to the birthday boy. I patted his beer barrel tummy, untied my belt and slid out of an oversized red skirt. When I unzipped and slithered out of a purple blouse, my red and gold necklace broke. Beads sprinkled the floor.

I reached into the shopping bag, threw chocolate candy into the crowd, swiveled forward and reverse to remove a pair of satin shorts. The purple and white bathing suit came into view. I yanked a long purple feather shawl out of the bag and twirled it around my neck. I threw a handful of chocolates toward the guests. I danced over to the birthday boy, rubbed his shoulders with feathers and planted kisses on the partially bald head and bright red face. The more I relaxed, the more fun I had.

My next performance was a 50th birthday party for Dick Throne. I rang the doorbell. Chris answered, "Well look here. We have a mystery guest; maybe a hobo." I peered from under the mask to see who was there. *No. I can't do this. That's preacher Davis over there.* Chris saw the look of surprise on my half-masked face. *I'm out of here.* The music began. *No turning back now.*

I shuffled toward the punch bowl and took a sip. Soon I was out of the coat and surrounded by church-going friends. I added a new twist to this performance. I yanked a black bra from my bosom, and threw it at the birthday boy. Laughter bounced off the walls. In fact I could hardly hear the tape playing. The guests had no idea who the bag lady was until the show was over. I removed the mask and sheepishly greeted the pastor. "I think I know you," he said with a grin. "Can't remember when I've had so much good, clean fun."

With each performance, I had more good clean fun—until I saw the video. My front had changed places with my back and the high school figure was gone forever. After eight appearances, the Bag Lady became a has-been. A star has fallen. I know, that's a cliché, but I just had to say it.

Following my decision to hang up the act, our friends

booked a Caribbean cruise. "Would you be willing to do a comedy performance?" they asked. Lyle dressed as a big-boobs woman with big hips and long curly hair. Nancy, Mel and I wore dress jackets, jeans and ball hats. We lip-synced to the song "Elvira." Our "microphones" were Dixie cups. The director said, "I've headed up lots of talent shows on this ship, but tonight topped them all."

We were in great demand pantomiming on cruises, at family reunions and picnics. I have no idea how many videos are floating around the country, creating laughter and good, clean fun.

WE NO LONGER have children moving in and out, so we went on a simplification kick, removing junk that should have been gone ten years ago. Can't imagine how much we packed into the house, attic and garage. I can live without three sets of dishes. "Pitch it," I tell Mel. "If we kick off, the kids will back a dump truck into the driveway and tell each other to pitch it. I'd be embarrassed."

Mel lugged several boxes to the burning barrel. Dumping the contents beside a mountain of similarly un-needed stuff was not amusing or fun, but it did make sense. My "pack rat" hates to throw anything away. "Don't you dare bring anything back to the house," I warned.

Smoke tunneled through the backyard. He handed me a faded paper bag. "I think you overlooked something." The bag contained two yards of white satin fabric, leftover lace, and spare buttons Mel had covered when Wilma was making my wedding dress. A blue envelope contained the last letter I received from Yvonne. Remembering the last year of my dear sister's life was bittersweet.

Today is the fourth anniversary of her death. I just sang "Sweet Beulah Land" at the funeral of a friend. I'm riding in a funeral procession, taking notes for my journal, and thinking of the family's loss. Cars have headlights on and flags wave in the wind. The ride to the cemetery is slow. Some of the drivers are in a hurry. Other than the few in cars behind the hearse, no one is crying. As we move through town I look out the window and see children playing, lovers walking hand-in-hand. For some, today is just another day. For a few, today is the worst day of their life. I recall the worst day of my life. My grief seemed unbearable when I said goodbye. When I start to cry, I remember Yvonne's last bit of advice. "You can cry a little, but not a lot." She wants me to be in a happy room and I must carry out her wishes. Mom would agree.

Tomorrow I may meet someone who is reliving the death of a loved one. Someone may feel guilt and shame for acts of violence. Someone may have lost a job and retirement benefits. For every problem there is a treasure inside.

Laughing Out Loud

In April I acquire a longing for summer and warm breezes that slip through pink sheets hanging on the line. Flowers bring color to a bleak winter-ravaged landscape. Poplar trees bloom, cheery yellow goldfinches hug the feeder. Spring brings anticipation, a guarantee of renewal. Writers must convey their enthusiasm and fervent beliefs. In the spring I feel the need to get out of town, where I can gather my thoughts. I find an open road, but my vital ideas are crushed when the transgression of other drivers causes my blood pressure to soar. "Moron," I muttered when a minivan driver cut me off. "I hate minivan drivers. They block my view and I can't see if traffic is clear to turn right on red They drive the way fat dogs walk." I hit the brake and didn't get through the light. Mrs. Minivan made the light and sped away.

I pounded the steering wheel with my palm, and groaned like an old man with hemorrhoids. "Ohhh, jeeeez. I'm in a hurry. Got to get to the library before it closes." The light turned green and a Cadillac flew by. Her bumper sticker read PRACTICE HUMOR. Humor isn't for everyone. It's only for people who want to enjoy life and feel alive. I read that the key to happiness is to keep breathing, keep laughing out loud, and worry less. I will keep myself happy by keeping away from minivans.

In this day and age we're besieged with advice and information. Newspapers yawp, bumper stickers talk, television demands our time. Much of the information can't be used to help us. It's trashformation, useless mental junk food that clogs the brain and dulls the senses. My antidote for too much trashformation is a trip to the burning barrel. There, I light a match, burn my hand while trying to read the junk mail. I've prevented brainfill and landfill problems at the same time.

The radio yells about buying lottery tickets. Even poor people save a few dollars a week to purchase "the devils work," as Aunt Hannah used to say. In April my family vacationed in Florida. We stopped at a shopping mall, not to shop, but to get a glass of southern-style sweetened iced tea. A neon sign in large letters bellowed that I could suddenly become rich. "Hey gang, let's invest $5 each." Here I am, a grandmother about to submit to the devil's ways, about to buy my first ticket, about to lead my two sisters and our husbands into temptation. Would lightening strike me? Would a mighty rushing wind rip off the roof? Was there a chance that one of us would win $48 million? I would know the answer at midnight.

The lottery boom contributes to about 4.5 million households doing just what we did. The results: a new crop of sufferers of Sudden Wealth Syndrome, or SWS, lucky lottery winners. Would I suffer an array of symptoms surrounding a rite of passage as I move into new wealth? What if the money causes anxiety or depression, envy by friends and family? "Sudden wealth causes more problems than gradual acquired wealth," Wilma quipped.

I snickered. "Our friends will say 'You've worked hard. You deserve this.' I know one who will say 'must be nice' "

Herb jingled the change in his pocket. "Just think, I'll never have to say, Well, if I only had the money."

"Maybe I'd put some of it into the community and become a hermit." Arnold said with a crafty grin.

"You'll figure it out," I told him. "You'll come to terms with wealth—after family members become stewards of a portion."

Mel smacked his lips. "I'll order a porterhouse for every

meal. I'll be a different person. I'll accept having money." The waitress brought our order, the midnight hour approached and a corner television blurred the news: "Eighteen employees who worked in a Michigan factory were laid off a few months ago. That's the bad news. The good news is they won the Florida lotto, forty-eight million."

I was happy that someone who needed the money ended up winning. "Well, so much for our first and last try," I said. "At least we won't have to deal with SWS. I won't need an identity change. I won't have to buy a guard dog to protect my wealth. I've never had a yearning to be rich."

Wilma yearned for a puppy just like the picture she bought at a garage sale and hung on the bedroom wall. Every time she and Herb flipped the light switch they admired the nameless puppy. In February, when Ailene went for a visit, she said, "You two are lonely. You need a pet to pamper, something to keep you company."

"We've talked about that," Wilma told her. "My health isn't good. Herb isn't sure he wants the additional responsibility. As you age, you decide what you can handle and what you can do without. Besides, I watch the ads. Small dogs are hard to find."

The next morning the trio headed for the pet store. The French-speaking, slightly pompous owner leaned on the counter. "May I help you?"

"We're looking for a female puppy," Wilma said.

"Oh, dear ones, dogs make loyal pets. Loyalty is more valuable than diamonds. I'll never forget the first time I laid eyes on a dog with angel hair that I think you would absolutely adore." She made various hand gestures that showed off the dark red nail polish. "A salesman brought her in. He talked about finding a new home after she is spayed. The doctor just finished surgery, and she's still groggy. Would you like to see her?"

At first glance, three people fell in love with the tiny limp white Maltese, wrapped in a pink blanket and cradled in the doctor's arms. "She's doing fine," he said. "She'll be ready to leave tomorrow."

The next day the owner said, "My wife passed away, and I'm on the road so much. I hate to leave this little darling home alone, so I'll pack her things." After years of dreaming, Wilma held Angel in her arms.

That evening Herb sent e-mail announcements: *We have a new family member. She's eight inches long, weighs six pounds, six ounces. "Angel" is more valuable than diamonds. Her picture has hung on our bedroom wall for five years.* That day a new friendship began.

Friendship seems to blossom in the spring. In May my thoughts turn to Hoosier country. Shirley, Janie, Jeanette and I take a day to hit the small town of Shipshewana. Husbands aren't invited. It's the girls' trip. "Shipshe," is quaint, Amish. Restaurants feature down-home cooking. Stores are crammed with stuff described as "cute" and "darling." The tourist population (bus loads) is overwhelmingly female with an occasional male carrying packages and looking for the tool section.

We shop and shop and shop. The giant flea market equals crowds and fun. We spend hours going down one row after another, on a gravel walkway. We bargain hunt, and mentally decorate several rooms, touch everything and put some of it back. We try on hats, and make faces in the mirror. We try on shorts, tee shirts, and denim dresses. Lunch consists of an ice cream cone. We drive to Middlebury for a family-style chicken dinner, and purchase homemade items from the bakeshop.

During the ninety-minute trip home, we talk about girl stuff, silly stuff, kids, grandkids and husbands. We arrive home tired and broke. A corner of the trunk is designated for each person's treasures. My husband has enjoyed solitary time and caught up on projects around the house. He helps unload the bags of "necessities," and pretends to be interested, but can't figure out how we crammed so much into one vehicle. Before we go our separate ways we plan our next meeting, breakfast at Bob Evans where we catch up on all the news.

It's tough to keep quiet when you've got something juicy to tell. My friends don't gossip. Not much. Gossip is a pastime filled with pleasure and peril. Listening is a passive act. We desire to tell all in the name of frankness and honesty. There's a pinprick of pleasure over another's misery. We tell what happened. We find out what happened. We question if he left the job or if he was fired. Did she get pregnant because she wanted to? Is she really forty-eight?

Gossip has been associated with women, sharp tongues telling stories. My friends dish up straightforward information. I know a world-class gossip. Mrs. Chattermouth relays her information with innocence and impartial zest. She claims she uses gossip to relieve stress. "I find humor in gossip," she says. "It's not a cure-all, but it gets me through the day. I can't afford to ruin my day with anger over the job, so I ruin someone else's day with innocent gossip."

"There's no such thing as innocent gossip," I reply.

"Oh yes there is," she argues. "In today's fast-paced world people need a giggle or two. Humorous gossip nips negative thought patterns in the bud, makes you look at problems from a different perspective." She took a notebook from her purse. "Look at my glamorous gossip book. The world is full of odd stuff to laugh at," she went on. "Let me tell you what I heard the other day. Carmen's house is a mess. It smells. Both cats use the cloth furniture and carpets as their scratching post."

"Did you suggest double-stick tape? After a few hours the cats would get the message. Or she could put the cats in isolation for a year to see if they're allergic to people. My dear you must remember that gossip for therapy can create a river of tears. Gossip seldom leaves a sweet aftertaste."

The aftertaste of a few hours on the pictorial Au Sable River, drifting with the current, is better than therapy, better than soaking up the summer sun. The peak color season arrives during the last week of September, a perfect time for a canoe trip.

We rented four canoes. Our hosts, Janie and Neil, led the

way, and insisted that we hurry along before rain soaked our lightweight jackets. Shirley maneuvered through the gentle current, while John searched for plastic to cover his camera. Gray skies added mystery to the mood, mossy branches reached across the river. The smell of cedar filled our nostrils. Mel took a picture of Jeanette and me perched under bright colored umbrellas. "It won't rain on their parade," he said.

Jeanette was busy telling Chuck how to navigate; she preferred calmness to calamity. Around the bend, two men stood in waist-high water and tipped each canoe that approached. "No!" she yelled.

"Don't worry lady. We don't dump everyone, only our church group. They won't swear at us." Laughter, wet clothing, and dripping hair brought many smiles.

Within two hours the sky brightened and smooth, white clouds floated overhead. The quietness produced a dream-like stillness, except for an occasional birdcall and the steady rhythm of our paddles dipping into the water. I should say Mel and Chuck's paddles. Jeanette and I quickly became accustomed to the solitude and laziness of the awesome scenery. Fall sunlight looked like flames through the door of a wood stove. A palette of yellow, orange and red reflected in the clear water.

We meandered down a deeply twisted river loaded with history, ruminant logs of an aggressive lumbering that stripped the area of many trees. The forest provides seasonal homes for several bird species. During the breeding season, the area is rich in songbirds.

Croaking sand hill cranes, squawking kingfishes, and a variety of ducks attended our picnic lunch on the sandy beach. We turned in the canoes and headed back to my favorite camping choice "roughing it" at the Holiday Inn.

The major problem with going on a trip is coming home. The refrigerator is empty, the cupboard is bare, and the only alternative is eating out three times daily or going to the grocery store. With gas prices at an all-time high, we sometimes combine errands; however, taking a husband grocery shopping is hazardous to your health.

"Lock all the doors. Someone stole my purse!" I told the gal at the grocery store service desk.

"What does it look like?"

"It's beige, has two short handles and small beige leaves on the nylon mesh side."

"Where was the purse?"

"In my grocery cart, which is also missing."

"What aisle were you in?"

"Where the olive oil is. I was helping a woman in a wheel chair. She wanted something from the top shelf. I got it for her."

"Go back where you came from."

"Do you expect the purse to be lying on the floor?"

"I'm trying, lady."

"You're no help." I headed back to the crime scene. The wheel chair lady was still comparing olive oil prices, trying to decide if imported extra virgin or cold pressed was best.

The attractive blonde I had seen earlier was still making a decision about Jell-O pudding. She flashed a pleasant smile, which I didn't appreciate at the moment.

"Someone stole my purse. Did you see anyone close by?"

She pointed toward the hardware department. "A man came from over there. I saw him eyeball your groceries. He grabbed the cart with purse in it and headed for the door. He was carrying a tube of caulking."

"Describe him please."

"He was wearing on a short-sleeved white shirt—quite a nice looking, expensive shirt—blue dress pants, black shoes."

Gee lady, I didn't ask for a flawless investigative report. I just wanted some speedy, bare facts. "Yes, yes, you've been helpful. Thanks very much." *A man dressed like that was in my house this morning. A man dressed like that sat next to me in church a short time ago. He bought my dinner.*

I quickly headed toward the service desk. A security guard and two associates recognized me as the lady with a booming voice. Standing nearby was a man in a white shirt, blue dress pants and black shoes. My booming voice went into a six-sharp key change. "Arrest that man!" The associate nodded toward the security guard. I waved my arms in the air. "Arrest him. He's a criminal! He took my purse!"

From five feet away, Mel held the purse in the air and looked at me with a gleam in his eye. "Does this belong to you?"

"Arrest that man. I want to see him put in jail. He's my husband, but he took my purse!"

"We can't arrest your *husband*."

"Why not? He committed a crime." I grabbed the purse and began lashing it across his back. By now, a small crowd had gathered, but that was a minor milestone. "I hate you. I've never been so mad at you. And if I had kept my big mouth shut and not claimed you as the man in my life, they'd be carting you off to jail *right now.*

"I'm trying to teach you a lesson, dear."

"Well, I'm not learning." The criminal grinned all the way home.

A GIFT FROM Mel's daughter Betty spiced up our life. The cedar bird feeder attracts chickadees, blue jays and too many blackbirds. Cardinals catch the eye like a bright scarf on a gray dress. A skittish female cardinal pokes at the seed on the ground. The brilliantly colored mate scatters smaller birds that dare to come into the pecking area. Tiny yellow finches scarf up thistle seed at a dollar a pound. With more time to stand still and enjoy what's going on around us, we've found the pleasure of feeding birds. It's a show well worth the price.

We also became acquainted with Stash, a small gray squirrel that often crashed the buffet line. He first claimed the back yard during a blizzard, when I tossed out bread scraps every morning. He took over the territory. Gourmet corn and sunflower seeds conveniently appeared on a wooden platform that was located just a jump from the maple tree. Stash slapped at the feeder, tried to embrace the swaying object, and fell to the ground, only to scramble up and try again.

Even though I favored feathered over furry creatures, I admired the gymnastic skill of the burglar who tried to walk the metal tightrope. Stash dangled upside down, holding the hanger in his paws, circling the feeder with his front paws. Instead of feeling remorse that Stash was defeated, I felt mean-spirited enough to evict the squirrel.

Hauling home sacks of sunflower seeds tote up the cost of keeping our birds and buddies in a fat and sassy condition. Now we have five feeders. The songs last until late evening. Feeding the birds gives a new idea for the often-asked question, "Dad what could we buy for you?"

Instead of the usual answer, "Socks," Mel tells them, "Lots of bird seed." Last year his stash was 100 pounds. Hundreds of sparrows arrive and eat everything in sight. Reminds me of feeding teenagers again. You can't fill them up, and they hang around all year.

The air around me sounds and smells like spring. Daffodils wave cheerful golden topknots. I gaze at the first sign of spring, Mom's purple iris waving in the breeze. I recall the day Herb and Wilma visited a few years ago.

He opened the trunk. "Ailene dug the iris bulbs your mother planted at the long cabin, and put them in the family cemetery. I brought these for you." Before long, our children, nieces, and nephews' yards embraced Mom's favorite beauty and fragrance. Gee took bulbs to California and most of his children have planted and told their children the "Purple Iris Story." Mom's flowers grace lawns in at least a dozen states. Perhaps my grandchildren will keep the plants and the story alive.

Gardening is a satisfying benefit of retirement; having time for things that the business of earning a living doesn't allow. The kid's sandbox became a flowerbed filled with forget-me-nots and pink coral bells for hummingbirds to enjoy. Lilac bushes perfume the air. For summer-long color, I purchase geraniums, the "Big Bloomers" from our local greenhouse.

Our new adventure brings challenge. Wandering deer herds consider blossoms a convenient buffet. We enjoy our three-tier fountain, and pond of water lilies, goldfish and Koi, but fighting algae has been a challenge. Cutting grass is an eight-hour weekly job, but gardening is a form of meditation that allows you to stop thinking and tune in to the moment. We sit and admire the handiwork, satisfaction that money can't buy. Perhaps the grandchildren will recall "Grandma's garden" as a spot of beauty.

After a few years, the bedrooms become an office supplied with computers, viewers, scanners and printers. After all, the family room has soft carpet and a long couch. Both fledglings return periodically. They want desserts, hamburgers on the grill. "Coming back home is a real treat especially when I'm greeted with the aroma of homemade bread," Leisa said.

The children offered to buy a bread machine for me. "What?" I asked. "My friends tell me that if you want warm bread in the morning you prepare everything at night, the machine does its job, but you have to pop the bread out of the pan when the oven shuts off; otherwise the warm setting activates the machine and it doesn't shut off for hours." I told them, "I'm through with 5 o'clock feedings. I enjoy combining ingredients, kneading the dough, feeling it spring to life at my touch. I nurture the embryo loaf, place it on the counter and watch it expand."

When Teri bought a bread machine, Gary found out that Mom was right again. I met him for lunch on Thursday. "I'm tired today, couldn't sleep well," he said. "That bread machine woke me from a sound sleep. I moved to the couch. The machine chugged into another cycle. I awoke, moved upstairs, drifted off to sleep and the buzzer rang. The smell and taste is good, but the machine belongs three houses away."

The grandkids see commercials featuring Poppin Fresh, the Pillsbury Doughboy. I told them about the death of their friend.

The obituary read:

> Veteran Pillsbury icon, Pop N. Fresh died of a severe yeast infection. Fresh's funeral was held in Bakery stadium. Mrs. Butterworth gave the eulogy. "Fresh was a man who never knew how much he was kneaded. He was a crusty old man. He folded in at the age of 75." Aunt Jemima shed buttermilk tears as she talked about her friend. "Fresh rose to high honors in business. He never had egg on his face. His life was full of turnovers." The California Raisins sang, "Ode to Cinnamon Twist." Hungry Jack read a poem about Fresh's half-baked schemes. He said Fresh was a smart cookie that rolled in millions. Betty Crocker prepared the funeral dinner. Hostess Twinkies provided the dessert. Many flours were displayed. Fresh was cremated at 350 degrees for about twenty minutes. He and his third wife have four children and one in the oven.

I wonder what Aunt Margaret would have thought of a computer making bread, and the quick work of sending a letter that we used to pound out and re-type on an old typewriter, electronic greetings, e-mail, and clicking a button to accept an instant reply.

When my button-pushing chores are done, I sit and think of the olden days. We drove the car until it died. The price tag on a Chevy coupe was $6,000, but who could afford one? Gas was eleven cents a gallon. In the olden days we got married first, then lived together. Weddings didn't cost a year's pay. We had a life without the threat of AIDS and IAD, Internet Addiction Disorder, a medical problem that is as real as alcoholism. I think we've outdone civilization.

My grandchildren realize that a technological canyon exists between now and then. They ask about life without cablevision, remote control, camcorders, and CD players. "Without VCR's how did you watch movies? You didn't have a dishwasher?"

"The children were dishwashers. We survived with only

one television. Moms were family barbers and cleaning ladies. Birthdays were celebrated in back yards. Your grandpa was not ashamed to take lunch to work. Well, one day he was mortified."

"Mortified? What's that?"

"He was embarrassed. He had gained too much weight, so I packed a sack lunch with one sandwich, fresh carrots and a large tomato from the neighbor's garden. Co-workers invited him to eat out, he offered to drive; he would devour the packed lunch during afternoon break. His boss, Mr. Valentine climbed in the back seat. He felt something wet, squishy, and discovered red fluid on his backside. Mr. Valentine didn't have a happy heart."

"That was a good one! Tell me more," Joshua said as several grandchildren sat at the table with watercolors, paintbrushes and poster paper.

"Your parents didn't always have garage door openers, Nickelodeon, Play Station, and Nintendo. They didn't have carbon monoxide detectors and airbags. They didn't have answering machines. We never heard of HMO. We were before credit cards, Frisbees, artificial hearts, tape decks or yogurt."

"Golly, my parents lived halfway in the olden days," Lauren said.

"You're half right. You don't realize, sweetie, but a revival is going on. The spiritual revival is one thing, but the ironing revival is another. Gone are the polyester days. Cotton is in. With cotton comes ironing. Our neighbor gave me *one dollar* to iron a basket stuffed full of frilly dresses that her twin girls wore to school."

"They wore dresses to school? She paid you only a dollar?"

"I hated ironing, but a dollar would buy twenty candy bars. The clothes had to be dampened using a water-filled pop bottle with a sprinkler head stuck in the top. Each piece to be ironed was rolled up and stacked in the basket to set for an hour or so. Steam irons were unheard of."

Some people do their most creative thinking during a long

drive or by shutting themselves in the bathroom like I used to do when the children were young and I needed to gain ten minutes of "me" time. Others do their best thinking while reclining in an easy chair. Give me twenty minutes at the ironing board and I can sketch out a story or resolve the national debt. I use this solitary time to think about last Sunday's sermon, talk to God about my family or confess my faults, (or those of others). My ironing sessions are shorter these days. Maturity also brings instinctive refusal to maintain perfection and wrinkle-free clothing. I've even been known to remove jeans from the dryer and hand press the crease.

MARRIAGE IS at the top of the list for life's moments of contentment and happiness. Second is the birth of children. At the end of the happiness scale is aging parents with random thoughts, snagged on branches of a dying brain. As I mature, I have only memories of my parents, but I watched Mel's mother reach the point in time. She lived through a Depression, a recession and an economic boom, two World Wars, a conflict in Korea, wars in Vietnam and the Persian Gulf.

Her health was excellent, but her mind was in a cage. Her rumpled brain swirled, dashed against the permanently locked door. She couldn't find the key. "Can't you give me a pill that will help me remember?" she begged. "If only I could think clearly." A blank stare replaced the look of assurance. Her once pleasant personality faded into the distance. Some of her grandchildren preferred to remember the good times. Their visits faded into the distant.

"I don't know if I want to live long enough to walk with a cane, incapable of driving or using my woodworking tools," Mel said with a frown.

"You sure do. Just keep that table saw hot, the camera clicking, and the golf clubs swinging. You need to put a positive spin on life. Negative thinking destroys inner peace that we need as we age. I read that pessimists have a shorter life span than positive thinkers."

"So I'm a pessimist? Okay, I'm smiling. Well, I'm sort of smiling. I heard that smiling keeps you young."

We attended an Ameritech breakfast. I told Mel, "I'm glad you're not old like those other men. You can tell we're at a retiree meeting. Men leave the room more often than women."

People tend to forget that you must adjust to the changes brought about by age. The urologist is important. When you age, your eye doctor, internal medicine man, pharmacist and the dentist become your best friends. A television commercial advertised a brand of false teeth glue. In the past, such commercials featured an old grandpa trying to gnaw on an ear of corn. The implied message was, "Here's another example of what to expect down the road." The new false teeth glue commercial sings a different tune.

Imagine the scene, a breathtaking shot of a couple galloping on horseback across the plains of the west. Time has hardly laid a finger on this flawless couple. They are wrinkle-free, clear-eyed and bulge-proof. Each sports a head of lustrous silver hair.

The ravages of age have missed them, but each knows the other's secret. They reached the age when they must wear false teeth. They canter along and flash happy smiles. Suddenly both horses buck and halt. She reaches into her saddlebag, produces an apple and takes a bite. The false teeth glue has done the job. They make old age glamorous and see themselves as glamorous. They race toward a picturesque ranch house. Once inside, I suppose they swallow three Tylenol and take a hot bath in Epsom salts.

I've notched up a half-century, but I remember, and can still smell fresh mowed grass sweet with life. The wind is sweet with possibility. So if I become toothless and saddle sore from my gallop through life I will take Geritol and greet you with a smile.

When we reach sixty, we tiptoe carefully through a minefield, hoping we won't blow our dreams to bits. Some of these mines explode unexpectedly despite our best efforts to prevent destroying our hopes. Growing older requires tolerance and the ability to be charitable toward self. We must avoid dwelling on what could have been, what should have been, and what might have been done differently.

Thoughts of the good ole days—driving a stick shift on two-lane roads, feeding dripping clothes into a wringer washer, freezing my buns hanging clothes on the line—make me appreciate modern conveniences. I'm perfectly content to put clothes in the machine and watch television while waiting for the buzzer to tell me the washing is done. Clothes dryers became common household appliances in 1950. I love the smell of freshly laundered sheets dried by the sun and wind, but I also love the dryer's musical "ding."

Technology crept into my generation, and the ability to make wise choices was a necessary component in the process. Like the author of the first Dr. Seuss book, my first one involved a thousand hand-written pages. Cutting and pasting required scissors, transparent tape and lots of desk space. I refused to succumb to having someone else print the finished work, so I entered the new world. I'll spare you the boring details, but I learned that maturity doesn't bring patience. Many times, I wanted to drag out the old Royal pica typewriter. I knew how to set margins, tabulations, compute page and space requirements. But Leisa insisted, "Hang in till Saturday and I'll help you." I did and she did.

With technology comes an increase in noise decibels. We live in a fast-paced modern age. The sound of an ax cutting into a tree has been replaced by the whirr of a chain saw. We hear the shattering blasts of the modern day diesel railroad engine. The train whistles I remember as a child carried all kinds of dreams. The sound seemed to say, "Come away with me."

Our smoke alarm goes nuts when it suspects danger. The shrill warning shatters eardrums and frail nerves. It goes into hysterics if a pie drips a teaspoon of filling. The kids used to yell, "Dinner is ready."

"The fire alarm works," Mel says as the dog howls and the family rushes down the hallway flapping towels in the air.

The alarm is one of many noise aggravations in my life. Cars beep at you, speak to you. "Remove key from ignition before you lock the door. Fasten your seat belt. Put your foot on the brake to start me." My iron buzzes and turns itself off if I'm on the telephone too long. The toaster tells the bread when to pop up.

Sometimes I long to bathe in quiet and the solitude of night where a symphony of cricket chatter and the shadows whispered secrets that no one else heard. I contact my Internet carrier late at night and a deep male voice says, "You've got mail."

I FOUND A COPY of Mel's first letter written on the computer:

To my dear sister, Reva: I will try to write a letter on this new machine. Typing with one finger is slow. My wife or daughter would have typed a whole page before I got started. I don't know how to make paragraphs. Sorry. Last night we played cards. Chuck and I didn't do well. We wonder if Jeanette and Patty have secret codes. I asked Patty to get me a glass of water. She told me to say the magic words. I said, "NOW!" Aren't you proud of me? I figured out how to make a paragraph! Hope I didn't spell any words wrong.

I'm having a hunger attack. My wife made toast and coffee this morning. I think she might be putting me on a diet. Well, I don't know if I have typed right, spelled right, or if the words fit the page when I push "print." I think that's what you do. Will write again when I graduate from my self-trained computer class. Wish me luck! Leisa types "LOL" sometimes. I think it means farewell. Maybe I should use it. So here goes: LOL!

We laughed out loud many times while on family vacations. I can still visualize running barefoot on the beach with our children. The silt between my toes was like moments caught from novels. Serious moments came when we listened to the rhythm of thirty children's voices chiming: "I pledge allegiance to the flag of the United States of America and to the republic for which it stands; one nation under God, indivisible, with liberty and justice for all." Some of them stood tall and proudly saluted the flag. A few squirmed, bit their lips, or hid behind the taller ones.

Over 200 braided their voices in the song, "America," that opened a three-day bash, the National Association of Lively Families. In addition to patriotic gestures, our meeting included golfing, swimming, shopping, a touch of history and a genealogy search that began in 1937 when fifty Livelys of America met for the first time. A friend told me, "No way will I join with family members who sit around in rocking chairs discussing their arthritis condition, their children who have gone astray, and their financial woes."

This group is upbeat, positive. Since many arrive early, we now make unofficial plans for Wednesday and Thursday evening activities. Friday afternoon we pick up nametags, get information regarding activities, discount tickets, pay yearly dues of $15, and purchase tickets for the hotel's fabulous Sunday breakfast buffet.

At the Friday pizza pool party, the Youth Vice President encourages teens to participate in the activities scheduled throughout the weekend. A special treat this year was homemade ice cream. The president calls meeting to order. After an invocation, motions are made and voted upon. Minutes are recorded. This year's hosts, Russell and Tonya from Georgia worked for several months collecting information, recommending restaurants, museums and entertainment. Chattanooga Holiday Inn Choo-Choo was the location for this year. A trio from Georgia sang, "The Chattanooga Choo Choo." The secretary read last year's minutes. We heard reports from the editor of the newspaper, the historian, genealogist, treasurer, and vice-president.

The next morning the President appointed committees: resolutions, audit, and reunion location. He took care of old and new business and talked about plans. Some prefer to sleep in and skip the Saturday morning meeting, but most show up for a group picture. Many opt for tours, swimming, factory outlets, or amusement parks.

With feelings of animosity, and attempts to divest ourselves of hatred and revenge, we toured Chickamauga Military Park, the nations oldest and largest, the site of a two-day Battle of Chickamauga. I thought of the ones who marched with a sword or musket in the ranks of the Confederate and Union armies. Many who were once united in the strongest family and friendship bonds were ready to kill each other. They waited for the word from their leaders.

After dinner we headed for the Saturday night entertainment and auction. The talent search should carry the title "Star Search," for it opens up the stage to vocal and instrumental groups, skits, pantomimes, writers, poets, dancers, and jokesters. A few of the Lively children have recently appeared on stage and screen.

The silent auction for children featured toys, trinkets and books. Parents and their grown children outbid each other for the hand-made crafts. An oak rocking horse, crafted by Randolph Henderson from West Virginia, went for $1,000. Zen Lively from Michigan hand carved a duck that netted $150. Proceeds from the auction benefit the third supplement of the 12,000-page Livelys of America books.

Sunday morning after breakfast we heard committee reports, and voted on new members. Everyone looks forward to the "States Report." When the president called " Michigan" eight stood, the audience applauded and we vowed to have better representation next year. The winner never changes. Ninety from Georgia wallowed in pride and declared, "The South shall rise again." We had attendees from the fifteen states. Traveling from the west coast was a distant cousin who accidentally hit our WEB site: www.livelyfamily.com

The last item on the agenda was the location for next year. If two or three hosts present suggestions, we vote and majority rules. Our whirlwind weekend came to an end. We formed a large circle with chain of hands and lifted our voices in the song, "Blest be the Tie That Binds." After the closing prayer and sharing e-mail and snail mail addresses we went our separate ways, taking with us new friendships and new memories.

Moments slip away, but you'll never regret taking time out of your busy life for a well-planned family get-together. Next year we travel to Charleston, SC. Many have already made plans to meet in Myrtle Beach to "practice our vacation."

MY MUSIC TEACHER says, "Practice makes perfect." I don't want to brag; wasn't raised that way. There is nothing to be gained by bragging, but I'll put aside ego lessons Mom taught me in time for a book signing. She would be proud of my accomplishments. On Saturday the waitress interrupted a book-signing luncheon to tell me that a local radio station was calling. "I see in the paper that you're at the Cascades Manor House, and that your book is out. Why didn't you call me?"

"Sorry, Rocky, things are moving too fast."

"How about a live interview? Readers want to know about how over 500 people trusted someone so much that she robbed them of a half million dollars."

"What the readers found was a warm story about the people involved, a story about the victims' strength and courage to put aside mistakes and move on with life."

During court proceedings a local television station, WLNS, interviewed the prosecutor, victims and attorneys. The reporter came to a book signing party and announced, "I'd like you to meet the author who capably and explicitly gave the world a new view of the Denman case." Friends at the prosecutor's office arranged for me to attend and discuss scams at civic organizations. They're wonderful people, the kind who read my books.

A few days later WILX-TV, an NBC affiliate, featured an interview. Radio Station WJR in Detroit requested more detailed information because the protagonist lived in that area. Marketing my books to consumers is easy, like attracting hungry birds to a full feeder. As with anything we do, we must keep the feeder filled.

The local daily, the *Jackson Citizen Patriot* schedules photograph sessions with Corey Morse, a journalistic intern from Michigan State University. He will follow me around for three hours and take three rolls of film about a day in the life of a writer.

I told him, "I take pleasure and pride in reaping rewards that come from effort. If you can dream it, you can do it. It's all about possibilities. You *can* go anywhere from nowhere. I was once a nobody, but there was somebody who knew about me and took me far beyond my own imaginings."

In November Mel had hernia surgery at Foote Hospital. One of the nurses saw a copy of *Sweet Dreams...Bitter Awakenings* in my briefcase. "The author of that book was here a few months ago visiting a patient. She's a young celebrity."

Mel said, "That's my wife. She calls herself a writer, not a celebrity. She's a grandmother."

On Grandparent's Day at Nathan's school the teacher read my book for children to her first grade class. Grandparents gathered around Nathan, the main character in the story. Additional benefits resulted from that story. I became acquainted with writers from Spring Arbor University. The professor of my creative writing class at SAU invited the students to his home for a cook out. After a delicious dinner we turned in portfolios. Dr. Metts prayed that each student would take their creative talents to the highest level. I was proud and pleased that a busy professor cared enough to pray for his students.

I often expose the grandchildren to campus life. We sit by the water fountain and watch students hurry to class. After

286

lunch in the cafeteria, we head for the sale table in the bookstore. I write down "wish lists" and when the family comes to our house for Thanksgiving dinner, we write our names (and wishes) on slips of paper, put them in a bowl and everybody draws. Leisa searches the bowl for Lauren and Lindsay's name. "I deserve the privilege of buying for girls," she says.

Mel has a talent for shopping. The associate in a dress shop told me, "I've never seen a man watch his wife try on dresses for an hour, give his expert opinion as to color, bulges or style, then willingly pay for the item." But holiday shopping is a different story. I've heard that male stress levels skyrocket when faced with crowded stores, choosing gifts and standing in checkout lanes. A study was conducted in London. Male shoppers wore monitors and every man in the survey registered increases in blood pressure and heart rate, something you'd expect to see in a fighter pilot going into combat, or policeman going into dangerous situations. Women did not register a significant change. Women are more comfortable with shopping, if they wear proper shoes. Men shop for tools and computers.

Mel's surgery and recuperation kept him from spending untold hours prowling the malls. Nor was he able to climb a ladder to string Christmas lights on our roof. Slowing down gave us extra time to savor the real meaning of the holidays. The truth is, people have so much stuff there is nothing left to buy. During my Depression years, the gifts were neither grand nor expensive, but were chosen with care and received with pleasure. Currently, children are overwhelmed with expensive gifts. Mel has the gift problem solved. He goes to the garage and selects maple or oak boards. He designs, sands and varnishes shelves or plant stands.

The holiday season is a time to reflect and enjoy, a time to witness the trusting innocence of the small child and the loving expression on a youthful parent's face. It's a celebration season that remains a part of me all year long. I gather the grandchildren close and tell them about shepherds tending flocks on a hillside near Bethlehem.

"On a night two thousand years ago, the wind was cold. It seemed to be quite an ordinary night, much like hundreds of other nights spent beneath that vast star-lit sky. Without warning, an angel of the Lord appeared saying, *"Fear not. For I bring you good tidings of great joy which shall be to all people. For unto you is born this day in the city of David a Savior, which is Christ the Lord. And this shall be a sign unto you. You shall find the baby wrapped in swaddling clothes lying in a manger."*(Luke 2:12-13)

"Was Jesus a small baby?" Lauren asked. "Or was he a tall guy like my dad?"

"There are facts we don't know. But we know that He came. We've experienced a thrill that many people around the world have never known."

"What's that, Grandma?" Lindsay asked. "I know. We have lots of houses and cars and toys that other kids don't have."

"That baby offered the world a new beginning," I said. "I remember the summer day in a little country church when I was fifteen. I accepted Jesus that day. Wilma, Herb and I stepped into the water of baptism and promised to live as near to God as possible."

In 1997 we began worrying about a weather pattern called "El Nino" (a Spanish phrase for the baby Jesus) that might cause droughts, floods, hot weather, cold weather, too much snow or not enough snow. The theory is that warm water builds up in the Pacific Ocean, causing winds that disrupt normal weather. The periodic winds were called El Nino because they hit Latin America in December.

El Nino brought tornados, hurricanes and heat waves. In 1998, the Christmas-time phenomenon caused evaporation, a jet stream with winds high above the earth. Snowmobiles gave way to golf carts and sweaters replaced snowsuits. We sold the snowmobiles, but not the memories.

Winter, like rich coffee, is an acquired taste. It's a taste you have to force yourself to re-acquire every year. The season's pleasures are enhanced by spending time with friends, tossing another log on the fire and letting the cold stay outside.

In December Mel decided to remodel the kitchen. We planned a simple task of tearing down and ordering new cupboards. Mel sketched plans. "Modern counter tops have moldings that are too high for these outlets," he said as he cut holes for new ones. We spent two days ripping up carpet that been glued to the floor for ten years. One job led to another. "We need an ice maker."

"Definitely."

"I'll have to run water lines twelve feet. But that's all right."

"The stove and refrigerator are thirty years old. Time to bid them farewell," I said. "And this sink won't match the new furniture. The white sink requires new white faucets. The microwave takes up too much space on the counter."

Might as well get an above-the-stove microwave. We need a new garbage disposal."

"And the splendor of a new kitchen necessitates new window treatment. The dining room opens into the living room so the drapes have to match." We headed for the J. C. Penny store. The sales associate was putting up a new display. "I want to order Victorian swags in antique satin fabric. Could I have a better look at that one?"

"Sure, but this style comes in only one size."

Mel knew my next brainstorm. "Get out your tape measure, Mel. Use your engineering expertise. I need four sizes. Swags are easy to do." Each idea required several new items and lots of extra work.

The kitchen, for the most part designed by my multi-talented perfectionist, proved to be just what we wanted. After twenty days, my husband had created a picture-book showplace. Light oak cupboards, black and white furnishings, accents of blue with white counter tops, white sink and faucets, country blue and mauve carpeting and hand-designed window treatment. We dared not repeat our former do-it-yourself paper-hanging project that ended just short of the china-throwing stage. We remained friends throughout the kitchen project.

In March Mother Nature's mischief returned us to the 19th century living. At three o'clock I awoke to the sound of sleet pounding the tin roof on the patio outside our bedroom window. The light on the bedside clock blinked. Limbs on the maple and honey locust trees were scattered in the yard.

At daybreak Mel called the power company who had already received numerous calls. He brought in logs for the fireplace, and within a few minutes the family room was toasty warm. Gary Scott was spending the weekend. He liked the "old-fashion game" we were playing. "Let's go out to breakfast," I suggested. Many other power-deprived people crowded into every restaurant in town. Standing room only. After satisfying our caffeine crave and with full tummies, we headed home as the snow-covered roadway began icing over. The interstate looked like a parking lot, stranded motorists wondered what to do. We waited in line at the local supermarket to purchase a supply of milk, spaghetti, soup and bottled water. The motels were all full.

Gary Scott did his homework. We read until evening. Mel lit candles and a kerosene lantern. We played canasta and ate popcorn until nine. "I haven't been in bed this early since childhood," I said while stacking more blankets on the beds.

We awoke to snow piled three feet high in the driveway, and halfway up the windows. I lit the gas stove and poured bottled water into a pan. "The inside temperature is fifty. Twelve outside. I'd give $5.00 for a decent cup of coffee."

"Just hold on, dear. The power company agreed to have everything taken care of by evening."

"Hope so. You can see your breath in the kitchen. The bathroom stool needed fur lining if we were to reach success. I'm barely able to move around. My wardrobe includes pajamas, sweat suit, jeans and a wool sweater."

We climbed into bed at eight-thirty and awoke at five. The paper cup and plate supply was depleted, along with my will to survive. "We can't go out to eat today. Limbs are all over the roadway." I wrestled with the crank can opener. We had apple-sauce, a slice of bread heated on the fireplace coals. The noon menu consisted of slightly warm spaghetti, crackers and sweet peas. "I've worn the light switch out, forgetting that it went on strike," I laughed. We dined by candlelight had herb tea, and went to bed at eight. By now I'd give my ruby ring for a decent cup of java.

"I must be getting used to pioneer living," I said the next morning. "Slept in until 5:30." I realized the sacrifices my an-cestors made and felt a bit guilty about being ungrateful and unthankful for material things that now seemed essential. By now I'd almost trade my husband for a cup of coffee.

That evening the hum of the freezer, the blinking of a dozen clocks scattered throughout the house, and the gentle clicking of the forced air furnace reminded me of the wonder of electricity, the beauty of flushing. Before long the kitchen was warm, filled with the smell of cinnamon from a just-sliced cake, and the best cup of coffee I've ever had. So long to the simple life and the good ole days.

THE GRANDCHILDREN call often. "Grandma, will you come to my game on Wednesdays and Fridays?" Of course, I must be there. Gary Scott is an avid soccer player. So far I've learned about volleys, goalkeepers, spikes and saves. I used to think a rainbow was something we see in the sky, until I wit-nessed his rainbow kick. He placed the ball between his feet, leaned forward, the right leg in front, the left leg turned side-ways. The left foot faced right heel and while running he jumped into the air, flipped legs up. The bent knee threw the ball in the air and it soared in front of him.

Gary Scott was goalie at the next game. Teammates had the ball. They ran toward goal, the opposite team got the ball and opponents pressed closer. A hard kick came from thirty feet away, into the top right hand corner. He dived for and grasped the ball pressing forward, crashing into the goalpost. He saw stars; his team saw victory. When he regained consciousness, teammates were standing over him yelling that he had saved the goal and won the game.

Even though I'm older I still enjoy the grandchildren, especially taking them to Cedar Point in Sandusky, Ohio. Parking a great distance away and riding a tram stirred up memories of my family's arrival at the park when the gates opened. Gary and Leisa loved thrill rides with a passion, particularly roller coasters. Each year they stood next to the YOU MUST BE THIS TALL sign. Finally they give a high-five and a broad grin. They spent the day in a mad frenzy to pack in as many rides as possible. Leisa had the focus of an army general plotting strategy for attack and conquer; knocking off favorite rides one by one. All too soon Gary began noticing the teenage girls with short-shorts, skimpy halter tops and bare shoulders glistening with oil as they braved the hot sun. Pimply-faced boyfriends sprinkled conversation with a rare form of English and course vulgarities.

We enjoyed everything about Cedar Point, even the shimmering heat that rose in waves from the asphalt midway, the clatter of metal rides and screeches of riders. "This is the best day of the year," Leisa said as we headed for the *America Sings* production at the theater. The best treat that became a tradition was following our noses to the elephant ears booth. Leisa and I purchased one to share while people-watching from a park bench. The summer Leisa left home, the nostalgia of amusement parks and county fairs took on new meaning. "There's your favorite thing, elephant ears," Mel said as we walked past the yellow and red booth. "I'll get one for you."

"No thanks, I'm too full. The truth is, they don' taste the same because Leisa isn't here."

After the children grew up, we watched the grandchildren bounce from ride to ride with the same passion and Cedar Point stamina their parents possessed. When the sun set over Lake Erie and night arrived, twinkle lights and starry skies blanketed the hearts of children and adults. A touch of magic came into being. At eleven, as we shuffled through the exit gate a small tired and sleepy voice said, "Grandma, this is the best day of my life."

I wonder if we used up all the good old days, or are there still some left over for the next generation. I want the memories, but I don't want to go backwards, unless I put my Cadillac in reverse while laughing out loud.

Historic Moments

Since childhood I've been fascinated with castles, princesses and royal families. I followed Princess Diana's life and longed to be charming, poised and sophisticated like Princess Diana. She personified a dream come true, a big house, new dresses for every occasion, and more shoes than she could wear. I share her interest in shoes. Recently I counted forty-five pairs, including well-worn and wrong color.

Princess Diane kept company with the rich and famous. She knew how to party and preferred nights on the town to evenings with her sons. Diana had every luxury and convenience imaginable. She was psychologically fragile, sometimes suicidal and plagued with an eating disorder. She smiled on the outside, cried on the inside.

My fairytale image melted when I discovered that Diane was no heroine, no model I'd want to imitate. Yet an unsaintly immoral person was used for good in a hurting world.

The miracle associated with Princess Diana is a self-centered individual bringing relief to victims of land mine warfare, hope and encouragement to common people.

In November 1997 a car crash in a tunnel under Paris claimed the life of Princess Diana, her boyfriend Dodi Fayed, and their driver. Mourners raged at photographers who chased the car at high speed. Legislators talked of prohibiting public photographers. Tests exposed the driver as legally drunk. I learned in Business Law class that in this case the courts used the Napoleonic Code and there was no prosecution.

A week after Diane's death, Mother Teresa of Calcutta died of a heart attack at eighty-seven. Her last words were, "Jesus, I love you." She launched over 500 missions in 100 countries. She touched the world. A frail old woman opened millions of eyes dimmed by glitter. To accept the Nobel Peace Prize, she wore a familiar white sari edged in blue, valued at one dollar.

The truth revealed in the lives of Diana and Teresa is one truth. God uses worldly power and selfish people to bring good news to the poorest of the world. One woman had everything money could buy and one had nothing. One woman had beauty and charm; the other had internal gifts of a big heart and a gentle spirit. When Princess Diana and Mother Teresa died, commoners and royalty all over the world grieved. A million bouquets bloomed in London, near Westminster Abbey where Diana's body rested. Reports via radio, television and the Internet caused tears for days.

A corner of my mind relates to graduation day. The principal said, "Character is what you are in the dark; what you are when no one is watching." The statement remains true when the matter of discussion takes an unprincipled direction about what happened in 1998, in our nation's capital.

I've witnessed many historic news moments in my lifetime: the shot that wounded President Reagan, Challenger blowing up, the Berlin Wall coming down, the explosion of the federal building. But when television broadcasted a pathetic middle-aged guy apologizing for doing what some middle-aged guys do with willing women, it was the grand scheme of sex overshadowing our society. It was President Clinton's mea culpa.

On the world stage the president was speaking about the perils of terrorism. On the television set, he was being asked to define sexual relations. A grand jury demanded answers. In millions of offices cars and homes, the drone of testimony ran for four hours. A fifty-year-old world leader tarnished and diminished the office of the president, the highest office in the land.

I grew up seeing politicians rise and fall for a variety of reasons. Presidents have lied to the people. Roosevelt lied about getting involved in World War II. Lyndon Johnson lied about Vietnam. Reagan lied about the Iran Contra. Other presidents have fooled around, Roosevelt, Kennedy, Ike. I grew up believing that to tell the truth was paramount. Being truthful wasn't an option, but a requirement.

The grand jurors had bonded with former White House intern, Monica Lewinski, and extended a comforting hand to the tearful twenty-five-year-old. The jury forewoman said, "We wanted to offer you a bouquet of good wishes that includes luck, success, happiness and blessings." Was this a courtroom drama we watched?

The grandchildren asked for explanations. "President Clinton has not developed the moral character and self-discipline we learned in high school," I told them. "A young woman put sexual gratification over a sense of self-respect. Voters decided that character didn't count. Character and self-respect may be old-fashioned, but never outdated." Some say that in a perverse way, the president and Monica knew the end. Others thought Monica sensed that Bill had a split personality.

I helped my son study the Scout Oaths. Bill Clinton would not be admitted as a member of the Boy Scouts of America. If he were already a member, his admitted lies would be grounds for expulsion. The Scout Law declares: "I pledge to be morally straight." The public seems to be less concerned about the character of the president than the strength of the economy. The president may have never been a Boy Scout, but he twice took another oath, required by the Constitution. The words, as do the Scout Oath and Scout Laws, have meaning. They presume the oath-taker will live up to his pledge and accept the consequences for violating them. He undermined and redefined our most fundamental document by lawbreaking and immoral behavior. We promote and admire Boy Scout standards. These constitutional standards are not vacated when a boy becomes a man. "Hang him by the appendage that got him in trouble," a reporter hissed.

During the sexual saga, The United Nations Arms Inspector reported that Saddam Hussein would resume development of weapons of mass destruction. He said the United Stated could no longer mobilize an alliance to stand against Iraq. Based on what we know about him and his behavior in office, some believe the reason for the statement was because world leaders did not highly regard the American president.

The story began a year prior, and in 1998 was ranked as the year's Number One story, a tale of desire, betrayal, broken vows and shattered careers. This was a true story. Shifting the focus from the Whitewater land deal, Independent Counsel Kenneth Starr turned the nation's curiosity to secret tapes and grand jury testimony. The House impeached the twice-elected president for lying to a federal grand jury and obstructing justice.

In a ninety-minute question-and-answer session before 4,500 ministers at a conference in Chicago, Clinton said he was trying to rebuild his life from the terrible mistake he made. He said, "My spiritual life is great, constant, and it's never going to change." He added, "I had to come to terms with a lot of things about the fundamental importance of character and integrity."

The sports world regards March 8, 1999, as an historic moment. The Yankee Clipper, Joe DiMaggio, died with Marilyn Monroe's name on his lips. We were saddened by strikeouts in Joe's marriages, especially the unlikely one to Marilyn Monroe. The Hall of Famer's lawyer and confidant said, "Just before he died of lung cancer at age eighty-four, DiMaggio whispered, 'I don't feel bad about dying. I'll finally get to see Marilyn again.' Joe never stopped loving Marilyn even after their nine-month marriage ended in divorce in 1954. She may have been the only one Joe really loved."

The Yankee team dedicated a monument to DiMaggio. On a sun-splashed afternoon at Yankee Stadium a crowd watched DiMaggio's former teammates—Yogi Berra, Whitey Ford, Phil

Rizzuto, Hank Bauer, Jerry Coleman and Gil McDougald—gather for the unveiling of a granite and bronze monument. Cardinal John O'Connor addressed the crowd and gave an invocation. Highlights of DiMaggio's career were shown on the scoreboard, including clips of his final visit to Yankee Stadium.

It wasn't necessary to know heroes back then. It was pleasurable to know they were common people. Kids could look up to him, and when they grew up, Joe DiMaggio made them feel like they were still kids trapped in aging bodies. When kids asked for autographs, he emitted star power in a gracious sort of way. Generations push ahead, but they left something behind, memories of a baseball great.

Tiger Stadium that opened April 12, 1912, was eighty-seven years old. To the very end, this was a wonderful place to hatch memories. Stadiums have come and gone over the last half of this century. Yet the love and affection that poured out from Tiger Stadium is unmatched.

I was about to give up on the Tigers. On Monday, September 27, 1999, Tiger reliever Todd Jones struck out Carlos Beltram. That night, at 7:07, the team that hadn't done anything memorable all season did something that no one will forget. Robert Fick hit a grand slam. Doug Brocail made a double play. The ghosts of Old Tiger teams smiled on the players and captivated 43, 356 fans.

The Tigers took the lead; hit a home run the first inning, tied in the third and regained the lead with Garcia's two-run homer in the sixth. Fick came to the plate in the eighth inning. He swung at the first pitch. The ball soared toward right field, hit the roof just over the World Series banners and bounced back onto the field. Flashbulbs helped illuminate the stadium. Jones struck out Beltram for the final out at the corner of Michigan and Trumbull. The Tigers beat Kansas City 8-2. The Royals were in last place.

The stadium that captured our hearts still holds its charm. Gary returned to Tiger Stadium, not as a child sitting beside

Dad, but as a member of Tiger owner, Tom Monaghan's security team. The Tigers have moved to Comerica Park, a sparkling new state-of-the-art stadium where memories will be forged at another corner, Adams and Brush.

AILENE AND I turned back the clock of remembrance the day she boarded a flight from Charleston and I flew from Detroit Metro. Wilma and Herb met us at the Orlando airport. We stopped for lunch; the waitress came to take our order. You'd have to know my brother-in-law to appreciate his humor. Herb said, "Sarah, I'd like you to meet my wife Cinderella and her two ugly sisters." Sarah gave a healthy laugh. "Buddy, if *that's* ugly, I'd like to hear your definition of beauty."

My sister-mom laughed as we recalled childhood, sharing work chores and nighttime hugs. Some of the unpleasant memories had been erased. Promises of the past, the fear of the present and the limits of the future were grounded as we sat on the patio listening to the water fountain and sipping French Vanilla Café.

Herb, our chauffeur and chef, created a variety of delicious food, provided curb service for shopping and kept plans moving on schedule. Every morning we awoke to the aroma of Folgers coffee. Unfortunately, the childhood maladies that Ailene encountered didn't stop at childhood.

Ailene is a daydreamer, a romanticist with a bit of Daddy's temperament. "It's been years since we spent Christmas together. Let's cook a traditional dinner, put up a few decorations and trim a tree. Would that be too much trouble?"

"Great idea. But are you up to doing all that? Fibromyalgia, chronic fatigue syndrome, and the air travel seems to have taken a toll on your energy." She said she was doing better. The next morning we piled into Herb's Oldsmobile station wagon. At Wal-Mart we went our separate ways and purchased items to put under the tree we had decorated in red and gold.

On Saturday we sat down to enjoy a turkey dinner with the traditional trimmings. But Ailene's Christmas dream came crashing to a halt. Halfway through the meal, she blinked several times, cradled her head in her right hand and closed her eyes. "Are you tired?" I asked. She didn't answer.

"She's probably just resting her eyes for a few minutes," Wilma said. "She's had a headache for two days."

About five minutes later Ailene said softly, "I can barely hear you."

After another minute or so l didn't think she was breathing. "Ailene, are you all right?" Several times I questioned and got no response. We applied a cold cloth, patted her face, and removed a fork that was still clutched in her hand. I found no pulse. We called 911 and notified a neighbor to watch for the paramedics. Ten minutes later the paramedics arrived. One lifted her arms, while the other grabbed her ankles. Her stretched-out body swayed as they transported her down two concrete steps. "You *can't do* that. She has two herniated discs," I warned while attempting to support her back.

"You'll have to move, lady. We can't get through the door," the short, sharp-voiced man said. They plopped her on a stretcher they had set up on the patio. "Did she just take medication? Let me see her meds." He followed me down the hall and into the bathroom. In a zipped cosmetic bag I found several prescriptions and the headache medication she had taken a few minutes ago. "She takes all of *this*?"

"No. She doesn't take all this! She takes blood pressure medication, an antibiotic and occasionally a sleeping pill. She brings all meds on trips in case she needs them." *He thinks she's a junkie!* He said he needed to take all meds with him. In the ambulance, tears welled in her eyes, fear of the unknown. "Whatcha cryin' for?" he questioned in a sarcastic manner. She didn't answer. The emergency room visit lasted four hours: inconclusive results. The paramedic had told me that Ailene's blood pressure was very high. Her chart said it was normal.

Later that week a neurologist asked about the chest bruises.

Ailene told him, "The paramedic became irritated when I couldn't hold my arm in the air. He hit me twice with his fist, to see if I reacted to pain."

Dr. Jacome hung his head for a minute. He gave Ailene a hug while questioning my health. "I've enjoyed a good life. I've been overly blessed." *Long ago I made a promise to protect my little sister. I still feel an obligation to do that. Perhaps a visit to the lawyer is in order.*

Our gift exchange was delayed, but our little Christmas party was more than we anticipated. Ailene continues to fight health problems, but I'm convinced that with courage, and strength from a higher power, she will win the battle. In the airport my sisters and I had a group hug. I waved goodbye, looked over my shoulder and said, "Remember, even when we're apart, we'll always be together."

Children and adults counted the months that led up to the year 2000. Babies were planned, parties and vacations scheduled. There were predictions of disaster, planes veering off course, computer crashes. People stocked groceries, water and lots of peanut butter.

The Eilers asked me to book a Panama Canal cruise. "I don't know where I'll be when the clock strikes a new millennium." I teased.

"Nothing will happen," John said with firm confidence. "It's just something to talk about."

"I believe only half of what I hear or read; the hard part is to know which half. Even thought I'm a glass-half-full gal, what if the doom-and-gloom predictions came true? Let's wait until later in the year," I told them.

Two weeks after the New Year began, we were the same as last year. The hoopla of what to expect had faded. That spring the newspaper draw attention to new laws, and amazing pictures of cherry trees blooming in Washington. Mel said, "With all the hot air blowing around in the nation's capitol, it's a wonder the cherry trees don't bloom all year around."

The year 2000 brought more numbers into my life. Do you

remember your first telephone number? In 1947, my number was 237R. My second number was 4188; three digits were added. Next came area codes and I needed help remembering ten digits. I accept changes, but after a few years, more access and area codes forced another change. The news left me reeling. Gary became a representative of a long distance telephone carrier. We signed a contract with his company. To call my hairdresser I dial two digits, plus five digits, plus one digit plus three digits, plus three digits, plus four digits. You'd think she lives in Ethiopia, instead of five miles away.

Surely life was never meant to be so complicated. When the U.S. Postal Service first began, they required a name, city and state on the envelope. Within a short time they added street address, a five-digit zip code and another five digits. Soon that number will be increased. This process is called enhancing the species.

Computer consultants warn us to avoid passwords with obvious identification numbers such as birthdays, names, or street addresses. I decided on a password, repeated it sixteen times a day, but forgot it the next. (Glad I wrote it in my address book.)

My address book is running out of space. In the olden days the most important and necessary information was Social Security numbers. I need five to fourteen lines to enter information for casual, social and business associates. For each entry I squiggled into a three-line block: home and business telephone number, address, Fax number, Web page, e-mail address and pager.

In case of emergency I need the children's business phone, pager number, 800 number and cellular number. In case I hear the recording, "The cellular customer is out of range," I need my residence answering machine code to check recorded messages. I'm thankful that my office is now in my home where I need one set of numbers. I hope I never forget my Medicare number. When my number is up, I hope family members know my lot number.

Twenty days after we celebrated the New Year, George W.

Bush was sworn in as the nation's forty-third president. On January 20, 2001 he said, "I'm ready to accept with pride and with honor the job of commander-in-chief." That day he issued an executive order to block or delay a variety of President Clinton's executive orders and last-minute rules. The front page of the newspaper also featured news of President Clinton cutting a deal. He reached an agreement with prosecutors that prevented him from being indicted after leaving office. Clinton paid a fine and surrendered his law license for five years. The agreement ended the Whitewater investigation.

ON SUNDAY MORNING, January 28, Ailene called. "Herb has been on medication for a urinary infection. Last night he had a high temperature and asked his neighbor Bill to drive him to the hospital. Patty, Herb had a heart attack in the emergency room. Joy is leaving Detroit Metro at 10:30 this morning."

In a rush to get Joy to the airport, her daughter Amy's car skidded on ice and dented a neighbor's new car that was parked in the shared driveway. She insisted that the damage was minor, but Amy was distressed.

Snow and ice threatened to close the airport. The pilot cautioned passengers to remain seated and wear their seat belts for the duration of the turbulent flight. The plane arrived safely. The passengers cheered.

When Gee heard the news he called his daughter Nancy. "I know you and Gary are on vacation, but Herb needs bypass surgery and Wilma has been having cataplexy attacks. That's a seizure-like condition. They desperately need you. Could you make a detour to Ocala?"

"I'm sorry to hear that. We're in Tampa, about an hour from them. We'll head up there right away."

When they arrived Joy told them, "You have no idea how pleased I am to see you. Mom's neurologist has scheduled a sleep study. He discontinued her medication because it could affect results. I'm afraid to leave her alone."

That evening Joy and Wilma visited Herb. As they were leaving the hospital, Wilma slumped to the floor. After a few minutes she gained her composure. Upon arrival home and while Wilma was taking a relaxing bath she passed out for about three minutes. "Sorry I pulled another one on you," she sheepishly grinned and said to her daughter who was standing nearby.

"Now, Mom, we have to get you out of the bath tub."

"Don't you dare call a neighbor."

"I wouldn't know which neighbor to call, but I do have an idea. I'll shove you forward and you crawl out on all four," Joy told her as they both laughed. The plan worked. Brenda Castle, who lived next door, came daily with delicious soups, pies and cakes. Wilma was having three to six attacks daily.

I called Joy the next day and detected a concerned apprehension. I told her, "I'll leave Metro at 10:30 tomorrow morning." Without fail, an emergency arrives when I'm having a bad hair day. I rearranged appointments while Nancy Sheets pampered me with a cut, shampoo and stylish hairdo. I thank God for friends, and for an understanding husband.

The next day I arrived at the Leesburg Regional Medical Center. As you know, I'm a curious creature and aging has resulted in additional inquisitiveness. Dr. Javad described the emergency unit procedures. Herb was checked and treatment began: blood cultures, antibiotics, Tylenol. He was alert and in no acute distress. Heart rate was normal and his color was good.

Due to Herb's history of peripheral vascular disease and hypertension, Dr. Javad ordered an electrocardiogram. The decision was made to admit Herb into the hospital, but before he was transferred to a room he began to have a sudden onset of chills. Although the monitor rhythm remained unchanged, his heart rate elevated. He experienced shortness of breath. A repeat EKG suggested that Herb could be having a heart attack. The next day a cardiac catheterization and angiogram revealed a triple vessel coronary artery disease—sixty to eighty percent plugged. An intra-aortic balloon pump was used. Herb was admitted to CCU and bypass surgery was scheduled.

On Wednesday Joy arrived at the hospital early, but Wilma's doctor advised her to stay home. Herb's pastor offered a prayer. Under general anesthesia, Herb was prepped and draped. One of the two chief veins in the left leg was harvested and the incision repaired. The breastbone was divided in the midline. A drainage tube was inserted into the ascending aorta and bypass was established. Three connections between blood vessels were surgically joined into the heart and sewn with suture.

Herb was weaned from bypass, drainage tubes were removed and the sites sutured. The sternum was closed with stainless steel wire. Herb tolerated the procedure well. The next day he said, "Patty. I'll beat you at cards real soon. In eight weeks I can get with my golf game."

Dr. Richardson told Herb, "You surely have someone up there looking out for you. Be thankful that you were on hospital grounds. Before you could get here you would have had a massive heart attack."

The therapist came three times weekly. Herb asked about the leg pain. The therapist smiled slightly. "Doctors harvest more vein than needed. After all, they can't stop the bypass procedure if they run short of supplies!"

In July, even though Wilma and Herb loved living in Florida, they sold their home and returned to family and friends in Michigan. Without technology, Herb's story would have had a different outcome.

Technology has taken over the world. The most important historical moment in my life is a computer that humbles body and mind. The monitor flashes humiliating messages about how dumb I am. I feel like I've been living on a desert island when conversations include terms such as ECC, SDRAM and GB.

Computer classes convinced me that floppies aren't beach shoes. A disk doesn't always give you musical selections. A mouse doesn't breathe. Windows aren't for spying on your neighbor. A drive isn't a Sunday afternoon pleasure. A tablet comes with a headset microphone. A laptop isn't for holding grandchildren. Storage is a zip drive not wooden shelves in a closet. Import is not a product from China. Bit is not a small helping of dessert.

My new computer has an IntelliMouse. My compassionate friend is the dictionary, but my Webster's New World printed in 1968 doesn't list words like: AMD versus INTEL processor, touch pad, subwoofer, pixel. Software, hardware, under wear – they all need to fit.

The year 2001 brought a historical moment that Americans will never forget. Nothing else mattered. On Tuesday, September eleventh, Gary called. "Mom, do you have the television on?

"No. I'm sitting at the computer. Writing."

"You won't believe what's happening. An airplane just plowed into one of the World Trade Center towers. It's simply horrible."

I pushed the "power" button and witnessed another hijacked plane crashing into the other tower. Within a short time, a plane struck the Pentagon, and one headed for the capitol, but crashed in Pennsylvania. There are no words to describe the incident. Horrible images leapt off the screen, falling bodies, bloodied victims and mourning families. Americans were under attack by forces we could not see, for reasons we did not understand.

The terrorist attack on America prompted postponement or cancellation of meetings, concerts and most athletic events. For the first time since D-Day in 1944, fifteen major league baseball games were cancelled. Fun and games seemed to be in bad taste. A local Christian radio station had sponsored a skating event. Nathan talked with the announcer. "We feel we should carry out our plans. Children need a break from the bad news we've heard all day, a break from the worry and concern."

Two hours later the phone rang. In the emergency room,

Nathan tried to be brave. "Grandpa, please come. I crashed into the wall. I may have broken bones." Nathan's fractures in the leg and ankle were insignificant compared to the injury and loss of lives in New York and Washington, D.C. We may never know the human toll extracted by this disaster. Displays of patriotism far exceeded what I remember from World War II. Flags were taped to bikes, cars, school buses, in yards and windows.

Early the next morning, rain soaked the bowed heads of several hundred students who went to school early for "See-you-at-the-pole day. Nathan, with crutches and an extra jacket covering his hip cast, joined them in the petition for God to bless America.

Emotionally, it could take years for Americans to recover. My hope is that as the healing and rebuilding continues, people will find comfort in the arms of our heavenly Father. Meanwhile, we should hold our loved ones especially near.

Now What?

The game of life consists of many valley and mountain-top experiences. Perhaps you want to know what happened to the other characters in this story. Who would have suspected, way back in those intolerant years that my siblings would be content with what transpired? John Adams wrote in February 1776, "We cannot ensure success, but we can deserve it." My family deserved and accomplished success. I continue to feel emptiness due to the absence of my brother Paul and sister Yvonne.

Wilma and Herb have various health problems, but they are content, happy and face problems with a smile. Wilma, a talented artist, coaxed me into sketching a teddy bear for my brother. A big heart on the bear's shirt tells Gee how much I care.

Gee and his wife Rada had nine children. Shortly after completion of their dream home she suffered a fatal heart attack. Gee met Lise; they are happily married and take pleasure in their blended family. Although he is semi-retired from the construction business, he helps family members build their dreams. A few weeks ago the phone rang. "Hello, sis," he said.

"Hey, Teddy Bear. What's wrong?" I asked. "You called yesterday."

"Darling, everything is fine. I'm enjoying the California sun and thinking about you. You're worth a bigger phone bill. You're worth a million dollars." I visualized his wide grin, his plump arms giving bear hugs. He ended our conversation with "Love you, babe."

I've mentioned Ailene and her husband Arnold's singing and recording success. They cope with health issues, but enjoy the children, grandchildren and the Gospel Tones. Ailene has written several songs, books and poems. At the age of fifty-five, she graduated cum laude with a degree in psychology and elementary education. I came across a letter she wrote. "I've never told anyone, but I would like to teach school at Pax just so the people there would know that I amounted to something."

Returning to Pax reveals that everything has changed. Very few of my descriptions could lead you into the places that now thrive, but vivid memories remain: The belief that Uncle Gil absolutely hated me, the feeling that I could no longer persevere. The mental picture of Mom's tiny arms and leathered skin that barely tolerated another morphine injection remained in my mind until prenatal visits convinced me that I must conquer the fear or struggle through life expecting the inevitable. By incorporating determination and will power, I conquered many obstacles, even facing a needle without flinching.

My life was shaped by hard work and complex challenges, promises to myself and to others. I have sent up the right message. Love floated back to me. I wallow in success while navigating through life's minefields. While putting these thoughts on paper I shared them with Mel, who was born and lived ten miles from me, his future wife. After forty-two years together, he's still my best friend. We have enjoyed life to the fullest, traveled, cherished nine grandchildren. Our children, who have lived in distant areas, now live within a few minutes of the same house where they grew up.

The driving time to visit our children and grandchildren ranges from seven minutes to three hours. It isn't easy for them to understand how I confronted life as a child. It isn't easy for me to describe my emotions. I have reflected on the past and focused on the distant past while describing interesting but painful events. There's adventure in writing a book. It begins as an amusement, a toy. It becomes a master, a tyrant. Like giving birth, it ends with delivery, with a feeling of pride like you get when children reach for your hand.

Memories float back. At the end of a Saturday night movie, Roy Rogers removed his hat, bowed his head and said a cowboy's prayer. "Lord, I'm not much by myself. I fail to do things I should do, but when the trails are steep and the passes high, help me to ride it the whole way through."

When I reach the end of life's road I hope I will have lived long and experienced much. When dusk falls and I get the final call, like the cowboys that sang about happiness, the happiest trail for me will be hearing the words quoted in Matthew 25:21: *"Well done, my good and faithful servant. Enter into the joy of the Lord!"*

Today, clouds are blown along by the wind, whirling snow against the kitchen window. Ice clings to bare branches of the maple and pine trees. In the near future their appearance will change, the signal of a new beginning, a new life cycle.

I watch the first ray of dawn turn the gray night into gold. I'm thinking of a bright summer and the years ahead.